IN ANOTHER WORLD

IN ANOTHER WORLD

THE FOUR SEASONS OF
TALK TALK

GRAEME THOMSON

new modern

First published in the UK in 2026 by New Modern
An imprint of Putman Publishing
Mermaid House, Puddle Dock, Blackfriars, London, EC4V 3DB

@newmodernbooks
@newmodern_books

Hardback ISBN: 978-1-917923-61-3
eBook ISBN: 978-1-917923-63-7

A CIP catalogue record for this book is available in the British Library.

Publishing and editorial: Pete Selby, James Lilford and Eleanor Porter
Typesetting: Marie Doherty

1 3 5 7 9 10 8 6 4 2

New Modern is an imprint of Putman Publishing

www.newmodernbooks.co.uk
www.putmanpublishing.co.uk

Printed and bound in Great Britain
by Clays Ltd, Elcograf S.p.A.

'The straight road had been lost sight of'

Inferno, Canto 1, Dante Alighieri,
translated by Seamus Heaney (1993)

*'Perfection is achieved, not when there
is nothing more to add, but when
there is nothing left to take away'*

Antoine de Saint-Exupéry, *Airman's Odyssey*

For Martha

CONTENTS

BEGINNINGS

(Wealth of Love)

I'm not sure exactly when I bought *The Colour of Spring*. Fittingly, perhaps, my engagement with Talk Talk's music has never been linear. It would have been sometime after the release of *Spirit of Eden*, in September 1988, but well before that of *Laughing Stock* in September 1991. It was most likely at some point in the second half of 1989 in Bristol, very possibly in Rayner's at the top end of Park Street. Vinyl, of course. I would have been fifteen, shading sixteen. Still ripe for miracles. Thirsting for them.

In which case, at the time of writing I have owned my copy of *The Colour of Spring* for around thirty five years.

For most of that period, the record has played cleanly, with one exception. Buried in the distended piano notes, hisses, creaks and Variophonic squalls of 'Chameleon Day', directly after the line 'breathe on me', my copy is afflicted with an aural tear, a Velcro *riiiiiip*, so loud and distinctive it is impossible to miss. With perfect syncopation, the sound recurs a few moments later, in the immediate wake of the same melodic refrain, this time after the vocalist, Mark Hollis, sings the words 'killing time' – although 'singing' doesn't seem quite strong enough a verb to describe what Hollis is doing here. It felt to me then, and sometimes still, that on these lines he was hymning the English gospel so clean, hard and true that his voice simply gouged its way into the vinyl, several layers deeper than the grooves. Absurd, of course, but this music tends to encourage such flights of fancy.

So ingrained are these two moments in my personal version of the song that, when I first heard 'Chameleon Day' many years later via a different medium – on compact disc, probably, but perhaps even digitally – I was startled by their absence. I realised that I missed them terribly. The jolting sound of needle on imperfect vinyl had become an intrinsic and beloved element in the musical landscape of the song. Random chance: the final overdub. I like to think that Hollis and his core co-conspirators Tim Friese-Greene, Lee Harris and Paul Webb might have approved.

This tear in the fabric of the music of Talk Talk is one of the factors which distinguishes what came during and after *The Colour of Spring* from what came before it. It is the crackle in the wire, the precarious fault line along which many of the words in these pages will run. The disturbance of sound in space, the upending of expectations, the meeting of spontaneous accident and laborious design. A mad kind of science to it all. In the pursuit of what end? Enduring beauty. Enveloping mystery. Art that lasts and shape-shifts, that is never heard quite the same way twice. Some kind of virtue. The case for the evidence? *The Colour of Spring. Spirit of Eden. Laughing Stock. Mark Hollis.*

While this book tells the story of a band and the people in it, it is above all a biography of these four records. They seem to me to first create and then explore their own worlds, but also to link together to form one amorphous whole. These records are puzzles which don't necessarily wish to be solved. That is a large part of their appeal. This book is therefore not about resolving anything, but rather immersing ourselves in the music and the various times and circumstances in which it was made, swimming around in the currents and seeing to what interesting places they might take us.

These records were not written or recorded by conventional means; or, at least, they were subjected to unconventional thought processes and practices which consciously disrupted their course. These are very particular artefacts. For all that I would argue they connect on a profoundly emotional, soulful and even spiritual level, they are, first and foremost, technical constructs. They are not mad jams, nor carelessly experimental; rather, they play with sound and space, manipulating notions of authenticity and spontaneity as cleverly and ruthlessly as any three-minute pop single. The consideration given to technology, to instrumentation, the recording environment, equipment, angles, distance, temperature, matters of millimetres and microseconds, is truly obsessive. The musicians who contributed to these records were subjected to a form of human sampling: used when needed, cast aside without any deference to reputation or ego when not. What mattered was not proficiency but *character*. Those that made the cut understood that they were just another tool in service of the chase for the correct feeling. The unimagined glimpse of some new beauty. Perfect imperfection.

The same instinct applies to Hollis's words, which play with distance, obfuscation, layered meaning, borrowings, effect. Their sound is perhaps what is most important within the wider tapestry. 'I treat my voice like an instrument,' he once said. 'I don't want to create this perfect ambience and then have the vocal ride over the top without any thought.'[1] But he can only get the sound, and the feeling, if he is singing something which has meaning to him. I listen, and I hear a search for something sacred. We need not put a name on it.

Writing about these records is further complicated, or perhaps simplified, by the fact that nobody who was a core member of Talk Talk will talk Talk Talk. The four men most closely involved in the making of this music have appeared sometimes to behave as though they were involved in covering up a series of grisly murders. Code: *omertà*. To be clear, the people who made this music *really* don't wish to talk about it. They never really did.

Mark Hollis died in February 2019, sadly prematurely at the age of sixty-four. Even when alive, he was not particularly forthcoming about these albums. During what might, at a push, be called the 'promotional cycle', he at least went through the motions and on occasion found a path towards articulating his aims and intentions. The meaning behind the music, however, was by necessity, and wisely, mostly left unexpressed. After releasing his eponymous solo album in 1998, for the final twenty-one years of his life, Hollis had no public profile whatsoever.

Having undertaken a couple of interviews which touched on Talk Talk almost twenty years ago, Hollis's co-writer, co-producer and all-round creative partner on these records, Tim Friese-Greene, now absolutely refuses to elaborate on his role. I have tried, and failed, to tempt him into print. His last communiqué, sent via his wife, Lee, said: 'I'm afraid it's a hard pass from Tim on this. He doesn't talk about those records, even the feelings of them.'

Bass player Paul Webb left the group after *Spirit of Eden* and has remained the most active former member, making music most recently as Rustin Man. Webb will acknowledge his past in Talk Talk and occasionally posts fond reminiscences on Instagram or Facebook, but reveals little of the inner workings of the band. He left in 1988. It was a long time ago. He has called Talk Talk 'a fun way to spend my twenties'.[2]

Drummer Lee Harris has maintained a fairly strict silence since he ceased to be a member of the band after *Laughing Stock*. He more or less vanished from view after he and Webb dissolved their post Talk Talk band 'O'rang, but still plays and records, most notably on Beth Gibbons' solo album, *Lives Outgrown*, released in May 2024.

The core quartet won't speak. There will be other reasons for their silence, but chief among them is a desire to let the music speak for itself. 'I don't know if that is the reason why no one [else has] talked,' said Webb. 'But for me it's been a thing that the less you talk about it, the bigger it is.'[3] I have become sensitive and sympathetic to their wishes. (Who am I kidding? I've had little choice).

In any case, I have grown a little uneasy about the mounting fascination and mythology surrounding the life of Mark Hollis. There is something unsettling about the cult of devotion that has grown around him, which built steadily in the silence that grew before his death and has only grown stronger after it. It feels prickly, uncomfortable – and diverts energy and attention away from the reason anyone outside of his private life cares about Hollis at all.

He was a man who made music, much of it wonderful, and most of it with the close assistance of other people. Away from his work, Hollis made no claims to be extraordinary. 'The man and the artist, I would say that the two sat in different worlds,' says Nigel Reeve, who in the late 1990s worked as head of repertoire at EMI, where he collaborated closely with Hollis on catalogue business and became a friend. 'The Mark that I socialised with was just a normal bloke. We would talk about all sorts of things. Then the music, the complexity and beauty of it, the instrument that was his voice … I felt they existed in separate worlds. When we would talk, you could tell the creative vision was part of his day-to-day life. We might be talking about the Chuckle Brothers, but there was still something … Certain things inspired him. But he lived in a very normal world. He just went about his business and people wouldn't necessarily recognise him. He was a quiet genius, such a pure soul, and that came across in his spirit.'

The music is where he gave us his all. He followed his heart with a great intensity and otherwise lived his life, by all accounts, well and quietly. Family. Friends. Travel. Golf. Motorbikes. Pub. Garden. As Hollis surely intended, there is little else but the music to hold onto – and not even much of that. From the period this book explores – 1986 and onwards – there are few available demos; one was released online in the wake of Hollis's death and there are some half-dozen others in existence that remain publicly unavailable. There are no meaningful outtakes. No bootlegs. I laid my hands on several snippets of studio chat from the *Spirit of Eden* sessions; they are closer to Derek & Clive than *Private Passions*. No live performances past 1986, no lyric books or documentaries.

Listeners to later-period Talk Talk have the released music and that is all. There is a clean, undeniable beauty to it.

•

I first heard Talk Talk in 1986. I have a clear memory of seeing the video for 'Life's What You Make It' on television one Saturday morning. I remember Mark Hollis's shaggy blonde mop, his colourised Lennon granny glasses and the way he pounded the piano and sang like a threat, a curse and a prayer, as an array of small woodland animals popped in and out of view. As a young teen feeling his way up and into the higher ground of the Waterboys and Van Morrison, the elemental, nocturnal, wood-smoked, outside-not-inside feel of the video, not to mention the pounding krautrock-on-the-farm drama of the song, would have appealed to me. I would have heard 'Living in Another World', too, around this time, a more dynamic, labyrinthine affair which I came to prefer.

To my recollection, there was no deeper immersion until a night in 1989 when a friend played me *Spirit of Eden*; I will return to that epiphany in due course. I recall later owning the album on cassette, the price sticker glued to the narrow spine of the case curling and yellowing over time. I went deep into it and, later that year, bought *The Colour of Spring* on vinyl.

Riiiiip.

I was late to the party. By this time, Talk Talk as a band was as good as over. There would be no more live shows, no more hit singles, no *Saturday Superstore*-friendly videos, precious few interviews, barely any sense of a unified group. All you could do was play the records – again and again and again. At that point, the world of Talk Talk, as far as I was concerned, consisted of just fourteen songs on two albums. In September 1991, with the release of *Laughing Stock*, that tally rose to twenty.

It was a long, long time before I circled back to the start of the story to listen to the first two albums, *The Party's Over* and *It's My Life*. When I finally did, they radiated a kind of jarring familiarity, like seeing your partner in the life they led before you knew them, with an odd haircut and wearing strange trousers, acting like a slightly different person. These albums, still, run counter to my understanding of what the band is. This is entirely my prejudice. This brighter, shinier version of Talk Talk is at times a fine one, but it's not the band I fell in love with, nor a group that takes me out of myself or builds the imagined worlds of this book's title. The likelihood is that our paths simply crossed at the wrong time. Grappling with the first two somewhat patchy Talk Talk albums after falling hard for *Spirit of Eden* and *Laughing Stock* felt frankly unnecessary. I already had what I needed.

By the beginning of 1985, and the making of *The Colour of Spring*, Hollis had sufficient resources, enough creative confidence and, crucially, a bedded-in collaborator to begin the work of fully bringing his ideas to fruition. This meant, perhaps perversely, a process of elimination. Over the next six years, Talk Talk were a band not just shedding weight but shedding form and literal meaning like blown blossom. Lyrics lose scansion and elude easy interpretation; song structures appear briefly only to dissolve. The process of addition and subtraction is not linear: you lose, you gain; you take to give. Absence is a new colour. Removal, an act of creativity. At the start of this process, there are three band members. By the end, only one remains.

One iteration of the band is not necessarily of more value than the other, but it is this version of Talk Talk that I am interested in. In addition to the band's final trio of albums, I have included Hollis's 1998 solo record, *Mark Hollis*. While being very much a work apart in and of itself, the album shares key personnel with *Spirit of Eden* and *Laughing Stock*, and also similarities in terms of the stringent working methodology, lyrical themes and musical motifs. And it's great, too.

Four albums. Four seasons. Together, they make a world.

SPRING

The Colour of Spring

i

('Come gentle spring / Come at winter's end')

It is February 1986 and the sap is rising early. A new beginning is being written in rhythm.

At the start of *The Colour of Spring*, Talk Talk's third album, we hear thirty-four seconds of unaccompanied drums and percussion.

It is a sound we can feel. It has the texture of good wood, quality carpentry. Something solid and artisanal. The rhythm, the grain, runs hard and true, but comes with characterful twists and knots, the steady pulse tricked out with fills and rolls, skipped beats.

What we are hearing is real, but also not quite real. You don't get a sound like the sound on *The Colour of Spring* by accident.

We join Talk Talk while they still resemble a conventional group and are still observing the orthodoxies of a traditional music career. Single, video, album, promo, tour. But the fault lines are shifting.

The work on *The Colour of Spring* stretched from March 1985 into the late autumn. The core creatives were Mark Hollis, Paul Webb and Lee Harris, joined by co-writer, producer and auxiliary musician Tim Friese-Greene and a further cast of session musicians and engineers.

Who are these people?

Where have they been?

We will get to that. For now, let's hear what they have been doing.

'Happiness is Easy' is where we start.

The song is, let's be clear, a monster. What a way to begin a record. Not only is it six-and-a-half minutes of magnificence, but it also acts as a kind of primer for many of the sounds, themes, styles and elements which will define later-period Talk Talk.

What hits first is the sheer plushness of the music; this is deluxe craftmanship. Big, roomy, precise; an idealised construct of what a great band should sound like in a good space. As will continue to be the case, no matter what our ears are telling us, we are hearing a carefully manufactured sound. Sonically speaking, this is as executive class as Talk Talk will ever get. In future, the music is subjected to concerted attempts to leave a little more of the grit in the pearl.

The instruction to the listener at the start of 'Happiness is Easy' is simple: keep your ears on the drums. They are, in any case, inescapable, as they are throughout *The Colour of Spring* and also the albums that will follow. They will, however, steadily lose their grid-like form. 'Mark once said something about the insistence of the snare drum being on the second and the fourth beat as being the whole central point of what record companies want,' says Laurence Pendrous, music master at Hall School Wimbledon, which Hollis's two sons attended; Pendrous was invited to play piano on *Mark Hollis* and became a personal friend. 'You have to build material around that, [even if it's] totally to the detriment of the artist and what he was passionate about.' We can, in fact, track Hollis's abdication from any intent to make mainstream music partly by the way in which the rhythm on Talk Talk records begins to divert from a rigid pattern, becoming more organic and fluid. Free time means just that: freedom.

For now, the drums are locked in. On 'Happiness is Easy', they are monolithic. Ansel Adams should have photographed them. Around them is a sense of space which will only grow in time to become perhaps the lead texture in the music of Talk Talk. Here, it is not so much 'space' as 'room'; each instrument feels as though it has the ability to stretch its arms out into the surrounding air without touching another.

After the drum prologue, the track rolls onto the rails. Blocky piano chords, enveloping organ, some busy fretless bass, lithe flicks of acoustic guitar. Hollis enters after a full minute. Instantly, this is a voice we can believe. No artifice. 'There is something just very special about his voice,' says Dennis Weinreich, one of three engineers who worked on *The Colour of Spring*. 'He is English from the moment he opens his mouth.' It is a voice that catches and breaks when it strives too hard, rising sharply before falling away at the edges of each line. There is a plainness that is both honest and heart-breaking. It's a voice with an ingrained ache, which speaks of restrained passions and inner struggle. Hollis's voice seems to be forever reaching for a place beyond literal meaning. It carries, always, the promise of compassion.

All this we can hear on 'Happiness is Easy'. And in the words he sings, as so often, a throughline of something sacred is glimpsed amid the interrogation of virtue, perhaps his great theme as a writer. Here, it arrives in the chorus via the voices of small children, shipped in courtesy of the Barbara Speake Stage School in East Acton, west London, which boasts a long list of famous alumni, including Phil Collins and Naomi Campbell. The credit for the choir on the inner sleeve – to 'Miss Speake' – is a nice play on words which presumably would have pleased Hollis.

The children are not singing as they might were they members of a trained choir doing their bit at a regional competition, say, but rather as they would at a primary-school nativity play. And, indeed, they are singing a hymn, about Jesus and Galilee and stars that shine. These wobbly young voices might easily at first be misidentified as ironic, their effect intended to mock piety, before we realise that they are being deployed as precisely what they are: missiles of innocence. Hollis is being sincere. Of course he is. The music of Talk Talk continually thrums with a tension between morality and mendacity, between what could be and what really is. On 'Happiness is Easy', this collision of values is articulated not just in the young voices, but in the music, through a tensile, unresolved hovering in the chorus. A single note on the acoustic guitar, scratching testily around a suddenly more primitive rhythm, represents the thin hope of the children. In contrast to the four-wheel drive smoothness on the verses, the drums turn mean, each *thwack* landing like a cynical slap in the face.

'Happiness is Easy' offers up more clues, other landmarks. The drifting wash of sound that arrives before the chorus is so quintessentially Talk Talk that it is practically a signature sound. In fact, it *is* a signature sound, as are the trumpet-like peals in the instrumental break which, not for the last time, reach out to Miles Davis's *Sketches of Spain*. The sound is a common connecting thread in so many of these songs, both intensely atmospheric but also a clever linking device, moving the music from one place to another.

It is made by the Variophon, an electronic wind instrument designed at the University of Cologne in the 1970s. The Variophon is controlled via a pipe and operated on the same principle as a brass instrument, the sound dictated by the force, control and resonance of the player's breath. It could imitate instruments such as trumpet, saxophone and clarinet not exactly, but with a strangely emotive blurred quality, a kind of sad drift that feels instantly nostalgic in the way that naïve imaginings of the coming space age during the 1950s now feel nostalgic. It sounds like a future that never happened.

'It was a German synthesiser, controlled via a mouthpiece,' says Dietmar Schillinger, who worked as an engineer on *The Colour of Spring*. 'You could select a sound on it, then play the notes on a keyboard, but the control was via mouthpiece. You would blow into it to give it the power and then play. It was really hard to get anything out of it. Those brass sounds we had on the record are from that. It's a very distinctive, absolutely brilliant instrument – and, of course, they made it their own. How lucky to find an instrument that sounds absolutely brilliant and nobody else uses it! It was a synth, but it's a very organic way of playing.'

Tim Friese-Greene bought a stockpile of them, just in case, because they were continually malfunctioning. 'It's amazing that nobody else saw the potential of it,' he said.[1] Perhaps not. It took a certain kind of ear to tune in to its possibilities. Yet another engineer on the album, Peter Woolliscroft, describes the Variophon as 'Mark's favourite instrument'. If there is a sound that comes closest to expressing the inarticulate longing at the heart of these records, the sounds that can be imagined but in truth cannot quite be made, then the Variophon seems to have been the favoured instrument of communication It offered a very particular synthesis of human and machine.

Talk Talk in 1986 still had some pop nous about them. Beneath the drums runs a thin click of percussion. It's *very* 1980s, almost dancefloor-adjacent. Indeed, in parts of this song, we hear premonitions of the coming Bristol sound; an intimation of trip-hop in the queasy grain of strings against rhythm that would soon come to fruition in songs such as Massive Attack's 'Unfinished Sympathy' and Neneh Cherry's 'Manchild'. Danny Thompson's nimble double bass motif winds its way high up in the mix, then a wild swirl of organ as the song ramps up. These are people who know how to build dynamics.

And then the music falls away. The drums bash-bash-bash, almost performatively surly. The guitar beadles around anxiously in a holding pattern. The children keep singing their hearts out as the song fades into silence.

'Happiness is Easy'. What a way to herald the new dawn.

•

'MIDI', said Mark Hollis in 1986, 'is a four-letter word.'[2]

If there was a creative mantra or guiding principle behind the creation of *The Colour of Spring*, there it is. Six strings good; Roland MC4 bad.

Hollis made clear several times in interviews during this period that the more synthetic sounds on the first two Talk Talk albums were a matter of economic expediency. 'People often say that there's this huge gap between *It's My Life* and *The Colour of Spring*, but we had a lot more money to make that album, so we used real musicians,' he said in 1991. 'I hate synths, they're horrible things, but if you want to make multi-textural music, they're a cheap way of doing it. When you get the opportunity to move on, you take it.'[3]

By 1985, Hollis had the opportunity to move on and he took it. Expressing how much he detested synthesisers, he dismissed them as a simulacrum of 'the real thing' – which is, of course, their entire purpose: to warp reality in interesting ways. Some artists simply use them more inventively than others.

The Colour of Spring would find little use for the old Talk Talk tool set: the Jupiter 8, the Prophet-5 or the Roland MC4 sequencer. Yet from the very start, this was an album created using cutting-edge technology. The writing process was completed, out of eye- and earshot, by Hollis and producer Tim Friese-Greene. Having started composing together on *It's My Life* using piano, they now graduated to using Page R of the Fairlight CMI, the all-in-one digital audio workstation, synthesiser and sampler which Friese-Greene had recently bought; the cost at the time would have been in the region of £30,000 – the equivalent of a decent-sized house.

Page R was a new innovation introduced when Series II of the Fairlight launched. Working in a similar way to a sampling machine, its great strength was the graphic representation of notes, layered in horizontal streams running from left to right, easily accessible and editable. With Page R, a range of sounds could much more easily be added to or removed from a piece of music. The innovation played a major role in the punkification of music's electronic age, a DIY step change that rendered more sophisticated or exotic sounds readily available to players who were not especially accomplished. Using Page R to write was highly impactful in opening out the potential palette of sounds and instrumentation for the next Talk Talk record.

There were more traditional inspirations, too.

Friese-Greene – who seemed to have something of the spirit of the Edwardian adventurer about him – had recently returned from a year-long sabbatical, driving 35,000 miles circumnavigating much of Africa. His trip exposed him to new sounds, instruments and textures; he was particularly enamoured of Congolese soukous. From the start, a strong, cyclical rhythmic underlay was embedded in the vision for the record.

While his partner was bringing these ideas to the table, Hollis had become more or less obsessed with early twentieth-century music. He had been listening to classical music since long before the band formed (the first song he ever learned on piano was 'Moonlight Sonata'), but his tastes sharpened in the year leading up to *The Colour of Spring*. 'I do think that there's an area of classical music which I have an affinity for,' he said in 1986, as the British music press guffawed behind its hand. 'The impressionist period, around the turn of the century, is something I love very much. I love the textural quality that it has. But equally, there's a hardness to soul music and gospel music that I like.'[4]

The way Hollis frames these two elements, almost as opposites, outlines in the most basic terms the binaries at play in Talk Talk at this time. At the bottom end, the direct, spare beat of soul and gospel – to which we might add the motorik pulse of krautrock. Laid over that, layers of textural nuance and painterly detail. Both sides have inbuilt space; they are, at heart, minimalist.

In terms of Hollis's classical tastes, the big hitters largely didn't land a punch, nor the showpiece symphonies. Almost nothing he admired pre-dated the late 1800s. He was wary of anything grandiose or bombastic. He talked particularly about Frederick Delius's later works, the exquisite miniature tone poem 'On Hearing the First Cuckoo in Spring' and the larger orchestral piece 'In a Summer Garden'. He loved Béla Bartók's six string quartets, written between 1909 and 1939, some of the most influential classical music of the century. Robert Fripp and Steve Reich are also admirers of these pieces, which use two violins, viola and cello, and had their roots in Hungarian folk music.

When Hollis referenced the 'Impressionist' period of classical music, he was talking about composers such as Delius and Bartók, but also Maurice Ravel; not the chest-puffing Ravel of *Bolero*, but the writer of the string quartets and more reflective collaborations with the poet Stéphane Mallarmé. Mallarmé's poetry had earlier been set to music by Claude Debussy, who would have loathed being called the Monet of musical Impressionism, but the phrase captures something of his vast influence on the loosely affiliated movement.

The classical branch of Impressionism followed in the wake of the Impressionist art movement. As a label, it was never a perfect fit. With its analogue in visual arts, musical Impressionism placed an emphasis on instrumental timbres that created a shimmering interplay of musical 'colours', melodies that hovered rather than resolved and a disruptive intent towards traditional musical forms. The emphasis was on creating atmosphere, on conveying the moods and emotions aroused by the subject rather than a sharp portrait of it. Colour, timbre, pointillism.

It is not especially difficult to hear where some of these features play out – consciously but also quite naturally – in the music of Talk Talk from this point onwards, nor where the sound palette of Impressionism is reached for: small clusters of strings, brass and woodwind instruments, nature-in-sound, folk inflections and pastorals, not forgetting the treatment of the piano, an instrument both Hollis and Friese-Greene truly loved. Erik Satie, Ravel, Debussy and Gabriel Fauré, the latter another artist better known for his earlier, simpler, more accessible music, such as 'Clair de lune', rather than the more harmonically and melodically complex compositions he wrote later in life. Hollis also liked Anton Webern and Olivier Messiaen, two sons of Impressionism, even if they weren't quite rooted in that source.

All this came into play when he and Friese-Greene started writing loops on the Fairlight and then began to build up the songs for *The Colour of Spring*. In early 1985, they spent time in Nomis

Studios, the vast rehearsal and recording facility in west London, mapping out the foundations which included, early on, rough melodic outlines.

'They did all the basic backing ideas on the Fairlight,' recalls Peter Woolliscroft. 'It was just a working basis. They changed quite a lot. We went through and replaced the sampled sounds in the studio, the drums, the piano, things like that. The task was to run the Fairlight parts into the mixing desk live. The next step involved replacing the sampled sounds with live instruments, as the initial samples were not satisfactory.'

Many of the real instruments played on the record to replace the Fairlight parts were then manipulated using the Fairlight once again. Sections could be cut, flown out or dropped in, sampled and repeated multiple times, straightened and called to order. Most of the string parts, meanwhile, were synthetic, courtesy of the Kurzweil KC88 synthesiser, new on the market in 1984. More organic than the Fairlight CMI, it delivered a particularly crisp and clear piano sound. When that great beast of burden of 1980s electronic music, the Jupiter-8 synth, was called into service, which wasn't often, it was bent into almost unrecognisable shapes – but it is still there.

The Colour of Spring, then, offers a glistening facsimile of naturalism. This was the new game – to conjure a roomy, organic ambience which sounded somehow *truer* by fixing it up with all the latest fittings. 'Mark always was very insistent that this should sound like it's a live band, [to] keep it very simple, keep it organic,' says Woolliscroft. 'So, we have a whole studio full of electronic equipment to give that impression!'

It is a point worth remembering as we listen to these records. We are being told a story. *Nothing we are hearing really happened.*

Talk Talk recorded *The Colour of Spring* over the course of many months, primarily in three different London studios. In each one, they worked with a different engineer: Woolliscroft in Battery, Dietmar Schillinger in Wessex and Dennis Weinreich at Videosonics. Talking to each of these men individually, I am sometimes put in mind of a poor spouse who discovers that her ne'er-do-well husband has been juggling a secret family for years. None of the three engineers seemed to know much about the existence of the other sessions. Each thought the album was more or less finished at the point where they stopped working on it. There were other quickie overdub sessions, too, at Capital and Roundhouse. There is the distinct whiff of creative infidelity about the making of *The Colour of Spring*.

There is a temptation – perhaps because this was the last time Talk Talk were a truly commercial proposition, or perhaps because the album sounds just a little more ordered and well behaved than what came later – to suppose that it was recorded in a more or less conventional fashion.

Instead, many of the changes that would define the working practices for *Spirit of Eden* and *Laughing Stock* were beginning to be implemented. There was already a dedicated attempt to build a 'vibe'. At one studio, an oil projector was set up in the control room, spilling multi-coloured textures over the mixing desk and into the live room. It was also the first album where all the material was written entirely by Tim Friese-Greene and Mark Hollis together, with no input from any of the other band members. Much of it was played that way, too.

This process began in March 1985. For several months, Talk Talk had exclusive access to Studio 1 at Battery Studios in Willesden, north-west London. Studio 1 was located in a separate building across the road from the rest of the complex and came complete with its own kitchen and social area, as well as a three-quarter-size snooker table. These were the glory days of record company largesse; they had the run of the place for as long as they liked.

Woolliscroft initially found Hollis a dominant and somewhat peculiar presence. He 'called everyone a cunt' and, shortly into the sessions, began to refer to the engineer as a 'smackhead', half-jokingly implying that the frequency with which he left the room meant that he must be disappearing to shoot up in the toilet. In reality, Woolliscroft doesn't remember any drugs at all being passed around at Battery. 'Certainly nothing in the studio. If anybody did anything, it was away from there, but I don't remember it ever being an issue. Alcohol, yes.'

Instead, the sessions ran on a drip-feed of Fox's biscuits, which arrived by the box each day and would be decimated by the evening's end. The exception was Friese-Greene, who was on a 'grape-only diet' at the time. Both he and Woolliscroft were trying to quit smoking. The air-con was on full blast all day; little wonder the atmosphere could get chilly. Hollis's temperament tended to run hot and cold without warning; sometimes he appeared tetchy and standoffish, while on other days he was upbeat and friendly. Paul Webb and Lee Harris were more amenable, but 'clearly operated in Mark's shadow'. When it all got too much, Friese-Greene would retreat to the flat upstairs where his girlfriend was living, often with Hollis and co in tow, leaving Woolliscroft and tape op Paul Schroeder to continue labouring over those magnificent drum parts, which took an inordinate amount of time to perfect.

They had set up the kit with the aim of getting an ambient sound to replace the sequenced parts from the Fairlight. Harris spent a day experimenting with various snare drums before settling on a Ludwig Black Beauty worth £600.

It was not simply a case of mic'ing up the kit and then letting Harris play to a click track. On *The Colour of Spring*, we are hearing live drums deconstructed, with each component part played separately. Drumming along live proved challenging due to the machine-driven nature of the tracks. It was therefore decided that Harris would have three attempts at playing a full take on each song. Otherwise, they would sample each individual drum from the live kit and drop it into the track. Extensive timing adjustments were required to ensure synchronisation with the other instruments. For a track such as 'Happiness is Easy', those unforgettable drums fills at the start are an illusion of a complete live drum take. In reality, Harris would play the fill separately from the rest of the drum track and it would then be sampled and dropped in where desired.

During the sessions that later took place at Wessex, engineer Dietmar Schillinger recalls even more focus being placed on the drum parts. In keeping with the working methods for an album that sometimes sounds as though many of the songs were recorded afresh on three separate occasions, in Schillinger's recollection, at Wessex the drum and bass parts were created from scratch again.

'Lee and Paul were playing their parts when we laid down tracks at Wessex,' he says. 'There was a lot of work getting those drum sounds. That was not easy going. There were [many] snares in the studio and Lee would sit out there half a day, maybe longer – *boing boing boing* – tuning and testing one snare after another. In order to get those drum sounds on several tracks, we did all the drums separately. You couldn't get that kind of separation by playing the drums at the same time. You get spill from the hi-hat, you get spill from ringing toms … You can only get that [sound] when you do instruments apart.'

First, Harris would play only the bass drum and snare; a table tennis bat was placed where the hi-hat would normally sit, in order that he could keep the basic rhythm driving along without creating any splash or spill. Cymbals, tom-toms, hi-hat and fills would then be recorded in a similarly separated fashion.

'Lee is a great drummer, by the way,' says Schillinger. 'The drums on that record are just incredible. A lot of people think that in order to have good drums, you need to be a good drummer and be able to play everything at the same time. But sometimes I used to think you needed to be an even better drummer to play the drums separately than all of them together. Trying to get that groove going playing a snare drum or a bass drum at a time, that is really hard.'

To give the bass drum sound extra depth, they would sample the deep *thwump* of a thick, rubber yoga-type ball slapping the parquet floor in Wessex's capacious live room. 'If you blend that thump with a bass drum, you get a really good sound,' says Schillinger. 'There was quite a lot of that experimentation going on.' At Battery, the drums were subjected to another twist. The tracks were played at high volume through the Bose PA system in the studio and then re-recorded to achieve a more live feel.

All this, just for the drums.

In the end, the album contains only one song on which Harris actually plays a full kit in a conventional manner: 'I Don't Believe in You'. After all the weeks and months of struggle to cut and paste the drums on every other track, 'you can't tell, really, I suppose,' laughs Woolliscroft.

There is barely a breath of a pause between 'Happiness is Easy' and 'I Don't Believe in You'. That silvery shiver of harp at the start of the second track on *The Colour of Spring* is archetypal, a glimpse of Hollis's pure love of the unrepeated sonic 'moment', something he always sought out and appreciated in the music that he loved. Those moments will, in some ways, come to define all these records. Here, announcing 'I Don't Believe in You', it arrives as a chimeric presence, one of God's smallest creatures rising and shaking off the dew. Then bang, and in. Those drums again. You would follow them into war.

The song, said Hollis, has as its subject the propaganda films in which the new postwar Labour government of 1945 promised the British people that 'everything would be as fantastic'.[5] The reality, the lyric suggests, was somewhat different. Hollis returned to this idea several times. 'A New Jerusalem' on his solo album, ruminates on more or less the same theme, this time in the aftermath of the First World War, while on 'After the Flood', the key phrase is 'Lest we forget, who lay'. Originating from Rudyard Kipling's 'Recessional' poem, from 1897, 'lest we forget' is of course now more commonly associated with the Remembrance Day memorials, a warning to be mindful of the sacrifices of battle. There seemed to be something about the betrayal of those who gave so much during wartime that touched Hollis and somehow illuminated the eternal stand-off between good and bad, right and wrong, 'between expectation and reality'.[6]

Knowing this, the voice he uses at the beginning of the song can be regarded almost as actorly. It is suitably sly, a foxy croon. 'Promises so golden / Years have proved them wrong,' he chides. We will hear a similar vocal again, interestingly, on 'After the Flood'.

This is Hollis at his most world-aware, coolly suspicious of those doling out some poor facsimile of goodness. Yet when he reaches a higher register, his voice betrays him. It aches for humanity; it cannot hide. 'I'm trying to leave some self-respect,' he sings, as 'the charade goes on.'

That instrumental break is quintessential Talk Talk, the quasi-symphonic sound of flight, of release. The 'guitar' solo is actually a synth played by Ian Curnow, whose presence, or lack of, was indicative of the fresh start *The Colour of Spring* represented. A new dawn, with new rules and new faces.

Curnow was an absolutely central figure on *It's My Life* – and he played in the touring band and was involved in the demo stages for *The Colour of Spring* – but he found himself marginalised when it came to recording the album. 'By then, Mark was much further down the road towards his absolute control of things,' he says. 'He was passionately against any synthetic sounds whatsoever, anything that wasn't completely organic. There was no dialogue given to the musicians that this change was intended, so we all found the change pretty hard to understand, especially after making such a great album as *It's My Life*. I do think it was a further step on the journey from the first album being branded as synth-pop. As I was basically the "synthesiser" player, that left me with a much reduced contribution.'

In the kind of perverse/enlightened move which in some ways characterises the thought processes behind these albums, Curnow was brought in only to solve the problem of finding the right sound for the 'guitar solo' on 'I Don't Believe in You'. The solution was to use a synthesiser, but make it sound as unlike a synth as possible by feeding it through a Mesa Boogie guitar amp, then through a full-size PA rig and mic'ed up back into several faders on the desk. '[It was] very experimental, very intense,' says Curnow, who recalls one other twist that could be interpreted as ritual humiliation. Hollis secured Curnow's hands together with gaffer tape, leaving only the thumb, first and third fingers exposed on each hand, the idea being that this would force him to play the part in as unschooled and spontaneous way as possible. '"What would this solo be like if you played it like a Rhesus monkey?" It took me hours and hours to put together a decent part.'

Steve Winwood is credited with the organ solo on 'I Don't Believe in You', but it's not actually him. Unless it is. Most likely it's Friese-Greene. But maybe not. To Winwood or not to Winwood, that was the question. His presence on the entire album remains open to debate. He has performing credits for three songs listed on the inner sleeve, which is perhaps no surprise, given Hollis counted Traffic among his all-time favourite bands and revered Winwood. Nonetheless, both Woolliscroft and Curnow insist that his Hammond parts didn't make the final cut. He had been invited to come to a session at Battery, but instead summoned Hollis and Friese-Greene to his home studio in the Cotswolds. 'Mark and Tim disappeared for the weekend,' says Woolliscroft, 'because Steve said, "I'll do it, but I'll do it at my place." I came back in [to the studio] on Monday morning and said, "How did it go?" and they said, "Nah, didn't get it." Mark was quite disappointed. Steve was his hero.'

In Curnow's understanding of the narrative, Hollis went as far as travelling to the US to record Winwood playing organ on many of the tracks for *The Colour of Spring*, before returning to the UK and deciding not to use any of it. 'Bold…' Whatever the actual course of events, to remove the parts of such a venerated figure from the album was a further example of Hollis's dedication to the pursuit of the ideal, regardless of the reputations of those involved. In this case, Winwood's flamboyant freeform style was not what they envisioned for the track. Or perhaps his character did not quite align with theirs.

Whoever is playing that organ did a fine job. 'I Don't Believe in You' builds up an impressive head of steam. By the final bridge and chorus, the song is smoking. It was odd that, when visiting EMI executives heard the album initially, they could identify no obvious singles. This song, surely, would have stood out, though perhaps its stately tempo felt a little sluggish for the radio.

In the event, Hollis and Friese-Greene came up with 'Life's What You Make It' to fill that hole, if not quite to order, then close. In July, following a short break in the album sessions during which Talk Talk played some overseas shows, it was time for the record company men to pay a visit to hear the album, which most of the participants felt was close to completion.

When EMI A&R man Dave Ambrose came to listen, he conformed to the stereotype of A&R men the world over by telling them none of the songs would work as a single. While the band weren't thinking in such terms, according to Woolliscroft the pressure from the record company to return with a hit was 'palpable'. At this point, 'Living in Another World' was emerging as the frontrunner, but Ambrose deemed it insufficiently immediate for radio. They needed something 'catchy'. Hollis wasn't impressed. 'He wanted to push other people, but he wouldn't be pushed,' says Woolliscroft. 'He got really angry about that. "Single? I'm not doing a single."'

In a moment of frustration, Woolliscroft recalls that Hollis confronted the label executive, asking what exactly they meant by 'catchy'? They suggested, almost certainly as a joke, something 'happy, snappy, like that Bran Flakes advert' – leading to an awkward silence.

For those unfamiliar with mid-'80s pop culture in the UK, Kellogg's Bran Flakes campaign was a popular series of TV adverts for a cereal, tagged on an insistently catchy tune: 'They're tasty, tasty, very, very tasty / They're very tasty!'

Back at the office, a concerned Ambrose contacted David Munns at EMI and a crisis meeting was hastily arranged at a nearby pub. Talk Talk's manager, Keith Aspden, could see the label's point. Rather than dismiss the suggestion of writing a single to order – Friese-Greene concedes his initial instinct was, 'Fuck 'em!'[7] – he and Hollis accepted the challenge as a kind of artistic experiment. Could they come up with a 'catchy' single without selling themselves out?

They quickly created a circulating drum loop on the Fairlight and Hollis began playing a simple but effective repetitive piano riff over it, his interpretation of the Bran Flakes motif with a little 'Green Onions' thrown in for balance. The savant simplicity of the piano figure was, metaphorically, beaten out of him in response to what he felt was record company venality. A two-bar section was sampled and looped, and 'Life's What You Make It' was born.

For all that Hollis would often speak of the inspirational qualities of everyone from John Cage to John Lee Hooker, he was not averse to taking his cues from more prosaic parts of culture. Later, while working on the final stages of *The Colour of Spring* at Videosonics, everything would grind to a halt when he insisted on stopping work to go upstairs to watch *EastEnders*. 'We were breaking all this ground, we knew what we were doing was really interesting, commercial at the same time as being daring – and then everything stopped because *EastEnders* was on!' says Dennis Weinreich. 'Mark would go and everybody would follow. It was odd but also endearing. He wasn't difficult, but he would be single-minded. There would be something he would want and he would be quite myopic about it. "Oh, it's *EastEnders*. I gotta go." He was a complex character.'

'Life's What You Make It' had other influences. Friese-Greene revealed that the approach to the relentless Fairlight-driven rhythm track, as well as the challenge of writing a song on one chord, was partly inspired by Kate Bush's 'Running Up That Hill'. Bush's landmark single was released on 5 August 1985 and it is entirely feasible that, as fellow EMI artists and avowed fans of Bush, Hollis and Friese-Greene would have heard the single well in advance of its release.

In common with another Kate Bush song, 'Hounds of Love', as well as Prince's recent single, 'When Doves Cry', there is no bass on 'Life's What You Make It'. The piano does all the heavy lifting at the bottom end. It's a terrific pop song, the beauty of one great idea perfected and locked in. The blocky rhythm beneath the piano is both funky and contemporary. Immediacy, it transpired, rather suited them.

According to Hollis, the lyrics, or at least the sentiment, were inspired by Blanche DuBois in Tennessee Williams' *A Streetcar Named Desire*, the faded heroine living in the past, clinging onto the glory days. Yesterday's favourite. Don't backdate it. Perhaps. Hollis often claimed dramatic or literary inspiration, yet the results often seem to struggle to convey a sense of the source beyond a generic vagueness.

David Rhodes, one of Peter Gabriel's key collaborators, who had recently played live with Talk Talk at a summer festival in France, was asked to come to Roundhouse Studios in Chalk Farm to add what became a memorable guitar part to 'Life's What You Make It'. His spiralling notes punctuate the title phrase, effectively serving as a second hook. 'They played me the track and it was pretty much there,' says Rhodes. 'It just needed some moments. I remember Mark saying he wanted it to sound "pox", which was his favourite [expression] – as though it were on the edge of just breaking.'

'Pox rock': the logical successor to punk. For all the riches and time at their disposal, Hollis craved sounds that surprised him, which often meant one that wasn't sonically perfect or even conventionally 'good'. For now, this notion remained a work in progress, something to be explored further on *Spirit of Eden* and *Laughing Stock*. Rhodes set up his pedal board, plugged in, switched on and started to play around. 'I was trying some things and Mark turned to me and he said, "Can you play like Acker Bilk?"'

One wonders whether that was a helpful instruction.

'It was, in a way, because you start thinking about a bloke in a bowler hat and a stripy shirt and you are away from where you are, I suppose. He did that a lot [with musicians], trying to play with their idea of themselves in the studio. Mark was always challenging people like that and he would do it in different ways.'

'He was just pushing all the time,' says Peter Woolliscroft. 'If you give somebody a ridiculous request, they either say, "Piss off!" or "That's interesting, I'll try this." He probably didn't want it to sound like Acker Bilk. He just wanted somebody to do something different. The whole idea was it had to be different.'

'It was fun, I really enjoyed it and it worked,' says Rhodes. 'It was always a pleasure to be in the room with them but challenging. And, for my trouble, I was paid 120 quid.' Rhodes would return to play guitar on 'Living in Another World' and 'Give it Up'.

Meanwhile, 'Life's What You Make It' continued its evolution almost to the very end of the album sessions. Dennis Weinreich says it was largely recorded from scratch again at Videosonics. Stuart

Stawman, at the time the chief engineer at Wessex, recalls being asked to help out as tape-op on what he was told was the final day of recording for *The Colour of Spring*, in late 1985. 'They were (re)recording the piano for "Life's What You Make It" and [trying to] lock in the groove of the Bösendorfer grand piano, played by Hollis, against the drum track,' says Stawman. 'Once that was done, he wandered off into the studio to play the solo. He played it once, said something like "Yeah, that'll do" and came back into the control room. It is a beautifully simple, even child-like solo but, with the exception of a saxophone solo I'd once recorded with Mel Collins, it was the only time I saw anyone record anything, let alone a solo, in a single take.'

Stawman later worked again with the band on *Spirit of Eden*. He laughs. 'This was not something I would ever see Talk Talk do again!'

·

For the first and only time in the decade span of their working relationship, Mark Hollis sent James Marsh, the artist responsible for all Talk Talk's album and single covers, all the song titles and lyrics in advance of him coming up with the design concept for *The Colour of Spring*. 'I think it was going to be called *Chameleon Day* originally,' says Marsh. 'It was all about spring and change.'

Talk Talk music is seasonal (it is also tidal). Spring is a perennial point of reference, in both sound and words. *The Colour of Spring* is, to borrow from a song which the band had yet to write, the 'April song', the 'glistening foal' of Talk Talk albums. It was born facing forwards, gazing towards spiritual rebirth and seasonal regeneration. Easter is coming.

Nowhere is this more apparent than on 'April 5th'. 'When you first hear that track, you think it is about a woman, or a girlfriend or partner, but it's obviously about spring itself,' says Marsh. 'It's another ambiguous thing.' Emerging from a steamy concoction of hisses, squeaks and sighs, this fragile ballad contains the album's title phrase. Titled for the birthday of Hollis's wife, Flick, it personifies the newly arriving Spring as a woman filled with promise, landing 'fresh upon the ground'.

Singing towards the bottom of his register, Hollis bids farewell to winter and hymns the changing seasons as 'a promise that's nature's gift' – one promise, at least, that won't be broken. The song is anchored by a lovely but ominous piano figure, around which the music hangs. The gently decaying outro is a tapestry of glistening piano, tenderly probing saxophone, acoustic guitar and Sunday-best organ. The sheer loveliness of it all inspires Hollis to trip over himself in the kind of metaphysical trance – 'Let me breathe you' – that recalls Pharoah Sanders' cosmic multiphonic breath rippling through time and space or, in intent if not in voice, Van Morrison at his most transported. He becomes at one with the saxophone, yet still, there is something held back. Hollis is aching to become unmoored, rather than entirely feeling it. He is seeking transcendence, you suspect, rather than experiencing its full effect.

And what about Paul Webb's hesitant little bass pulse right at the end – a love-pumped heartbeat in hushed conversation with the rising sap, a living bloom communing with the elements around it.

'April 5th' is a murmuring come-hither to the muse, and here she is working overtime.

ii

And breathe.

The stylus circles the run-out groove at the end of the first side of *The Colour of Spring*. Let's lift it, let it rest a while.

Who are these people?

Where have they been?

During the making of Talk Talk's third album, Mark Hollis was thirty years old.

What took him so long?

He was born in Tottenham, north London, on 4 January 1955, between brother Ed, who was three years older, and brother Paul, seven years younger. When he was still at primary school, his family moved thirty miles east of London, relocating to Rayleigh in Essex, an unremarkable, medium-sized town on the northern fringes of Southend-on-Sea. They were a peripatetic family and would move house many times again within the area. Hollis nevertheless recalled his upbringing, in the rare occasions he discussed it, as stable and loving, and his parents as supportive of him pursuing his creative interests.

He dropped out of sixth-form college before sitting his A-Levels, but later completed them as a part-time student. He dropped out of the University of Sussex in the first year of studying for a degree in child psychology. 'It was really boring,' he said.[1] One boon of university life was meeting his future wife, Felicity Costello, known to all as Flick. They were married in 1985 and remained so until Hollis's death in 2019.

So far, so standard; few great musicians last the distance to graduation. By then, Hollis was twenty-one and, like so many of his peers, found punk to be a galvanising force for someone with a creative mind, a deep love and knowledge of music and an already keenly developed distaste for working mundane jobs. All he was waiting for was permission. Punk granted it. 'Finally, music belonged to everyone,' he said, proving perception is always far more important than reality.[2] Skiffle, Bert Weedon's *Play in a Day*, more than one folk revival, Beat music and garage rock were just some of the innovations in the recent lineage of popular music which encouraged a democratic DIY ethos, and while the industry's gatekeepers did not magically disappear in 1976, the psychological impact of punk was nonetheless an exciting catalyst for those of Hollis's generation.

'Punk said, "If you think you can play, you can play",' he said some twenty years later.[3] Though the music he made changed drastically, there would always be, buried deep within it, an adherence to the punk mentality. Its enduring legacy was a commitment to 'chance, and randomness and spirit' being the most important things, not technique.[4]

'The thing about punk rock, the idea behind it which for Mark gave it legitimacy, was that the artists didn't themselves need to be technically adept,' says Laurence Pendrous, Hollis's friend and the music master at his children's school. 'Their desire to be there making music was their [sole] qualification. For someone who brought out the work that Mark did, you wouldn't think that would be their philosophy, [but] I think it really gets to the core of what he wanted to talk about, that a punk rock philosophy was one of the most valid. And yet, in his own writing, he achieved a level of perfection musically which was actually far greater.'

Hollis already had his own punk hero in the shape of his older brother. A catalytic figure in his early life and career, Ed fulfilled the role of mentor, spirit guide, musical taproot and highly connected contact. Almost every tributary in Hollis's early musical development winds back to him as the source.

Ed Hollis was a man-about-town with many fingers in many pies, savoury and otherwise, around the grassroots music scenes in both London and Essex. The music journalist Tony Parsons once described him as a 'megalomaniac Canvey Island Kim Fowley'.[5] Who could resist? He was a well-known figure on the Southend pub-rock scene, as part of Dr Feelgood's entourage and manager of Eddie & the Hot Rods. In addition, he co-produced their records and contributed lyrics to several songs, including their biggest hit, 'Do Anything You Wanna Do'. Ed Hollis knew everyone, and everyone knew him, and despite Parsons' put-down, most people liked him. He was eccentric, wildly excessive, motor-mouthed and unreliable, but he was also regarded as kind, energetic, enthusiastic, friendly and definitely in it for the music rather than the money.

There was more to him than pub rock and punk. He was renowned for his extensive record collection. On the Southend and Canvey scene, Ed was dubbed 'one thousand Eddie', on account of the vast mass of vinyl which filled half the caravan in which he lived and which grew to some 10,000 albums. These reflected extremely catholic tastes. Sun Ra gambolled happily alongside the Osmonds. Kraftwerk made way for the MC5. He was the only person anyone knew who possessed Charles Manson's album. He owned 150 LPs of obscure live jazz recordings from the New York loft scene. His compilation tapes for friends became legendary: mixes of eight different versions of Culture's 'Two Sevens Clash', Abdullah Ibrahim, Stones bootlegs…

His younger brother soaked it up and would later earn a similarly well-deserved reputation for his eclecticism, as well as for forming his tastes with a breezy disregard for trends or the critical consensus. '[Mark was] definitely someone who didn't run with fashion,' Paul Webb later recalled. 'Me and Lee had come from Southend … lots of mods, lots of electronic music, lots of soul boys, but it was all fashion-orientated. But the first time I met him, he was playing Otis Redding, he was playing Delius. His idea of electronic music was the soundtrack to *A Clockwork Orange*. He just came from a different place and I think always that's a good engine for art.'[6]

'Mark loved many different kinds of music,' says Simon Brenner, Talk Talk's original keyboard player. 'We would listen to King Crimson and Miles Davis and big choral works like "Carmina Burana" by Carl Orff.'

From an early age, Hollis displayed a fascination – perhaps even an obsession – with the *record* rather than the *song*. He started playing guitar on the cusp of becoming a teenager and even then, learning the rudiments of the recordings he loved on a cheap guitar, he was frustrated that his efforts sounded nothing like the studio versions. Paul Webb recalls that when they listened to music together, or rather when Hollis played him things, he would laser in on particular parts. 'With Burning Spear, it was all about the lazy vocal phrasings. With *In the Court of the Crimson King*, it was all about the heaviness of the mellotrons. With Marvin Gaye, he focused in on the bass playing.'[7]

'Mark had rather large ears which I was jealous of,' says the American composer, producer and musician (and Hollis's later-life friend) Brian Reitzell, with great affection. 'I knew he could hear better than I could!'

A man with such tastes could have spun off in so many directions – as he did, in time. But for now: punk. By 1977, Hollis had started writing several of the songs which would eventually appear on the first two Talk Talk records. He had also started a band, the Reaction, a Jam-lite outfit which he led on vocals and guitar.

Here again, Ed was a conduit. In 1976, Island Records, the pioneering label run by Chris Blackwell which had made its reputation originally releasing reggae and folk-orientated records, remained philosophically and creatively more closely aligned to marijuana than amphetamine. Speedy Ed was invited to run an ill-fated and short-lived punk subsidiary, with the intention that, through his knowledge and contacts, he would offer the label a direct line to the younger, noisier artists coming through in the slipstream of the Damned, the Clash and the Sex Pistols. He called it Speedball, a name, sadly, with an all-too-literal aptness.

Hollis often hung out with his brother around the Island offices and studios in the late '70s. He met a lot of people, watched, learned and gained a feel for the lay of the land within the music industry. Indeed, it was Ed's connections that kickstarted his music career.

●

'Talk Talk' was a song long before it was ever a band. The opening track on their patchy 1982 debut, *The Party's Over*, and released as their second single, it dated back to the early days of the Reaction. Ed was credited as its co-writer and also as its producer when the Reaction recorded it at Island Studios, although a young Steve Lillywhite did much of the technical heavy lifting. Originally titled, rather wonderfully, 'Talk Talk Talk Talk', it sounds today like a generic, off-the-shelf, stop-start punk 45, but the bones of the song proved sufficiently sturdy to survive the transition into a shiny new decade.

The title and words of Hollis's first significant composition established a theme. Both can be viewed as a repudiation of the efficacy of language. Communication, its impossibilities and its obfuscations, became one of Hollis's enduring preoccupations. Did he ever sound happier than when burbling at the end of 'April 5th', contentedly lost in a wordless reverie? On 'Living in Another World', 'Speech gets harder / There's no sense in writing.' 'Should have said so much / Makes it harder,' he sings on 'Watershed'. Communication as complication and confusion; knowledge as distraction. Hollis struggled with articulacy as a collaborative artist, and even as a lyricist, you get the sense of a man wrestling with meaning – and often losing. It began early on.

'Talk Talk Talk Talk' was licensed for inclusion on Beggars Banquet's 'sound of '77' punk compilation. *Streets*, which featured John Cooper Clarke, the Adverts, and Slaughter & the Dogs among its seventeen mostly obscure acts. Shortly after, largely through Ed's influence, the Reaction signed a six-album recording contract with Island, although there is little evidence to suggest they merited such a momentous deal. For a spell, the game was afoot: promotional photos, a tour, reviews. In the end, the only fruits from the relationship was the band's sole single, 'I Can't Resist', released in August 1978. Melodic and punchy, with decent vocal harmonies and ringing guitars, 'I Can't Resist' was heavily indebted to the Who. Somewhere in the Island vaults there are masters of songs recorded for the Reaction's debut album, but it was not to be. Ed Hollis's already excessive hard drug use and chaotic working practices put an end to Speedball before it had barely began. The band were dropped by Island and Hollis had to regroup.

The Reaction ended in late 1979. Hollis recorded a number of demos paid for by CBS which included 'Mirror Man', 'Have You Heard the News?', 'Renée', 'Candy', 'Cara Lynn' and 'I Keep on Telling You'. Some of these songs fell by the wayside. One was the lovely 'Crying in the Rain', which on the demo has a sense of space and a gentle grace closer to the landscape of *Laughing Stock* than anything else Hollis did for several years subsequently. Many others ended up being recorded by Talk Talk.

CBS didn't pursue their interest, but in late 1980, Hollis was offered a deal with Island Publishing. Ed once again played his part, physically placing his brother's demo tape in the hands of a junior at the Island offices. It made its way to Keith Aspden, creative director of Island Music Publishing, whose job it was to find and develop promising artists. Hollis was signed as a solo songwriter and paid £2,000 a year.

In order to record his songs for Island, a group of simpatico musicians was required. One candidate was Hollis's fellow north Londoner, Simon Brenner, a piano and keyboard player with a classical background who was working in a record shop near Hampstead Heath. The owner, Robert Greenfield, was a guitar player with a band called Cayenne and acted as an informal fixer for the local musicians who came in to buy records. One of them mentioned that he knew of someone locally who was looking for a partner to write and perhaps perform with.

'I thought it worth a go and rang Mark,' says Brenner. They met at the flat in nearby Muswell Hill where Hollis now lived with Flick. 'We really got on and shared a love of classic songwriting, anything from Sinatra to Prince,' says Brenner. 'He had this amazing voice which I instantly thought had extraordinary potential and was the main reason for my working with him.'

Not untypically for an aspiring musician scoping out their place in the landscape, looking for any breach in the industry's defences, Hollis's earliest manoeuvres were somewhat scattershot. There are moments that feel entirely incongruous. He and Brenner would sometimes write together in one of Island's tiny piano rooms. One of the A&R staff instrumental in bringing Hollis to the publishing side of the label was Clive Black, the teenage son of the renowned lyricist Don Black, who wrote the words to such staples as 'Born Free', 'To Sir, With Love' and countless others. Clive told his father that Hollis and Brenner were looking for lyrics to two songs. An invitation was extended. Thus, we must picture Hollis in a room in a plush Knightsbridge flat, festooned with gold discs and Oscars glistening atop the piano, composing with the man who wrote 'Diamonds are Forever'. The songs that Black helped complete were called 'She's Not You' and 'And Then I Think of You'. Brenner and Hollis recorded them as demos, with just voice and grand piano. 'At that point, we were thinking more Burt Bacharach than Duran Duran,' says Brenner.

Yet certain traits and clues to Hollis's artistic temperament were already in evidence. Brenner recalls in those early days in that flat in Muswell Hill, heavily stoned, 'we would sit on his sofa and listen to tracks and study the details. He and I both loved little touches that you don't usually hear at first, like a small bell or a strange trumpet noise – unusual stuff that was only played perhaps once or twice on the track.'

One might say that Hollis eventually made entire records following this philosophy, as his desire to write a 'classic song' diminished and his determination to string together records filled only with unique and unrepeatable 'unusual stuff' took hold. In some ways, it would always be about the record, not the song.

•

To help Hollis demo his material, he and Brenner were joined by Paul Webb and Lee Harris, two teenage friends from Southend. Despite their youth, they were adept musicians and already had experience playing in a local ska band called Eskalator. 'We were fuckin' tight,' Harris later recalled. 'We had been playing music together since we were fifteen. We were the band glue.'[8] Ed Hollis had scoped them out via his Essex connections.

The line-up was Hollis on vocals, Webb on bass, Harris on drums and Brenner on Wurlitzer piano and Roland Organ/String Machine RS09, later augmented with a very simple Moog-type synthesiser. They had no name and no guitar. In an early interview, Hollis insisted the lack of the latter was because 'the whole idea is to have a small jazz line-up'.[9] The first rehearsal took place in a school hall in Canvey; Webb and Harris's fathers dropped them off. In the coming weeks and months, the two new recruits would travel up to London from Southend on the train and stay at Hollis's flat. Brenner would pick them all up each morning in his orange Mini and drive to rehearsals. 'They liked to play silly games,' he recalls. 'I would drive around a roundabout ten times with the windows open and we'd all scream. It was great for the first ten times…'

Quite quickly, they became a proper band rather than a singer-songwriter plus hired hands. Keith Aspden finagled the fledgling group time in the cavernous rehearsal rooms beneath Island's offices in Chiswick, where they rehearsed solidly for months. Usually, the presence of the previous occupants would still be pungently evident: fetid sweat and smoke lingering in the air, the bins full of old joint roaches. Already, there was a thirst in Hollis to create an atmosphere of abandon or disturbance in which the musicians could lose themselves and simply surf on the sounds they were making. 'Sometimes we would turn the lights off so it was pitch-black and all you could see were the red lights on the amps and keyboards,' says Brenner. 'Things got pretty wild and experimental at times in there and it is with some regret that I have no record of what it sounded like. We thought it was amazing and I think it probably was! I was the only instrumentation apart from bass and drums. It was just a joyous outpouring.'

Hollis was already twenty-five and the dynamic that would always define Talk Talk as a unit was quickly established. He was the eldest, the most experienced and, although Aspden signed the other three band members to the same Island publishing deal in the summer of 1981, the entire project was really his baby. Brenner was in his early twenties, the classically trained 'sensible one'. Harris and Webb were barely nineteen and stamped with the unruly enthusiasm of youth. They partied all night while Hollis went home to Flick. They were also more in touch with current trends and alternative music, such as Joy Division and Bauhaus, which Harris would listen to incessantly.

Having honed their sound, the search for a record deal began. In order to make a strong demo to shop around, at Island they recorded three tracks with the former Traffic and Rolling Stones producer Jimmy Miller. Miller was Hollis's dream choice, a chance-in-a-million punt which miraculously came off. Though he was still working, having recently produced Motörhead, it was the music that Miller had produced in the late '60s and early '70s with the Stones and, perhaps most significantly, Traffic, which prompted Hollis to seek him out. Traffic's *Mr Fantasy*, released in 1967, was a hallmark record for him, a kind of rock 'n' roll Rosetta Stone.

Indeed, his connection to the band was one of the key reasons Phill Brown was later hired to work on *Spirit of Eden*. Starting out in the business at the age of sixteen, Brown had been an engineer at Olympic Studios and had assisted Miller on, among other landmark records, *Mr Fantasy*. 'Mark was a massive fan of Traffic and Jimmy Miller,' he says. 'That was partly why I got the job. Pretty much the only [reference to other albums] he made when we were doing *Spirit of Eden* was, "If you can remember any of the mic'ing techniques or mics that you might have used back then, feel free to bring it to the table."'

The Miller-produced recordings of 'Talk Talk', 'Candy' and 'Mirror Man' offer a minor alternative subplot to the synthetic early years of Talk Talk. They were 'raw and had spirit and energy,' says Brenner. 'It was a real band, playing real music without frills and probably for me the musical high point. They had a Hammond B3 organ in the studio and a lovely grand piano and it was fabulous.' On the downside, Miller was another heavy drug user and, in Brenner's words, 'completely bonkers'. He would not become Talk Talk's producer when the time came for them to make their debut album. In truth, though the demos are more spirited than the eventual LP versions, they don't quite live up to the game-changing billing Brenner gives them.

Given their close relationship with Keith Aspden, and the fact that the band were already working for Island's publishing arm, the label seemed an obvious choice to sign them. However, Chris Blackwell wasn't interested. He was further put off by the group's association with Ed Hollis, who acted as their de facto manager in the early days.

'Ed was around a lot,' recalls Simon Brenner. 'We used to go on drives around Canvey and they would point out the houses where Eddie and the Hot Rods lived or the bass player for Dr Feelgood. It felt like a very odd place, kind of stuck in the 1950s. I really liked Ed and he liked me. He was quite bonkers at times, but in a very nice way. He had a wild enthusiasm about him which was very infectious.' However, his drug use was increasingly out of control, while his own attempts to produce a demo session for the band had been little short of disastrous. He was too far gone to be a manager or producer and, in the end, Hollis had to distance himself, at least professionally, from his older brother.

Island Records' disinterest in signing the band was a factor in Aspden deciding to leave his job as creative director at Island Music Publishing in order to manage them, which in the circumstances constituted an enormous leap of faith. He proved adept at creating a buzz around the band, but few labels were biting. In the end, it came down to London Records and EMI. The latter offered more and won. Talk Talk signed to EMI in late November 1981. By now they had a name, having briefly flirted with calling themselves 300 Cubs. A support tour with Duran Duran swiftly followed at the end of that year.

The connection to the darlings of New Romanticism would cling like poison ivy. Several years later, Talk Talk were still being described, rather amusingly, as 'a drinking man's Duran Duran'.[10] It was, then, perhaps an unwise choice to ask Duran Duran's engineer,

Colin Thurston, to produce their debut album, recorded at Red Bus in London and in a residential studio in the Oxfordshire countryside, where they slowly drove each other up the wall. Brenner in particular was subject to Hollis's inarticulate but very obvious disdain, as the singer stabbed a single finger repeatedly on the keyboard and insisted Brenner play it 'like this', without ever being able to explain what 'this' was.

There isn't much on *The Party's Over* to suggest that Hollis was a future paragon of pioneering post-rock expansiveness. For all his later repudiation of synthesisers and synthetic instruments, he gravitated fairly speedily towards the prevailing commercial sounds: fretless bass, electronic drums, drum machines and synthesisers. He proved adept at grabbing the tools of greatest convenience; he was happy to use roughed-up guitars for his punk band and he also tried writing standards on a grand piano with Don Black. Now that post-punk was giving way to the New Romantics and electronic music, he saw the sleeker vehicle of the synthesiser as a means of packing his more grandiose musical ideas into a smaller – and cheaper – package. There was an expedient, pragmatic quality to the way the band sounded – and also to how they presented themselves. The branding was off-centre, as well. An infamous photoshoot and subsequent TV appearances where they dressed entirely in white came back to haunt them.

Hollis's reasoning – and to an extent it has become the orthodox critical take – is that he *had to do this* in order for the band to gain the profile and the means to be able to pursue their true aims. 'Mark believed in the songs, it was just [finding a way] to get them out there,' says Nigel Reeve of EMI. 'The band had to go through the white-shirt-and-trousers looks, touring with Duran, getting sales in

Europe, to get the money to be able to pursue artistic freedom. It became a natural progression.'

It's not a criticism – many young bands are hungry for their big break and will take it whichever way it comes – but this perhaps lets Hollis off the hook. Plenty of artists, never mind ones signed to a major label, follow their hearts from the get-go, regardless of the financial struggles. Plenty of groups, then and now, used horns, strings and Hammond organs. If that was how you wanted your music to sound, you brought in the players to do so, whatever the cost, literal or otherwise.

Hollis followed a different path, perhaps as a means of exerting greater control over the music and the musicians. I get the sense he knew it was a gamble, one that creatively didn't pay off. The feeling among the band was that their debut album conveyed little of the depth or texture evident in the rehearsal room or at their early gigs, which had an energy and freshness that stirred audiences. 'In truth, it wasn't a great success,' says Brenner of the album. 'As is often the case, great engineers don't necessarily make for great producers. None of us had experience of recording at this level and with so much at stake. Although everything was correctly recorded and sounded pristine, it had very little depth and failed to convey what we had done in the rehearsal room.'

Starting with the first single, 'Mirror Man', and following through to the album, most of the reviews were poor or dismissive. The songwriting occasionally received a gentle pat on the head, but Hollis's voice proved divisive, while nobody *at all* seemed to like the way the record sounded. For the next few months, tracks were constantly being remixed, the music biz equivalent of desperately trying to resuscitate a body on the operating table that's already clinically dead.

In commercial terms, at least, *The Party's Over* did the job, reaching a respectable 23 in the British album charts. The single release of 'Today' was a bigger success, climbing to 14, at which point 'Talk Talk' – which had already been released and failed to crack the Top 40 – was swiftly remixed and reissued on its heels, this time entering the Top 30. In the States, the song reached the Billboard Hot 100.

Hollis and Talk Talk enjoyed their landmark, rite-of-passage, Big Pop Moments almost immediately, whether hearing 'Mirror Man' on the radio for the first time, courtesy of the estimable David 'Kid' Jensen, or supporting Elvis Costello on his Imperial Bedroom tour of the US, where they sat at the front of the bus as it took them from the airport into Manhattan and made them feel as though they were living in a movie. They even had their very own 'Beatles-at-the-George-V' moment in July 1982, bouncing on the beds and screaming with joy in a hotel in Los Angeles as news came through that 'Today' had hit the charts in the UK. A few hours later, they had been bundled onto a plane and packed off back home to appear on *Top of the Pops*.

These were most musicians' childhood fantasies. If any of that had ever motivated Hollis, by 1985 it did no longer. 'He was ambitious,' says Ian Curnow. 'Not for success or glory, but simply for achievement.'

Hollis's creative journey can sometimes appear almost unfathomable, but Simon Brenner sees a connection between the frustrated synthpopper and the later uncompromising artist. 'Sometimes when we were playing around in the beginning, you had a sense of what was to come. He would spend hours and hours bashing out the same chords on the piano over and over again. His evolution surprises me in its sophistication, but not in its almost obsessive detail.'

The extent to which Hollis's aims, his ambitions, were in plain sight from the very start is striking. In the first-ever major Talk Talk interview, which appeared in *New Musical Express* in January 1982, he is, somewhat ludicrously, already talking about the band being more like a jazz quartet than a rock or pop group. Meanwhile, the spartan creative ethos, the commitment to a painstaking process of elimination, is also in place.

'I heard Anthony Burgess talking about his writing recently and he was saying he can spend six hours writing thousands of words and then throw almost all of them away,' he said. 'It's the same with songwriting. It's worth it for the stuff you're left with at the end. The last thing in the world I would want is to be thought of as a disposable group. I want to write stuff that you'll still be able to listen to in ten years' time [and] still think of as a good song then.'[11]

By the time Hollis sat down with *ZigZag*, on the occasion of the album release, he had hit full steam: 'My basic idea was to have the same line-up as someone like [John] Coltrane … What I like about Shostakovich and music like that is that total oppressiveness in the force of it and then, at other moments, that pure sort of tranquillity. It's between those two extremes.'[12]

Yes, the 1980s were different times, with peppy pop stars routinely throwing the names of Gramsci and Barthes into *Smash Hits* interviews like unpinned grenades, but it still feels like a painful stretch from Hollis's high-falutin' reference points to the dreamy and rather generic wine-bar pop of 'Today'. And yet … how brilliantly and precisely that last quote describes the albums Talk Talk would make at the other end of their trajectory. The notion of those two

Shostakovichian extremes – the oppressive force meeting the equally devastating power of pure tranquillity – held true. Think of the yin and yang of 'Desire', recorded only a few years later.

Hollis already knew exactly what he wanted; it was just that, in the beginning, the claims he made for his music were almost laughably at odds with the wider perception of Talk Talk as the latest bunch of gloomy synth-pop chancers. 'I knew that we both thought about writing something more important and more long lasting than just any old pop song, and he would tell journalists this during our first album,' says Brenner. 'It never seemed to ring true to what we were actually producing at that time, though.' It led to a confusion between Talk Talk and the music press which never quite cleared – and a mutual suspicion. His earnestness was at odds with the tone of the times. At best, it was often deliberately misconstrued for comic effect; at worst, ridiculed. Hollis was a deadly serious artist pegged as a pop tart with ideas above his station.

It's little wonder that, in these conversations and many more like them over the next few years, he presented as a man alternately frustrated, depressed, surprised, superior and dismissive, someone rankled by the fact that no one, or hardly anyone, is hearing his true artistic vision come through in the music he is making. Also in 1982, talking to *Record Mirror*, he said: 'Tragedy's what I feel most at home with … It's just the conflict between trying to attain something more than you are, which is a good thing, and the parody of actually doing it.'[13] He is talking a game that he is not yet able to play, exasperated – as he so often would be – at the space between reality and perception.

Yet his vision came good. His words in these early promotional skirmishes made perfect sense, but only much later.

Simon Brenner left Talk Talk in 1983. In truth, his face didn't fit. He was a nice middle-class north London boy mixing it up with three Essex lads who regarded calling everyone a cunt the zenith of comedic genius. Brenner was the first major victim of Hollis's inability to express what he wanted and an early example of a rather unbecoming tendency to direct his frustrations towards a human target. He would not be the last. 'I was definitely aware toward the end that he was looking for something more, but he wasn't sure what that was and I couldn't provide him with it,' he says. 'I think I became the focal point of his frustration.'

Talk Talk henceforth continued as a trio – although, of course, it was never that simple.

•

Early on, much of the excitement and untrammelled experimentation in the band seemed to get mislaid between the rehearsal room and the studio. How to get that sense of thrill and spontaneity onto a record? The answer, perhaps, lay in an already evident need for collaboration.

There is a point worth making and remembering throughout: *Talk Talk was not Mark Hollis and Mark Hollis was not Talk Talk.* There can be a tendency to render the two synonymous, but while it is fair to say that it was Hollis's overall vision for the music which shaped these records, and his voice and his words which stamped a unique identity upon them, the music was a hugely collaborative endeavour in every aspect: writing, playing, recording, producing. I wouldn't want to hear Talk Talk without the countless mesmerising contributions made by Lee Harris, whose playing on these records includes some of the greatest drums parts I have ever heard.

Paul Webb is so important to the melodic hooks and the texture; he fills in the bottom end while Hollis floats on top. Both Harris and Webb were for so long essential to the group's overall sound. And that is before we even begin to measure the impact of the many dozens of musicians, from hardened industry pros to rank amateurs, who added unique and heartfelt parts, as well as something of themselves, to the records.

In terms of composition, as well as performance, the extent to which Hollis required a collaborator can't be overstated. 'He *needed* other people,' said Keith Aspden. 'But he didn't *want* other people.'[14] This slightly awkward dance was in evidence as early as *The Party's Over*, which features one song written by Paul Webb, one by Hollis and his brother Ed, three composed by Hollis alone and four credited to the entire band. 'Someone would start playing some chords or a few notes and the others would jam with it,' says Brenner. 'Mark would start singing melodies and phrases to the music pretty early on and it just grew from there. Although it was clear that Mark was the lead, the writing of the music was very much a collaborative effort. The songs grew organically and then we would play them over and over again to perfect them to the stage where they seemed complete and ready to gig with. This period was the best time of all. Mark would write nearly all of the lyrics after the song was set, although some of the choruses and phrases came from the rest of us. He would spend hours writing words and then bring them in.'

Hollis was never what you would call prolific. Many songs on the first record, as well as the second, had been kicking around for several years before they were definitively recorded. Arguably, he was never quite so productive again. When it came to writing for the second Talk Talk album, *It's My Life*, Brenner was gone and Hollis was already struggling to come up with material by himself. Thereafter, every track on the final three Talk Talk albums was co-written by Hollis and Tim Friese-Greene. After Friese-Greene departed the scene, seven of the eight tracks on Hollis's solo record were co-writes, using three different collaborators. The only song released after 1984 solely credited to Hollis is the beautiful and abstract 'Inside Looking Out', released in 1998.

Hollis clearly needed someone to bounce off; to surprise him, challenge him, start the engine, back him up. An accomplice. In this sense, his relationship with Friese-Greene is especially key. It is comparable to the one enjoyed by David Bowie and his long-term producer Tony Visconti, had Visconti also co-written all the songs; or Bowie and Brian Eno, had Eno, not Visconti, also produced those three 'Berlin' records.

In short, let there be no doubt that Tim Friese-Greene is absolutely essential to every aspect of the final three Talk Talk records.

interlude 1

(The 'Mark & Tim Show')

There is something of the enigma about Tim Friese-Greene: strikingly tall; comfortably middle-class; a little reserved; technically skilled; a gifted musician, particularly adept on the piano and organ; and an original and perhaps slightly eccentric thinker. 'I have nothing but the highest regard for Tim,' says Dennis Weinreich, who worked with Friese-Greene many times, before and during Talk Talk. 'He is phenomenally creative. He has an interesting perspective, both on life generally and in musical terms. His ideas really did come out of leftfield and I think that is the reason that Tim and Mark got along very well, because Mark thrived on that leftfield input.'

He has some impressive and artistic antecedents: his grandfather, Claude Friese-Greene, was a British filmmaker working in the 1920s and '30s, while his great-grandfather, William Friese-Greene, was an inventor and photographer who played an innovative role in the development of moving pictures.

He had started out as tape operator at Wessex Studios in the mid-'70s and relatively quickly worked his way up to engineer; rather wonderfully, one of his earliest credits in this role is on the Wombles' *Superwombling* album, released in 1975. It is no coincidence that every Talk Talk record Friese-Greene worked on used Wessex, a converted late-eighteenth-century hall attached to St Augustine's Church in Highbury New Park, north London. It had the emotional pull of home. When he began working with the group in Studio 1, Friese-Greene brought a touch-sense memory of the studio's Hammond organ and outstanding Bösendorfer grand piano. 'I used to play around on those quite a bit,' he recalled. 'I never used to take it at all seriously though … All the time I worked in the studio as a tape-op, an engineer and then a producer, I treated keyboard-playing as a hobby. I started playing on people's records quite by accident.'[1] His first recorded appearance as a musician was on a single by the punk band 999, produced by Martin Rushent, and there were several others.

As a producer, Friese-Greene started – and in some ways continued – as a jack of all trades, a technically gifted hired hand who could bring his objective skills to everyone from the Nolans to Stiff Little Fingers. He made a name for himself producing Tight Fit's 'The Lion Sleeps Tonight', which was a UK number one single for three weeks in March 1982. The band were a loose agglomeration of dancers and session singers, while the song was a more or less novelty version of a much-covered South African tune dating back to the 1930s and sometimes known as 'Wimoweh'. Friese-Greene not only produced the accompanying album, *Fantasy Island*, but also co-wrote one of the songs on it.

Commercially speaking, it was a purple patch. He also had hits with 'Cry Boy Cry' by Blue Zoo and Thomas Dolby's 'She Blinded Me With Science'. But it was not especially satisfying work. 'Tight Fit had no credibility at all,' he said in 2006. 'One of my big issues at that point was that I wasn't really getting the bands that I wanted to produce, and I didn't really see how Tight Fit being number one was really going to further my cause. It was more a thorn in my side than anything else. I just knew from that point onwards that being offered the stuff I wanted would prove even more difficult.'[2]

How did this fledgling career in eclectic, not especially soulful or highly invested-in record producing end up piquing the interest of Mark Hollis? Hollis had noticed that Friese-Greene had produced three chart singles that sounded nothing like each other and that, therefore, he did not come pre-loaded with a signature sound. 'I think that was quite important to him,' said Friese-Greene.[3] Even so, it was an interesting choice, one that in some ways debunks Hollis status as an artist disdainful of the pop charts.

As for what attracted the producer to Talk Talk, in a sense the connection was equally underwhelming. 'There was nothing remarkable about Talk Talk at that point,' he said, with some justification. 'I thought their first album *The Party's Over* was okay. I didn't particularly rate the songwriting at that time, but I thought that Mark sounded okay. I took it on because there was nothing else around that I wanted to do more at the time. And there was nothing I disliked more than not working at that stage.'[4]

So, a marriage of convenience. What shifted the dial was the beginning of a writing partnership that first provided material for *It's My Life*. When work began on the album in the spring of 1983, Hollis was struggling to come up with songs. Friese-Greene looked like he could provide a solution. 'We both clicked quite well at an early stage and [Mark] suggested that we try and write together. I would never have had the temerity to do so myself, because it is not a thing that a producer does, puts himself forward as a co-writer. It would have been pretty lairy.'[5]

They began writing together on the piano in the front room of Friese-Greene's house in Stanmore, on the north-western fringes of Greater London. They came up with the album's memorable title track, on which the verse, bridge, chorus and bassline are all memorable melodic hooks. It became a big song for the band, eventually. For Friese-Greene, who sometimes gave the appearance of being terminally underwhelmed, if not quite jaded, it was 'nothing to get excited about'.[6]

'It's My Life' was one of two co-writes, the other being 'Dum Dum Girl'. On the album, Hollis finally found a home for 'Renée', Talk Talk's first truly epic exercise in melancholy, integrating touches of Roxy Music's lush grandeur, the Cure's glowering angst, Simple Minds' dreamy elegance and Kate Bush's ECM experiments. Caught between bitterness and affection, Hollis relays the hometown tale of a girl he cares for being played by some local Lothario, but what he's really up to is encapsulating the pain of lost innocence and the ebbing away of youth.

The album was a step-up in terms of the variety of sounds, atmosphere and texture. The songs were better, mostly. The music thickened and became more stylised. Others played their parts, but in his roles as producer, co-writer, keyboardist, sound-shaper and de facto fourth member in the studio, Friese-Greene must take a lot of the credit.

The creative interplay between him and Hollis seemed innate, instinctive. Musically, they dovetailed well. In broad brush-stroke terms, Friese-Greene was the more accomplished musician. He could read music, he was comfortable using the terminology and he also understood the technical and harmonic aspects of recording inside out. Hollis was coming from a more instinctive, emotional perspective. 'At a certain point, technique is something which can be annoying,' he said in 1986. 'I write music with Friese-Greene, who understands music. I don't. What I do is love music. He understands it and loves it. We are working from a common love for certain things.'[7]

Hollis was being consciously faux-naïf here; he understood music, all right. But it neatly illustrates what perhaps each viewed as their core strengths.

'I think Mark relied on Tim hugely,' says David Rhodes. 'Tim is a very clever bloke, properly disciplined, he has knowledge of music theory and knowledge of sound and [musical] ability. Just a clever guy. They had a good chemistry between them. In the studio, Tim would suggest more specifically the harmony, whereas Mark would occasionally sing a little line, just a suggestion of what notes you might like.'

'They were very much on the same wavelength,' says Martin Ditcham, the English drummer and percussionist who played a significant role on all four of these records. 'Very much like brothers, if you like. Tim wasn't the employee to Mark being the employer. They contributed equally, I would say. It always seemed that Tim had a huge contribution and he plays many instruments. They were both master of the ship.'

Continuing the nautical metaphors, Peter Woolliscroft describes Friese-Greene as 'a good anchor. He knew what Mark meant and he would set it up. He wouldn't force anything. He would let Mark explore every idea and do what he wanted, and then at the end, Tim would say, "Oh, just let me do it. We've explored it, so I'll do the organ part." Then Mark would say, "Yeah, yeah, that's what I meant. Feedback. Fucking good that, innit! Yeah, well done." Or he would say, "That's shit. What are you doing? It's nothing like what I meant." They never fell out. It was a good partnership and they worked well together.'

On a personal level, they appeared friendly and interacted easily, if never quite as bosom friends; close but still with some professional remove. They would go to the pub and sometimes out to dinner together while working, but between albums, there was little contact. They were very different but with certain shared traits. Dennis Weinreich offers one perspective. 'I think one of the reasons they may have got along is they were both … not socially awkward, that's just not fair. I had a really great social relationship with Tim. He was fundamentally shy, but a big presence. Like a man who is six foot four slouched down trying to be small, because he doesn't want to be noticed. That was kind of how I felt about him. He deserved to be noticed, because he was talented and interesting and intelligent and fantastic.'

'I do find it hard to imagine them as "pals" outside of the studio,' says Stuart Stawman. 'But I can easily summon memories of both of them where – to me – their love for each other was apparent. I don't know if they were friends, I feel certain they loved each other … When I stop and think, I realise I have Tim as quite an affectionate guy in general, towards Mark and others, including myself. I don't know how else to put it, but you could feel his affection, not always but often enough to summon a fondness from me. I wouldn't say that of Mark – at least not in the studio – but that's not to criticise him. He was perhaps more ensconced in his creative act. But I do think their mutual love was apparent.'

By 1985, Hollis + Friese-Greene had become a very forceful equation, greater than the sum of its parts, driving Talk Talk through *The Colour of Spring* and beyond.

iii

Side two.

Nothing on *The Colour of Spring* hits quite as hard as 'Living in Another World'. The portion of the song close to the end where Hollis sings the title phrase repeatedly without any affect or adornment, as David Rhodes unleashes a volley of slashing electric guitar chords, is a rare moment in the Talk Talk catalogue of sheer rock dynamism.

By then, the song feels fit to combust. 'Living in Another World' starts already in fourth gear, as though we are entering the movie halfway through the car chase, the adrenalin already running hot. By the time the (second) key change kick-starts the chorus, the song is a mile high and rising. Some unholy force takes hold of it. It's almost frightening, the propulsion. Hollis is in characteristically racked form, singing so hard he seems fit to burst as he digs around his romantic and cosmic alienation.

It is a powerhouse vocal performance on an ingeniously constructed track. The song is built as a hairpin ascent, a Jenga puzzle, an 'Escher staircase'.[1] We climb with the music as the key keeps rising, the same simple, relentless two-chord pattern transposed in each of the three sections to an ever higher pitch, from Am/F to Bm/G to Fm/D flat. Hollis, either cleverly or intuitively, sings of finding a way 'through this maze'. It is a song where the sound is perfectly expressed in the words.

The track had its roots in an early unreleased demo called 'Cara Lynn', which features the original lyrics and melody of the opening two lines of 'Living in Another World'. Again, the thesis is the sheer impossibility of communication: 'Better parted … speech gets harder / There's no sense in writing.' And later, 'Truth gets harder / No sense in lying.' Hollis was a dedicated truth-teller, quite often to the point of social discomfort – for others, if not for himself. 'The degree to which he could be direct really did take out the social politenesses at times,' says Laurence Pendrous. 'I spent hours with Mark, we played golf, I had an enormous amount of contact with him and spent an enormous amount of time talking to him. He was never really difficult. The thing with Mark was that he was so honest. Just *ruthlessly* honest. He always told you what he thought. But, then, is that not the same personality that permeates every aspect of Mark's work, that is at the core of what he was as a musician?'

Hollis later said the lyric was inspired by Jean-Paul Sartre, which would suggest a connection between the line 'Did I see tenderness where you saw hell?' and Sartre's maxim that 'Hell is other people'. Certainly, existential dread leaks from every pore of the song – '*Help me!*' – but it's the unstoppable whirlwind-ing lifeforce that wins out. This is a tour de force ensemble production, from the crisp congas to Mark Feltham's bluesy harmonica huff, soon to become a Talk Talk trademark. There's the swirl of organ, conspicuously Traffic-like whether it is Winwood at the keys or not; the voice like a weather front; Paul Webb's outstanding intuition, keeping the bass bumping on a single note during the first section, then mixing it up on the next two. The more immediate groove of 'Life's What You Make It' delivered EMI's much-desired Top 20 hit, but nothing signals the transition of Talk Talk into a band harnessing an energy somehow mightier than all its parts quite as magnificently as 'Living in Another World'.

'Give it Up', by contrast, is equally powerful while being arguably the most conventional-sounding track on the record; a well-heeled country cousin to 'I Don't Believe in You', all expensive upholstery, leisurely tempi and a big, surging chorus. The drums are sent into the Fairlight and sent out again sounding like a million dollars – or, at least, £30,000.

The bass and organ are hooks in themselves. Hollis works up from a croon to a shout, and although the lyrics could be interpreted as a shadowy forewarning of the explicit anti-heroin feelings expressed two years later on 'I Believe in You', they read more like a rare instance of Hollis's interest in environmentalism being articulated plainly: 'Watching rivers run black / By the trees that are vacant to greed.' There is another crazily doctored synth solo from Ian Curnow before the song ends with an assuring wash of organ. How they loved this sound and that easy swing between two simple major chords, like lake water gently lapping on the land.

•

By now, Talk Talk had become 'an extendable orchestra … malleable'.[2] Are they still a band? Kind of. Maybe. Not quite. Talk Talk remain a trio in terms of how they are presented to the world, and they are a band that will keep playing live for another year, albeit bolstered by a raft of session musicians. But as they toil at length in the studios of London during most of 1985, the writing is already on the wall.

'On *The Colour of Spring*, Lee and Paul were around to get the backing tracks down,' says Peter Woolliscroft. 'Once they had finished that, they were gone, really. Which is a shame because they were nice lads. I think they wanted to be involved. Once the backing tracks were completed, the project became a collaboration primarily between Mark and Tim.'

From the start of his association with the band, Friese-Greene had been clear that he had no wish to officially join its ranks, despite being invited to do so quite early on. He wanted to keep his professional autonomy and wished to stand just a little outside the process. 'When I was the producer, I was happy to respect the sovereignty of the band – i.e. Mark – in terms of what it did,' he said. 'To work, it had to accommodate his worldview, if you like. That is what I saw the producer's job as being. I thought that it would be very dangerous for me to see myself as a band member because I felt that it would give me extra rights and would create difficulties.'[3]

This makes practical sense, but the point became increasingly moot. During the recording of *The Colour of Spring*, the partnership between Hollis and Friese-Greene fully coalesced. They had written all the material together and became increasingly autonomous in the studio. Friese-Greene began to take a more active musical role, particularly on the keyboards, playing Wurlitzer piano and his forte, the Hammond organ. Winwood be damned. Rather than rent one, Hollis had opted to purchase a Hammond C3 and L122 Leslie cabinet for £750, a magnificent old beast which initially malfunctioned but came good.

'Tim is a fine musician,' says Dennis Weinreich. 'There is absolutely no question about that. But like a lot of engineer/producers, who are also musicians … How can I explain this? Particularly as an engineer, because he *was* an engineer, you play mixing console and microphones. You don't play piano. That's the band's job. There is almost a barbed-wire fence between the control room and you as an engineer/producer going out and sitting at the piano and saying,

"I think we should do this" … Tim started to do that more and more. If you start to impose yourself in that dynamic, what happens is the artists' confidence starts to become marginalised. Musicians are already funny about the people in the control room. There are two or three people in there judging you the whole time. Some people will respond well to that. Other people just shrink.'

As Friese-Greene asserted himself, Paul Webb – never the most confident musician – shrunk. 'I never felt like a natural bass player,' he said. 'It took me days at home with the demo or backing track to come up with something I liked … Sometimes Tim or Mark had a bass part in mind, so I learned that. Other times I came in with a section they liked and we collaborated to finish the bassline off.'[4]

Some of Webb's parts are among the highlights on *The Colour of Spring*, but his status as a core original band member did not prevent Hollis and Friese-Greene bringing in other bass players if they felt a new approach or technique was needed. One of them was Alan Gorrie from the Average White Band, whose 'funky style clashed with the band's needs,' says Peter Woolliscroft. 'His energetic performance in the control room was ultimately deemed unsuitable, leading to the erasure of all his parts, which prompted laughter among the team.' Gorrie is, nonetheless, credited on the sleeve and we certainly hear electric bass on the track. Perhaps he was resurrected from ridicule.

Gorrie was one of a 'revolving door' of external musicians brought in to add their spontaneous contributions to tracks. They were given little in the way of conventional direction: 'Bring your gear, get your sound, we'll play you the track and you respond.'

Adding to the roll-call of bass players was the renowned double bassist Danny Thompson, a veritable walking history of great British music. The former Pentangle member had, in the 1970s, struck up a remarkably simpatico musical partnership with John Martyn, with whom he had toured and recorded extensively. Thompson had also recently recorded with the likes of Kate Bush and David Sylvian. He was a force of nature, big and rambunctious, and armed with an endless stream of tall tales, quips and badinage, all of which were warmly welcomed into what had become an often fairly solemn work environment.

Thompson's contributions to the song 'Footprints in the Snow', later retitled 'Happiness is Easy', were particularly fine, his funky, Brubeckian stabs vying with the busy electric bass. Even then, his riff was sampled and dropped back into the song to maintain a sense of perfect sound and tempo.

Thompson would be called back to work on *Spirit of Eden*. It's notable how many of the musicians that Hollis connected with and used extensively were of a similar character type: often Londoners (or near enough), down-to-earth, humorous, excellent musicians who wore their proficiency with extreme lightness and little ego. Thompson certainly fitted the bill. Martin Ditcham and Mark Feltham were cut from similar cloth.

Session guitarist Robbie McIntosh was another who passed the character test. He had recently joined the Pretenders' live line-up and had worked with Friese-Greene previously on 'The Lion Sleeps Tonight', as well as playing on *It's My Life*. Upon arrival at Battery, McIntosh was handed a guitar made from an old, rusty petrol can, one of a variety of odd, homemade instruments Friese-Greene had collected during his travels in Africa. This particular creation comprised a plank of wood inserted into the petrol can and strung with piano wire, a set-up which proved challenging for McIntosh, to the extent that the tips of his fingers started shredding. Nevertheless, as required, he squared up to the challenge and coaxed a tune from it, though very little of it was retained.

'It is still a bit of a mystery as to what I actually did [on the album]!' he says. 'I still get people telling me how they love the guitar solo on "I Don't Believe in You" and it's not a guitar solo, it's a synthesiser. I did some acoustic guitars on "Happiness is Easy" and "I Don't Believe in You".' The acoustic guitar work throughout *The Colour of Spring* is a thing of great beauty, alternating between percussive and expressive, between sitting back in the mix and darting out of it.

'Living in Another World' is me on the electric guitar,' says McIntosh. 'David [Rhodes] played some electric on that as well, but I did the solo, which has only got about three or four notes in it. I played it on my Gibson 335. Mark wanted me to use it because it was red. It was sometimes quite cryptic working with Mark – and Tim. He would get me to play maybe four or five passes for a track and then they would just pick the best bits.'

Some musicians found these working methods more palatable than others. The classically trained Welsh harpist Gaynor Sadler met with favour for her can-do attitude. The – all-too-rare – presence of a woman in the studio seemed to put them all on their best behaviour. Sadler was there with her husband and creative partner, Anthony. When Hollis and Friese-Greene asked if they would like anything, Anthony requested a pizza. In Sadler's recollection, either Harris or Webb – no doubt grateful for something to do – went out to fetch it. 'They were very, very sweet, nice individuals,' she says. 'There was no pretension. It was very calm. Tim and Mark were clearly on each other's wavelength. They were very experimental and they liked the idea of the harp being turned the other way around, so you sat at the column end, nearest to the bass strings. We worked out some interesting stuff. It was great fun. It took a lot of takes and then they used the bits that they wanted.'

Percussionist Morris Pert grew frustrated, however, at having to play countless ideas for people who were uncertain about what they wanted. Friese-Greene, for his part, suspected Pert of coming to work inebriated. After a few days, he left under a cloud, though some of his playing remained – which was not the case with every guest.

'Mark's favourite tool was the 'erase' button,' says Peter Woolliscroft. 'We would get somebody in to do a whole series of overdubs and he would wipe them all out except for a couple of notes. That gives you an idea of the way he worked. He knew what he *didn't* want. It's all part of the creative processes. It's quite an interesting way of doing it.'

Hollis's idiosyncratic approach also included taking recorded mistakes, warm-ups and all manner of sonic throat clearing, and placing them strategically throughout most tracks. Capturing Danny Thompson's bass string twangs and fingering fluffs set the ball rolling; Thompson's antennae for innovation was acute and he was amused and delighted to oblige. The practice was repeated with every subsequent musician who came in. As a result, absolutely everything was recorded for potential use.

To the chagrin of seasoned saxophonist David Roach, who would go on to perform with Frank Sinatra and the Philharmonia Orchestra, his heartfelt overdubs, which originally flowed through much of 'Happiness is Easy', were gradually erased until all that was left was a rogue squeak and the sound of Roach blowing out the spit from his horn. 'I think Mark believed that mistakes were some of the best bits,' says Ian Curnow, 'something I completely agree with to this day. I maintain that all my best ideas are really mistakes.'

Roach may have begged to differ, although he made significant contributions elsewhere on the album, not least on 'April 5th'. Guy Barker's trumpet parts, meanwhile, were partially replaced by Hollis's beloved Variophon; so much for favouring 'real' sounds over synthetic ones. Mike Ratledge, the former keyboard player from the Soft Machine, was invited to take part but declined, citing ring rustiness. He may have dodged a bullet. The creators of this music seemingly had no lexicon with which to guide anyone else, which is why it took so long and would continue to do so. It was exploration guided entirely by the ear, rather than a map.

'Mark wasn't a poor communicator, but he often didn't know what he wanted until he found it,' says Dennis Weinreich. 'He was searching for something. Tim was the same, actually. This is very unfair and I hope it isn't taken out of context, but there is that thing about throwing all the shit against the wall and seeing what sticks. There was a tiny element of that. It was like, "I don't know what to do here, so I'm going to try stuff until something sparks an idea." The creative bit was knowing that something was needed. But he didn't know what it was. So, let's work on it and see.'

As well as entire parts being cut, sometimes whole songs went AWOL. At this stage in the sessions, they were simply building up backing tracks. With no melodies or vocal parts yet recorded, these acquired some unusual working titles: 'Edith', 'Earwig', 'Apocalypse', 'Rodney', 'Tony Davis', 'Berlin', 'Borf', 'Victor', 'Monkey' and 'Footprints in the Snow'. It is wise not to over-analyse these. 'Oliver Tambo' was named not in honour of the South African anti-apartheid activist but because it featured a tambourine. Hollis later claimed that the mysteriously named 'Myrrhman' on *Laughing Stock* was so called simply because its working title was 'Ethel Merman'.

Most of these works-in-progress evolved into songs that were included on *The Colour of Spring* or issued as B-sides. One that didn't was 'Nuclear Winter', much to the disbelief of Dietmar Schillinger, who recalls hearing it when he worked on the album during the sessions at Wessex and, forty years later, still pines to hear it again.

'One day they came in and played this track called "Nuclear Winter",' he recalls. 'I tell you – it fucking blew me away. My jaw was hanging on the floor. It was an absolutely brilliant song, but they didn't like it. They only played it once. "Yeah, we'll just give it another listen." It didn't sound like a demo. It sounded mostly finished, to a point where it might have needed a few more bits and pieces. It was very, very together. I just could not believe that this most brilliant song, in my opinion, never made it onto a record. It was probably too commercial. You could [already] tell this was going to be a big album. It would have been even bigger had "Nuclear Winter" been recorded. It was completely and utterly Talk Talk, with all the quirkiness in there, but it just had that commercial edge to it. It was probably too good, so they left it off, never to be heard again.'

I wondered whether this track turned out to be 'Pictures of Bernadette', the lively B-side to 'Give it Up', which is certainly catchier and more immediate than anything on *The Colour of Spring*. It was presumably sidelined for harking back too closely to the sound of *It's My Life*. But no, Schillinger is certain: 'Nuclear Winter' never saw the light of day. Many years after the fact, Friese-Greene confirmed as much when he mentioned the track in passing to a Talk Talk fan, intimating that he and Hollis had squirrelled it away with the intention that it never be heard again – until, perhaps, the event described in its name came to pass. 'A terrible title and not a great song' was his typically blunt verdict.

•

As the weeks in the studio progressed, and the guests arrived and departed, often none the wiser, the accretion of something – *anything* – became a case of often aimless experimentation. 'There was a pool table, so we spent a lot of time there, tearing our hair out,' says Woolliscroft. Quite a lot more time was spent in the bar next door. Often, it was tense and stifling work, and the atmosphere could be unpleasant. By now, Woolliscroft had started to see that the provocation behind Hollis's jabs and prickly demeanour was really just a demand for some form of response. 'After about six months, you just got on with him,' he says. 'You found yourself saying, "Fuck off, Mark, you twat." And he'd say, "OK". Towards the end, it was less hard work. It wasn't all bad. But in the beginning, it was difficult.'

One musical breakthrough was the arrival of the Kurzweil KC88, a new toy which provided most of the 'strings' on the record, its sampled violin, viola and cello parts recorded separately onto the tracks to give the impression of an expansive quartet. Its presets also delivered a crisp piano sound. Friese-Greene loved it. As the sessions wore on and they sought cohesion, 'the album really hung together on Tim's keyboard skills,' says Woolliscroft.

And, of course, it ultimately hung together in the revealing of the lyrics and vocals, which were entirely down to Hollis and tended to be addressed towards the end of the recording process. 'I don't think Mark ever did a guide vocal,' says Woolliscroft. '[During the album] we were all working on instrumentals a lot of the time and

I remember thinking, *How is this going to make sense because we don't know what the vocal is going to be?* And then it *did* kind of make sense. I think he had the words, actually, to most of them. He had it pretty much planned.'

Capturing the lead vocals was always a sensitive business. When it came to singing in the studio, some felt that Hollis's insecurities bled out. At Battery, he insisted on recording his vocals in the dark, which meant that, throughout the entire project, the studio team never saw him sing. They used the widest spread of a special AKG gold microphone with four independently controllable capsules to capture sound in various patterns, as Hollis tended to move around a lot while singing and often veered 'off mic'. The physical exertion of his efforts was evident. He would return to the control room drenched in sweat and often without a shirt. 'He would come back in wet through,' says Woolliscroft. 'He had given it his all.'

Dennis Weinreich recalls recording many of Hollis's vocal parts later at Videosonics. 'I don't remember any of the vocal sessions being in any way arduous,' he says. 'Sometimes he put dark glasses on or asked to turn down the lights. That's so totally not out of the ordinary. I don't remember him having his back to us. He would be in the studio and he could see us. He never said he didn't want to be seen. It was just, "Turn the lights down." I did a bunch of stuff with Scott Walker and he was the same.'

At Videosonics, they used a different microphone for his voice, an old 1950s valve mic, the Neumann U47. 'What everybody found with his voice is that, on the 47, it didn't need to be loud within the mix of the instrumentation for it to have presence, to cut through and have authority,' says Weinreich. 'It was there, but it didn't need to be loud. On that album, you can tell on certain tracks. The voice isn't very loud, but you hear every nuance. Those are probably the ones we recorded on the 47.'

Nowhere is Hollis's ability to cut through quietly but with authority more evident than on the remarkable 'Chameleon Day'. Robbie McIntosh describes *The Colour of Spring* as 'a very transitional record. There are elements that come to the fore on *Spirit of Eden* obviously, but then there are songs that are more structured and tighter.' If 'Give it Up' is representative of the latter category, 'Chameleon Day', the track that follows it on the album, is its most forward-facing.

Not coincidentally, perhaps, it is also the one song that features only Hollis and Friese-Greene. The pair tinker around on piano and Variophon, while those elegant Kurzweil strings are put to good use. This is a new landscape for Talk Talk, but one that will become familiar. The spare piano chords evoke that 'empty ballroom' sound of some of Hollis's favourite composers, but it is the melting of structure, the removal of rhythm, the overall telescoping of possibilities that feels really significant. On 'Chameleon Day', said Hollis, 'there was a definite element of simply feeling the direction it was meant to be going in and accepting what came out.'[5] He is describing a surrendering of control.

The song is an augury of a band weighing anchor and heading off into unmapped waters. It is the music of drift, unmoored, and it signposts quite explicitly towards *Spirit of Eden*. It would be entirely wrong to call a song as powerful as 'Chameleon Day' a work in progress or a rough sketch, but parts of it could blend into the beginning of 'The Rainbow' seamlessly, while the final fifty seconds could be dropped more or less anywhere onto that album and would feel at home.

For this reason, it could be said that the quietest corners of *The Colour of Spring* sing the loudest. Placed alongside the similarly chimeric 'April 5th', 'Chameleon Day' is a bridge between the more formal structure of *The Colour of Spring* and the looser, more experimental terrain to come.

'It's Getting Late in the Evening' is another signpost. The beautiful B-side to 'Life's What You Make It' was recorded early in the sessions and may have been earmarked for the album before its A-side turned up with sharper elbows. 'It's Getting Late in the Evening' is slow, pastoral, elliptic. There is an adherence to a conventional song shape in its first half, with its jittery keyboard pulse, simple piano chords and spiky bursts of guitar, before the form cracks and the music spreads out like an ink stain. An open-ended middle section brings a devastating rush, waves of dissolving sound and then a foggy sweep of Variophon, gesturing towards a drifting post-rock soundscape.

Hollis sounds anchored, happy, at peace, attuned to the healing power of contentment as the cares of the day drop away. 'Everybody's laughing,' he sings, and for once it's not at him. 'The tide shall turn to shelter us from storm / The seas of charity shall overflow / And bathe us all.' Intriguingly, he could be describing the cover of *Spirit of Eden*. Hollis was indeed already familiar with James Marsh's *Fruit Tree* painting, a personal piece which dated to 1975 and which would, in two years, come to grace the cover of the next Talk Talk album. Perhaps it was already inspiring him. Other influences on the song are less esoteric. The funky little keyboard motif which closes the song was a nod, said Friese-Greene, to the Doobie Brothers' 'What a Fool Believes'. Hearing the track again having been armed with this knowledge, it is impossible not to believe him.

According to Hollis, the basis of 'It's Getting Late in the Evening' was recorded with 'just one [microphone] up in the top of the room … It was just tambourine, drum, piano and organ.'[6] A similar set-up was used to record percussionist Martin Ditcham, who came into Wessex near the end of the album sessions to add his parts. Engineer Dietmar Schillinger recalls him and Friese-Greene (Hollis wasn't present) setting up 'a couple of ambient mics', then inviting Ditcham to sit in the middle of the floor with the exotic tools of the trade laid out around him and go to town.

For now, these innovations were filed under 'To Be Continued'. Ditcham would become an essential creative foil on the coming records, while a recording approach relegated to an experimental B-side would become an entire working methodology; the simple yet, as it transpired, horrendously complex ambient mic'ing technique became the default set-up for recording the drums on *Laughing Stock*.

Hollis spoke often about the meticulous way in which Talk Talk albums were sequenced, about the importance of each song and sound being correctly placed and sitting in harmony with those around it to ensure that the record flowed. It's one of the (many) reasons he hated the compilation albums that were put together without his input; the sequencing simply wasn't right and the flow was dammed up.

The movement from 'Happiness is Easy' into 'I Don't Believe in You' is one fine example of the art on *The Colour of Spring*. But the choreography at work as the ending of 'Chameleon Day' heralds the beginning of 'Time it's Time' to set up the album's finale is even more exquisitely achieved. The rising hum at the close of 'Chameleon

Day' merges with a ghostly pre-echo of the title phrase, before finally the perfect fall of Hollis's vocal, like a book softly closing. It is followed by a deeply cinematic blend of silence and drama, low clouds of unease hanging over it all. In the microsecond before 'Time it's Time' begins, a breath falls, a T.S. Eliot breath, 'between the motion and the act', worlds within it, moving the *mise en scene* subtly but powerfully from dark to light. It is a stunning transition and masterful sequencing. An eclipse. And then a sunrise.

The final song on *The Colour of Spring* is an epic production, another slow build through two shifting sections to a scything syncopated chorus. 'Time it's Time' is the only occasion that Hollis plays guitar on the album. The massed ranks of recorders, blown by whoever happened to be in the building, bring brightness and light, linking back to the schoolroom innocence of the children's voices on the album's opening track. Their touching amateurism is now contrasted with the stirring swell of the Ambrosian Singers, a venerable English choral group. Remember Simon Brenner recalling the young Hollis blasting out 'Carmina Burana'? Well, here comes the follow-through.

Again, the sense of momentum feels almost untethered. The track leaps up through the register and by the end the feeling is exultant, redemptive, as though heralding the end of some great ordeal. 'Now that it's over, rest your head...' Peter Woolliscroft could relate. The long, arduous process of making this record left him feeling shattered and uncertain about his future in the industry. For nearly a decade, he found it hard to listen to the immaculate work of art he had helped create. He would not be the last Talk Talk engineer to feel that way.

The first attempt at mixing *The Colour of Spring* began during the summer and proceeded relatively smoothly. Woolliscroft's notes from the time suggest that the album was finally completed on 7 October 1985. Or was it? The recording sessions at Battery were certainly concluded, but even when the mix was apparently signed off, it went through another spin cycle, at Videosonics, where much was added during a second mixing process.

Videosonics was a new facility owned and run by Dennis Weinreich, with an emphasis on film and TV work. Weinreich was an old friend and colleague of Tim Friese-Greene. 'I had just finished building my new recording studio in Camden and Tim called me up and said, "Could I do a few days on this project?" Tim and I had both come up by a similar route. We were both engineers who became producers and we found that we liked working together. If I had a project that I was producing and I wanted another set of ears, I would hire Tim. And, conversely, he would do the same with me. That's what happened with *The Colour of Spring*. They had most of the album mixed, but they weren't very happy. They thought that there was more there than they were getting out of it. In many cases on those tracks, all I was doing was remixing what was already there, but that wasn't the case on everything. They started to realise that a lot of what they had on the tape wasn't good enough. So we started to re-record.'

What was supposed to be 'a few days' turned into something significantly longer. Almost unbelievably, the drums were put through another process of manipulation via the Fairlight. Other earlier decisions were second-guessed. Songs that had already been finished, locked and mixed, they now thought, *It's just not right*. It meant more parts being recorded and more highly detailed faffing around on the

Fairlight as they worked track by track through the entire album, adding instruments, syncing rhythms, moving parts, taking things out. Rather than a sense of creative fatigue, there seemed to be a renewed vigour. 'It was very collaborative,' says Weinreich. 'There was quite a bit of focus. They kind of zoomed in as a unit.'

He found Hollis easy to work with: collaborative, open to suggestions, if a little aloof. 'He was certainly not a formidable personality when I was working with them, but he was very much a driver. Mark wasn't the kind of guy that had burnout. He was pretty high-energy. It was very positive. It wasn't tense. I had been brought in by Tim. I don't think Mark had any problem with me getting involved … but I always felt like he thought that I was "Tim's guy", not his. It wasn't unfriendly and we would certainly laugh and eat together and communicate when we were setting up sounds and so forth, but somehow or other there was that distance. When we were done for the day it was, "OK, bye" and then he would go. Tim was like that as well. Tim, when he's done, he's done.'

Recording and mixing at the same time can be a tricky process; they are two different skills and require different mindsets and processes. As an engineer, Friese-Greene recognised this. By the end, says Weinreich, 'there was a sense of holding the reins back on Mark because every time he heard the track, he had more and more ideas. All of this stuff was coming from Mark, not the other guys in the band. Tim was brilliant at saying, "This is it, this is the record, let's mix it. We're done."'

And Hollis?

'Oh, Mark would have kept going for ever and ever.'

Even by November 1985, Hollis and Friese-Greene were still going back to some of the original mixes from Battery. Everyone seems to have their own version of when *The Colour of Spring* was actually finished. I like this one. It comes from Stuart Stawman, which means we're back at Wessex.

'The first time I worked with Talk Talk and Tim Friese-Greene was when I was asked to fill in as tape-op on the last day of recording for *The Colour of Spring*, which must have been late 1985,' Stawman recalled. 'Towards the end of that day, Mark and Tim needed to check through all the songs on the album to make sure they had everything recorded. So, imagine this – my job was to keep changing the 24-track tape reels over for the next song and then watch Tim bring up the faders on the desk. We were listening to the whole of *The Colour of Spring* for the first time. The room was full of smiles. I particularly remember being "introduced" to Mark's sparkling grin for the first time. The guys were on a – totally natural – high, enjoying the fruits of their work. Everyone in the room knew this was special. They'd just recorded a classic album.'

And so they had. It had taken almost a year – at least a week for each second of those extraordinary drums that begin the record, the ones that sound so natural, so organic, so *easy*. Released on 17 February 1986, from those first moments on 'Happiness is Easy' to the final fade of 'Time it's Time', *The Colour of Spring* thrums with the tick-tock of new life. It is a hymn to regeneration, the sound of a fresh page on the calendar being turned.

Yet calling it a transitional record is, in a sense, understandable. It is certainly the last Talk Talk album conceived with even half an eye on the commercial music world, or where it is possible to hear the band at times marching in step with their peers. There are obvious parallels with Kate Bush's *Hounds of Love*, released a few months earlier and another widescreen, windswept, elemental record full of space and rhythm that harnessed an organic 'natural' feel to the most cutting-edge technology. Henceforth, the sense of Hollis and what remained of the band interacting with the cultural moment they were living in is tenuous at best.

On *The Colour of Spring*, we hear Talk Talk straining at the bounds of structure and songwriting, while creating something magnificent but monolithic within these perceived limitations. The songs are – with a couple of exceptions – built from the sturdy bricks of verse, bridge, chorus, while lyrically Hollis was still working within the parameters of meaning, albeit at the abstract end of the street.

It is a pop album, beautifully crafted, giving the impression that it is hewn from oak rather than plastic and steel. The sense of space is glorious. 'It doesn't sound like a 48-track recording,' says Peter Woolliscroft. 'It's not that big of a record. [The idea was to] give it space to make it sound full enough without having to add stuff, because on a lot of that album, the ethos was, *If you didn't need a part, don't put it on.* You don't need a rhythm guitar going through a whole track. If it's not doing anything, take it off.'

The erase button did its work well. Every sound is there for a good reason; nothing is gratuitous. 'If something happened and it was great, it doesn't necessarily get copied into the other choruses,' says Dietmar Schillinger. 'If the guitar is played *there* and not again, then there is a reason for that. Total control, that was the thing. It's that tension between control and creativity that is fascinating. Real artists can do both those things.'

That critical interplay between control and creativity was still a work in progress. *The Colour of Spring* soars, but it does not easily bend. On 'Give it Up' and 'I Don't Believe in You', the high-end gloss finish is breathtaking, but it also makes the disparaging description of Talk Talk crafting 'Anglo coffee table music'[7] fall within the realm of fair comment. Another reviewer described the record as 'a touch of class', as though it were a superior hire car.[8] This is beautiful music, but it is often safely locked and brightly polished. It is even possible to hear a formula developing, the idea of which would no doubt have kept Hollis awake at night.

What he and Tim Friese-Greene sought to do next was find more ways of playing with and against the rhythm, balancing looseness and structure, experimenting with arranging power and abrasion alongside beauty and silence without diminishing either side of the equation. Taken together, 'April 5th', 'Chameleon Day' and 'It's Getting Late in the Evening' represented a half-opened door, a hinge, to the next stage of Talk Talk. The possibilities of what they were doing had only really begun to present themselves. The minute, miniscule nuances of timbre, and rhythm, became an obsession. Like all obsessions, the likelihood is that the detail was in the end meaningful to only a handful of people, perhaps really finally only the two men actively pursuing it.

Every squeak, every creak, every pulse, mapped out in milliseconds.

Madness, really. But the payoff would be immense.

iv

To get some sense of how EMI must have felt when Talk Talk delivered *Spirit of Eden* to Parlophone in the early months of 1988, I invite you to set down this book for a moment and pull up the YouTube footage of the band playing the Montreux Jazz Festival on 11 July 1986, captured for posterity on the *Live at Montreux* DVD. Take a long look. Drink it in. You won't see this group again. Neither will their record company, who must have reckoned that they had in their grasp a band fit to conquer the world. Instead, they evaporated.

At Montreux, swelled to an eight-piece and playing a packed club rather than the now more customary 5,000-plus-seater arenas and even larger outdoor venues, Talk Talk were almost ridiculously potent. The comparison among their contemporaries that makes most sense is with the Waterboys, who at this point were very probably the greatest live band in the world. Talk Talk, even as they were disappearing from view, possessed a similar sense of dynamic range and possibility, of controlled surge, of scale, of barely contained need.

The Montreux performance was part of The Colour of Spring tour, a prolonged affair which began in modest UK venues before expanding to include two nights at Hammersmith Odeon, dates in Roman amphitheatres and at European festivals and a memorable summer evening playing Hangar T2 at the Imperial War Museum aerodrome in Duxford, Cambridgeshire, with the Fall as the very loud and somewhat improbable support act. The tour concluded in

Spain, on 13 September 1986. Plaza Mayor in Salamanca was Talk Talk's Candlestick Park, a final encore of 'Renée' their last goodbye. They would never play live again. Henceforth, they were an exclusively studio concept, barely even a band, perhaps closer to an idea than a solid entity.

What was gained? What was lost?

We were certainly deprived of a powerhouse live act. The *London 1986* live album, recorded at Hammersmith Odeon on 8 May 1986 and released twelve years later, is machine-tooled, the sound of a vast engine working at optimum capacity, every cog and wheel oiled and whirring. 'They've drafted in five extra musicians to boost the three-strong membership, and they are playing all these crashing great versions of their new songs,' said the man from *Smash Hits*.[1] 'Crashing' is a good word; the music does indeed come in huge, surging waves. Although featuring a different combination of auxiliary musicians from those on *Live at Montreux*, it is more or less the same set and the music is similarly full of thrust and dynamism.

In both cases, the power is impressive but – and perhaps this is hindsight doing its work – we can hear the music somehow thirsting for space, air, fluidity. The big 'rock' guitar solo on 'Living in Another World' at Montreux, played by sometime Talk Talk guitarist John Turnbull, feels both incongruous and illustrative. Here is a band entirely at ease with its sound, yet any appearance of abandonment, you realise, is actually artifice. The execution is tightly controlled. On stage, by now Talk Talk were in some ways emblematic of traits which seem almost anathema to how they have since come to be regarded. Meaty, thrusting, bombastic, even. Drilled. Locked. And for all the gear-surfing horsepower and the sweat-soaked intensity of Mark Hollis's singing, there is something oddly clinical about it all.

On stage, 'arrangement was king', said Turnbull.[2] Hollis was getting increasingly uptight about what he regarded as his songs being put 'through the mincer' every night.[3]

'When we were doing live stuff, Mark was very clear about how he wanted things to sound,' says David Rhodes, who first played with the band at a free festival in France in the summer of 1985, and many times thereafter. 'I learned all the material that they wanted to do and then we did two days' rehearsal with the band in Waterloo, in some railway arches. Mark came in for two afternoons and we just ran the set once each afternoon, maybe twice … Some people let a lot of stuff go, but he was pretty strict about the song areas, and then with the instrumental bits he just let people roll. That was nice. I thought it was an exciting band. It really rattled along. When Mark Feltham played a few shows, that was stunning.'

'It was my only experience of touring on that scale at that point,' says Ian Curnow of the 1986 tour. '[It was] sometimes fantastic and sometimes uncomfortable.' Curnow had been sidelined during the making of *The Colour of Spring*, 'relegated' from a previously much more pivotal role, which made his position in the touring band somewhat strained. During these dates, Talk Talk expanded to a small army on stage, featuring frequent changes in personnel, which by necessity was highly choreographed. 'We were certainly able to reproduce everything off *The Colour of Spring*,' says harmonica player Mark Feltham. 'It was fantastic live. It was totally reproducible.' Even so, the sets still routinely consisted of almost all of *It's My Life* but only half of their new album. The typical 1986 set list included, from *The Colour of Spring*, 'Life's What You Make It', 'Give it Up', 'I Don't Believe in You' and 'Living in Another World', the latter often prefaced with a fragment of 'Chameleon Day'.

The decision for Talk Talk to stop touring was solely Hollis's. He was hardly short of reasons, both musical and personal. In 1986, describing the band's material as 'extremely classically oriented pop music,' he continued that 'it is a great pity that you then deprive yourself of the ability to improvise. A little bit of improvisation is okay, but not nearly to the extent as you see with someone like John Coltrane.'[4] By 1991, he was clearer. 'Even at the time of *The Colour of Spring*, it was getting increasingly difficult to play the material live. We were looking at rearranging songs, but having spent a year and a half making the record, the *last* thing you want to do is go back in and rearrange it!'[5]

One can take various positions on this. You might argue that it implies some deficiency in Hollis's artistic make-up that he was neither secure nor relaxed enough to allow for a greater degree of live improvisation; to make the song different every time rather than preciously guard its studio arrangement. But his driving artistic impulse, which was by now beginning to be asserted, was to preserve numerous single acts of spontaneity, occurring only once, rather than seek to repeat them. That required a highly controlled environment – world building. His commitment to this ideal outweighed the imperfect rush of live performance. Thus, after September 1986, the studio became the only stage.

'Maybe he struggled with the sound,' muses Robbie McIntosh. 'He worked in a studio for a long time and everything sounds great. If you get on stage and try to make it sound the same, it's nigh on impossible. Maybe he wasn't prepared to make that compromise. He was a very uncompromising person to work with, that's for sure.

Not in a bad way. I never fell out with him at all, but he knew what he wanted. And he wasn't going to settle for anything less than what he absolutely wanted.'

By this point, Hollis and Tim Friese-Greene were bringing session bass players into the studio and submitting the drums to all that stringent precision-tooled manipulation. Did the singer even trust his two bandmates to do the business on stage? Talk Talk live was already an increasingly ad hoc proposition. Significantly, Friese-Greene was never an official member of the group and never performed with them, save for one occasion at the Montreux Golden Rose pop festival in May 1985.

From show to show, session guitarists came and went, as did keyboard players. It was never what you would call a *settled* group. Robbie McIntosh was drafted in for some gigs. 'I played [Rock in Athens, July 1985] with them. There was a fair bit of trouble there, I think somebody set a car on fire. I did two or three gigs in the south of France. That was me and Ian Curnow, Rupert Black on keyboards and Lee, Paul and Mark, and possibly a percussionist as well. I don't think Mark enjoyed it. He was going off playing live. He wasn't enjoying it very much.'

Touring was disruptive. The recording of *The Colour of Spring* was interrupted at various points throughout 1985 by one-off shows. It's not hard to imagine Hollis reluctantly having to wrench himself away from the job in hand and dragging himself onto the tour bus. Yet life on the road could, at times, be fun – or something close to it. David Rhodes recalls them all barrelling over to Germany to do a TV show and Hollis deciding that he wanted to drive the little VW van they were travelling in. 'He kept on seeing if he could start it in fourth gear…'

'Mark liked the camaraderie of the guys backstage,' says Mark Feltham. 'Loved it. But I always got the feeling he was uncomfortable on stage in the spotlight.' Perhaps some of the musical obstacles could have been overcome had Hollis loved performing, but his body language betrayed him every night. This was a man, as Tim Friese-Greene later acknowledged, who 'hates revealing anything of his true self'.[6] In terms of embracing the role of being the frontman in a rock band, it's hardly surprising that, says Rhodes, 'Mark didn't enjoy the process very much, though he was always great. He didn't really enjoy [having to] interact with the audience. He just wanted to deliver material and be gone. That being said, he was always fully committed and expected everybody in the band to be fully committed. As you'd expect.'

Hollis was neither relaxed on stage nor particularly engaging. In a damning live review for *Record Mirror* of a show at the Manchester Apollo in May 1986, the critic Dave Sexton wrote: 'As far as any preconceptions of Talk Talk go, there is just a blank space. Anonymous, to say the very least, they conjure up images of nothing in particular.'[7] Hollis would probably have applauded. He craved invisibility. Another reviewer, this time at the Hammersmith concert, talked of Hollis looking like 'a bit of a misery guts standing up there, hunched over the microphone and twitching his head. But at least his mournful voice and strange stage presence seem to be natural and gimmick-free...'[8]

That much was true. The misery was authentic. 'He hated touring in the end,' says Phill Brown, who first met up with Hollis following The Colour of Spring tour and became the engineer on *Spirit of Eden*. 'He was on the road for a year [it was closer to seven months] and it nearly killed the guy. He just had enough of all that and he had already had enough with the music business. He was already withdrawing from all of that. I think he liked the idea of being a studio band. He loved that environment. That was his big passion. To [now] be in the situation where we had unlimited resources, financially and equipment-wise – although we didn't use high tech equipment – [was ideal].'

As Brown suggests, with *The Colour of Spring* following up on the success of *It's My Life*, Hollis became financially secure enough to be able to call the shots. In his early thirties, recently married to his long-term girlfriend and contemplating starting a family, it was perhaps little wonder that he was growing weary of the more abrasive lifestyle that touring seemed to demand. David Rhodes recalls that Talk Talk was 'quite a heavy drinking band. Before going on stage, everybody was going to have a drink and Mark would take on a few tins of beer with him.' According to Brown, who admittedly was never with the band on tour but who was later regaled with anecdotes from this period, 'Mark had always smoked a bit of dope when he was on stage. They would eat a piece of hash, the three of them, before they went on, partly I think in the end just to get them [through] it. And they drank quite a bit.'

Jim Kerr recalls Simple Minds and Talk Talk crossing paths at one or two European festivals during 1986. He found them a lairy bunch, all 'Jock cunts' this and 'Jock cunts' that. At one point, the bands' two road crews began mustering for battle before tensions were defused.

EMI's national head of promotions, Malcolm Hill, had a reputation for trying to talk to his acts about moderating their drug use. Unsurprisingly, he was often ridiculed for his efforts. 'Mark was a bit of a stoner,' says Hill. 'How could he not be? It wasn't that heavy with Talk Talk, but there were a few things going on which I thought a bit unnecessary.' While performing on a TV show in Montreux, this time in 1985, Hollis, Webb and Harris, chaperoned by Hill, were invited to the house of Claude Nobs, who ran the Montreux Jazz Festival. The band prepared some treats for the occasion.

'I was unaware that there was some chocolate cookies laced with marijuana and the band, and Mark in particular, with great delight, kept feeding me these bloody marijuana cakes,' says Hill. 'I ended up being off my face and they thought it was totally fucking hilarious. Claude's house was up in the hills, quite a way out of town, up this winding track. There were just the four of us on this massive bus and they kept running backwards and forwards [up the aisle]. They were pretty stoned. The driver would stop the bus and say, "I am not going any further if these guys don't sit down and behave themselves."'

You can see how the thrill of it all might eventually pall. Reflecting in 1997, in his final interview, Hollis outlined a few of his reasons for stopping. Yes, the material got harder to play and he got tired of 'dealing more with recreating the past than ... looking into the future'.[9] He disliked the blinkered, bunker mentality that touring life demanded, where you go everywhere and see nothing. He was aware that alcohol was becoming a crutch to get him through it, which 'I don't actually think, mentally, is a good exercise'.[10] Lastly, and perhaps most significant of all, the imminent arrival of children was 'extremely important ... I don't think children and touring mix.'[11] His son Freddie was born in 1987. Charlie followed in 1990.

'He really didn't want to tour anymore,' says Mark Feltham. 'I was very close to his boys and his wife Flick. I think that he just didn't want to be away from them. Knowing the massive success that band could have had had they carried on, and if you think about the touring that that would have entailed, it just didn't suit his lifestyle.'

Although, as it transpired, making *Spirit of Eden* was a bit like spending a year on manoeuvres in the belly of a submarine.

Both Rhodes and Curnow use the phrase 'a necessary evil' to describe Hollis's attitude to touring. By the end, says the former, the feeling was 'just get it done – and maybe he was then very happy to let it go'. 'I think he hated it,' says Curnow. 'He was a very private person and didn't enjoy being in the limelight … As soon as he could, he turned his back on it.' Once something you don't enjoy no longer becomes a necessity, the game is up. After touring *The Colour of Spring*, Hollis spotted an open door with an illuminated EXIT sign and practically sprinted through it.

Clearly, he became creatively and personally ill-disposed to the whole idea of playing live and what it demanded. Yet it is likely he also recognised that dispensing with the very idea of Talk Talk as a live band after 1986 would be of some help, psychologically, in breaking down the more structured aspects of their sound. Simply knowing that, hereon, they were making music that need not ever be replicated on stage must have felt tremendously liberating. After quitting live performance, the Beatles immediately recorded 'Strawberry Fields Forever', 'Penny Lane' and *Sgt Pepper's Lonely Hearts Club Band*. Talk Talk made *Spirit of Eden*.

'That is one thing that did happen,' Hollis recalled in 1997, when asked what of significance might have changed between albums three and four. 'We stopped touring. Maybe that is the one thing that might have had an influence on [*Spirit of Eden*].'[12]

There is a logical extrapolation that the group no longer toured following the release of *Spirit of Eden* because they couldn't plausibly replicate the music they had made. But perhaps we should look at it the other way around. What if the only way Hollis could ever have contemplated making an album like *Spirit of Eden* in the first place was because he had already committed to staying off the road.

From now on, recreating music on stage would not be even a subconscious consideration during the recording process. He could go as deep as he wanted.

SUMMER

Spirit of Eden

i

Music is so much about the when, the where and the who. The point of personal impact is really the only release date that truly matters.

Spirit of Eden arrived into my world in the summer of 1989, delivered direct from a small bedsitting room in Montpelier, Bristol. I was fifteen, ripe for a miracle.

The record, and the room, belonged to Dave.

Dave had been the drummer in the school band formed by my brother Gordon and me. He had lived a few doors down from us in our village on the piratical fringes of Bristol. He wasn't much of a drummer, truth be told, but then none of us were much of anything. He looked the part, at least. Dave followed what might be called – at least in 1980s West Country Ruritania – a cool-jazz aesthetic: 1950s pleated bags with chunky turn-ups, striped granddaddy shirts, braces. There might have been, on occasion, a natty hat. Chet Baker stranded in Wurzel country. His black hair was greased back in a centre parting and his eyes were dark and heavy, hawk-hooded through weed and watchfulness. He carried with him at all times the whiff of romantic tragedy. Dave was the kind of young man sent to die for his country in slim novels of the 1920s or destined for a fatal car crash in the third verse of a '50s death disc. In reality, I have no idea what happened to him past the age of eighteen. He remains frozen and framed in the eternal Super 8 smudge of teen-dom.

Dave was short and sharp. Although you would never have called him book-clever, he knew a lot more than us about the ways of the world and I have since realised that this knowledge and our unaware-ness of it amused him. With his mod-like adherence to style, he disliked 'jitters' – a catch-all Bristolian pejorative which covered any-one falling into the categories of goth, crusty, metal, hippie or greaser. I often wonder what he really thought of teenage me, gloomy and pale, with my unkempt clumps of hair and holey rags. While our garage band was learning R.E.M. songs to cover – or steal – Dave advocated that we should play 'Lovely Day' by Bill Withers and 'Wild is the Wind' by David Bowie. He was a huge Pink Floyd fan and notably advanced of the rest of us in the field of chemical experimen-tation. He had, I suspect, romanticised junkie aspirations, along with two timeless responses to most situations: 'fuck shit' and 'no grief'.

Dave was staunch. He saved me on Corn Street one night when my quick mouth and short temper picked an argument with three punchy towners. I was actively seeking a beating. He bailed me out. And it was Dave who came with me to my first Glastonbury festival in June 1989. I was still two months shy of sixteen; by then he must have been seventeen. My mother, with an instinctive sense of Dave's innate goodness which neither I nor, I suspect, he recognised at the time, was reassured by his presence – and so off we went.

We had no tickets and five pounds. The pair of us mooched off on a sunny Saturday morning from Bristol bus station. On the way down, we met a sex worker (the phrase was not widely in use then; I'm afraid we would have called her something else) and her boy-friend/pimp. She had a lump of hashish stuffed down her knickers and burns and bruises all over her arms. Young me found all this scuzz pathetically glamorous.

The four of us jumped the fence after clambering onto the roof of a camper van and then scattered; she and I made our way towards the front of the Pyramid stage to watch Van Morrison. The air and the light at Pilton felt charged. Life for once conforming to the romanticised script forever running in my head, Van was halfway through playing 'Summertime in England'. I could hear that glorious, wildly eccentric, finger-snapping invocation of Avalon rolling towards us as we pushed closer and closer to the centre of the action. The past, present and future of the land we were all inhabiting – *claiming* – made sound, all in one and all at once. The sublime meeting of song and place stirred me, as it still does (*the when, the where, and the who*).

I can't recall where Dave disappeared to for the rest of that day. I spent a deep night in the company of people I didn't know, one of whom was dressed in some crude approximation of Native American headgear (cultural appropriation was another notion yet to find its footing in 1989). Elvis Costello played the knotty songs from *Spike* alone on stage while we sat and smoked around a campfire. The next day, somehow, my path aligned with Dave's and we went home. I don't know about him, but I was changed. At least I was convinced that I was, which is the next best thing.

Shortly beforehand, or perhaps just after, but certainly folded into that teeming time period, I had been visiting Dave's bedsit with Gordon. By this point, Dave had left our band, left school, left his silent, musty, unhappily broken home, and was working in town and living in a shared house in Montpelier in central Bristol, on the edge of St Pauls. It was an exciting area and an exciting era. Dave's chemistry class was continuing apace, though he could be almost paternal. I recall him once firmly refusing to give us a tab of acid. At the time, I was peeved. Looking back, I'm oddly touched by his care.

We visited one night. My brother recalls us driving around the city in Dave's Citroën C5 with the hood down. We would have been gently stoned on cheap, crumbly hashish the colour and consistency of earwax. To further enhance the mood, once back in his room, Dave played us a new record. I recall this being approached with a degree of ceremony. He had pulled the same move when playing us Serge Gainsbourg's *Histoire de Melody Nelson*. It wasn't slipped on casually mid-conversation; there was an element of 'OK, boys, listen to *this*' about it all.

The record was *Spirit of Eden*.

Do I remember how it felt? I think I do. The first song was a sense before it was a sound. A stir. When it finally loosened from its moorings, it carried the intimation of a great upending. It was both a leviathan cleaving the surface of the sea, arcing upward, and a vessel being dragged down below the waterline. 'The Rainbow' felt like a rending. Something opened. As the crescendo of the first section built, I fancy I can still feel the hairs on my arms rising with it, along with my senses pinging, as though coming up too fast on a chemical. Finally, the great wave broke in a clamour of clanging guitar and distorted blues harp, a harbinger of power and almost incalculable loss, and then the deadened drum tattoo emerging from it all, summoning us into a world beyond, a world turned upside down.

What can I say? I followed. I'm still there.

·

How did Talk Talk build an environment capable of nurturing a record like *Spirit of Eden*? Few albums have created a world as successfully and with such immersive mystery and power. As such, the 'how' is as important as the 'who, the why and the where'.

This music sounds like it could, perhaps should, have been made in some ramshackle country pile hidden out in the sticks, the exterior wildness seeping inside through cracked windows and ivy-choked chimney pots. Long jams and even longer nights curling into dawn. The air quality index reading 46 per cent unadulterated reefer smoke.

But no. For their fourth album, Talk Talk returned like a gang of helpless recidivists to Wessex Studios in north London. This time, they locked themselves away for the best part of a year. A casual passer-by during that period might have noticed two snazzy, jeep-style four-wheel-drive Toyota Land Cruisers parked next to one another outside the studio reception. One belonged to Hollis, the other to Friese-Greene. After five years of major label advances, publishing income, a handful of decent-sized hit singles (including a Top 40 showing in the States), hefty album sales throughout Europe and regular festival spots and arena shows, by now nobody associated with Talk Talk was slumming it.

Work began on 11 May 1987. They brought the bits and pieces of the music into the city and closed the doors. It was up to the technicians and the musicians (perhaps in that order) to bring the sun, the moon, the night, the world. This album, this extraordinary blossoming of possibilities, was created, counter-intuitively, in a dimly lit demi-monde, in an atmosphere of retreat and almost claustrophobic seclusion. The firm intention was to upend any sense of psychological stability or certainty.

Neither the control room nor the live room of Studio 1 had windows. The entire recording process took place, in the words of the studio's chief engineer Stuart Stawman, 'divorced from sunlight'. Hollis's stated aim was to recreate the mood of a late-night Traffic session circa November 1967. The main protagonists spent the best part of a year working in a state of altered reality. Engineer Phill Brown – who had actually worked on late-night Traffic sessions in

1967 and knew it was nothing quite like this – recalls 'an endlessly blacked-out studio, an oil projector in the control room, strobe lighting and five 24-track tape machines synced together. Twelve hours a day in the dark listening to the same six songs for eight months. As the months went on in the dark environment, with the technical requests and solutions, it became pretty intense.' In context, the dim glow cast by three Anglepoise lamps blazed like a solar flare.

There was a lucid thought behind this approach, which was an extreme extension of the mood-setting put in place when they had worked previously at Wessex on *The Colour of Spring*. 'I thought it was a smart move when Mark Hollis left a bubble-light projector in the control room for the *Spirit of Eden* album sessions,' Paul Webb later recalled. 'It was a good visual focal point that enabled your mind to go walkies when listening to playbacks.'[1]

There were plenty of laughs. It was not by any means all po-faced gloom and doom, but 'there was an oppressive feeling a lot of the time in the studio,' says the studio's maintenance engineer Richard Hill, who was called in to assist on the sessions from time to time. 'I don't really know how to describe it, but when you walked into the control room, you were *enveloped*. You were *in* something, an atmosphere – which at times, was lovely … They purposely made it slightly oppressive by the lighting and oil wheel projector and stuff like that. It's wearing when it [feels like] two in the morning all the time.'

It should be noted that these were not sessions which stretched on for days and days at a time. They worked from 11 a.m. until midnight or sometimes a little later, with regular breaks for curry, pizza and the occasional pub visit. Everyone went home at night – or, in Hollis's case sometimes, back to the flat he owned nearby in Noel

Road, Islington. They took weekends off. Still, the ambience seeped in and was especially effective when it came to throwing visiting musicians immediately off balance. David Rhodes, who was called in again but found himself this time a victim of the curse of the 'erase' button, remembers 'the oil wheel going in the control room. When it came time for me to do a take, they turned off the lights in the studio so I couldn't see. It was playful. And very challenging.'

'The oil-filled lamp was projected from the back of the control room and it was shining in between the speakers,' says Martin Ditcham. 'That was swirling all the time. And the drums had these three cheap kind of disco lights – red, yellow and blue – flashing on and off when the band was playing. It was very unusual.'

You get the picture. In time, everyone involved on a daily basis developed a touch-sense relationship with the music. To focus, Brown and Friese-Greene fixated on the shape of the faders on the mixing desk, although even they seemed to be in constant motion due to the rippling effect of the coloured oil projections.

The lengths to which Hollis and Friese-Greene went to build a disorientating immersive ecology during the making of *Spirit of Eden* and *Laughing Stock* can seem wilful at first glance, perhaps even a little indulgent in its head-shop extravagances: 'We do it because we can, man.' Some of the eccentricities and obsessions might appear as aimlessness disguised as artful exploration. Pranksterism, even. But these records exist in imagined worlds; they inhabit a realm beyond easy reach and such worlds require building.

To channel this music, you suspect Hollis was accessing a part of him that was seemingly not revealed in his daily life. 'I stayed friends with Mark after *The Colour of Spring*,' says Mark Feltham. 'Even when he decided to disappear, as it were, I still knew him through all that time and he would always be there as a friend if I needed him. But you always sensed that he was holding back that last 25 per cent. He wouldn't give it all away. That was part of his mystique, part of the attraction.'

In his work, Hollis held back nothing. The music had therefore to be made in an environment where such intimate access and revelation felt permitted, if not nurtured – and, furthermore, where any musician entering this world could also feel encouraged to go beyond the norm. The mood setting was imperative.

Phill Brown, who was driven to the point of genuine psychological disturbance and domestic upheaval working on *Spirit of Eden* and particularly *Laughing Stock*, ultimately stands by the way these albums were made. The idea, really, was simple: to create an all-enveloping environment which shut out everything but the music. Literally.

'We were under strict instructions not to let the A&R people into the studio,' says Richard Hill. 'They could get to the reception, but they weren't allowed past the door into the studio – and preferably not in reception either. It's the only album I remember like that.' Clearly, nobody this time was going to be allowed the opportunity to ask the downright impertinent question, 'Where's the single?' Hill found himself perfectly placed to man the barricades. For eight months, he was sleeping in the studio lounge and storing his belongings in the old live room following a nasty break-up with his girlfriend. At one point, one of the Talk Talk team inadvertently bayoneted his mattress with a microphone stand.

The spirit of musical rewilding which had begun on *The Colour of Spring* was let loose on *Spirit of Eden*. Now, every day was Chameleon Day. The sense-world of the album seemed partly to mirror what was going on in Hollis's life. The words to *Spirit of Eden* were written precisely where they sound like they were written, in the heart of the English countryside: the tiny village of Stanningfield in Suffolk, to be precise, where Hollis, his wife and a growing menagerie of animals had recently moved from London into the Old Rectory on Church Road, across the way from St Nicolas' Church and just down the lane from the village hall. It sounds almost like a parody of the pastoral English idyll and indeed a song such as 'Inheritance' feels like a man who has been unshackled from his plough and can finally rest a little. Without any more calls to leave home and go on the road, Hollis could perhaps more readily appreciate and access the peace and bounty of his immediate environment.

'I must have done the [final] sessions for *The Colour of Spring* in the autumn,' says David Rhodes. 'I remember Mark bringing in some apples from his garden.' Here is a glimpse of the man who wrote the words to these songs, the 'nature's son' whose heart has been coaxed out shyly by the sun. On the final Talk Talk tour, Rhodes recalls that 'I used to get up early in the morning and so did he, so I would see him at breakfast quite a lot. Mark would always look very neat and his hair was always, like, *giant*. It turns out before he showered, he always put on a shower cap. It was then that we talked a lot about more personal things. He had only recently moved to Suffolk and he was just getting into gardening. He was starting to know a little bit about plants. I had just got my first little garden and he was suggesting plants to me and that sort of thing. I have nice, happy memories of that.'

EMI's Malcolm Hill recalls a conversation along similar lines. 'Mark had bought this big place which had acres of land and I remember I said, "Well, who's going to [look after] all that?" He said, "No, no, that's not what's going to happen. I'm just going to keep a square in front of the back of the house tidy and the rest is going to go to wild."'

Apply your metaphors as freely as you wish. It is tempting to view *Spirit of Eden* as nature run riot, beyond its margins, the neat furrows and lines of the past dug up and grown over. But this was a planned disarray. Strategic spontaneity.

•

In the days, or perhaps even the hours, immediately after the news of the death of Mark Hollis was made public on the evening of 24 February 2019, Tim Friese-Greene posted a piece of music online. It was a demo of the *Spirit of Eden* track 'Eden' without any vocals or a bass part, recorded shortly before sessions for the album began. 'In memoriam,' he wrote. 'A late-stage rehearsal straight to cassette for reference. Recorded shortly before going into the studio, probably at John Henry rehearsal rooms. This is Mark on guitar, Lee on drums, and myself on piano and organ (the bass was always addressed in the studio once the basic track was down, which is why it doesn't feature here). It's best to take the eight minutes out and listen to the end, preferably in headphones, and in a quiet space.'[2] Though lacking lyrics or melody, this piece of music was immediately identifiable as the same piece which would eventually become the second track on the album.

Phill Brown caught wind of the demo surfacing and thought two things.

Firstly, that Hollis would not have been happy with it seeing the light of day, no matter the circumstances. 'Mark would have been really angry,' says Brown. 'Tim could have done it at any time in the last thirty years and he did it days after Mark died. I thought it was kind of weird … I never listened to it at the time because I was so annoyed. I thought, *I'm not going to go and join this party of listening to this demo*. I've always tried to very much support Mark's ethos. I was shocked when that came out.'

Secondly: There had been *demos* for these songs?!

The key phrase in Friese-Greene's note is that the recording of 'Eden' was made 'for reference'. Yet not only was it not aired during the sessions, but its very existence was also never mentioned, nor that of any other demos. Later comments from Hollis – one of which talked about trying to recreate a particular guitar sound for the song 'Desire' – implied that the entire album was demoed. Indeed, an early attempt at 'I Believe in You', at the time titled 'Snow in Berlin', was attempted during *The Colour of Spring* sessions.

'Before we started, everything was there as a basic structure, but the tracks themselves were all put down in a live format and then the overdubs were done at ridiculous length,' he said in 1991. 'Because, you see, the most important thing with this album was just for it to have the right feel, for it to have an absolute calm, but for it to have an absolute intensity inside of that.'[5] I like the 'ridiculous length' comment. The self-awareness is reassuring.

'It turned out that there were these [rehearsal studio demos] of Lee, Mark and Tim, with the basic structure of *Spirit of Eden*,' says Phill Brown. 'It's surprising. Certain elements [on "Eden"], especially the sound of the drums and the drum parts, are pretty much identical to the album. [So] they knew what they were after [all along]. I was there from day one, for nine months until we finished it, and not once was there any reference to the demo. We never heard demos in the studio. No one talked about the demos or referred to anything.

Certainly no musicians were ever played any demos. They weren't even played the whole track!'

It begs the question: if Hollis, Harris and Friese-Greene (and perhaps Paul Webb, though by this stage that may not have been the case) already had a clear idea of the sound and shape of the songs on *Spirit of Eden*, then why spend nine months giving the impression that they were painstakingly stumbling around in the dark? And why not give the engineer some sense of what they were trying to achieve by letting him hear the music?

Not playing any demos to outside musicians can be viewed as a legitimate creative tactic. Not playing them to their engineer could be seen as more a calculated power move, but most likely Brown ultimately was just another element in the recording process whose default responses Hollis and Friese-Greene wished to short-circuit: what better way to ensure that each sonic moment be assessed entirely on its own merits? 'When Mark went out to play guitar, he had parts, but it wasn't as obvious as it may seem,' Brown recalls. 'He might play a particular thing, which might be the verse, but he wasn't really playing it as a song – verse-chorus-middle-eight – because it was all pieced together. Because of the way we recorded, the [song] was an unfolding thing. It just seemed very random to me. Had I heard the demo, which I've now heard, then I would have known what we were going to be doing.'

In this case, foreknowledge was not the desired quality. The less anybody knew, the more they were compelled to come up with an interesting response. In this sense, *Spirit of Eden* was a marked devolution from *The Colour of Spring*. The songs may have again been sketched out in advance, but the intention this time was more obviously disruptive. Where the intrusive additions to *The Colour of*

Spring were most often augmentations to songs which were structurally robust, here the time was spent on making each and every moment of the album extraordinary.

The 'Eden' demo is a valuable insight into the rewards of this process. The 'written' song is already clearly there, albeit as a skeletal construct: guitar and drums, already echoing the Velvet Underground, alongside stark piano and, later, organ. The sense of space and silence rubbing against what we might call sonic violence is already implicit, though the dynamics are much flatter in the demo; it hasn't yet been roughed up.

What took so much time to locate, aside from the final garnish of the vocal melody and lyric, are the elements that could not be written by these three musicians alone, namely the dozens of moments of instrumental spontaneity, half-thoughts, last-ditch attempts, fuck-it-why-not tries, mistakes, tech glitches and found sounds which added the unique texture that Hollis obsessively pursued; not to mention all the failed efforts to add to the track that were discarded, which in their own way were also valuable, and which also inform the final version. The written song was a beginning, a basic necessity, but only that.

In Wessex, it all began, again, with the drums. The one thing Brown *was* aware of when they started recording *Spirit of Eden* was that Hollis and Friese-Greene had six rhythm ideas already written on a drum machine. There was no Fairlight this time. Harris then went into an equipment cupboard off the main studio, accompanied by six drum microphones and some disco lights. He began laying down the bedrock to the tracks, not simply replacing the drum machine parts but changing them, bringing in the vital human element. 'I created the patterns,' said Harris. 'I didn't think of them as complicated. How they were was how they had to be. All had to have "feel" and dynamic[s], as everything did.'[4]

His partner in crime was percussionist Martin Ditcham. If you recall, we left Ditcham during the latter stages of *The Colour of Spring*, sitting on the studio floor, surrounded by a kind of sacred circle of his percussive and rhythmic instruments, an ambient mic somewhere high above his head; Swiss-quality timekeeping by way of Ilford. Two years later, he's still there, this time with a pestle and mortar, children's toys, a glass tumbler and more than a few bright ideas.

'It got much more experimental on *Spirit*,' says Ditcham. 'I was in the studio with Mark, Tim and Phill Brown. They were in for a year and I'd go backwards and forwards doing bits and pieces as and when they needed it. As in most recordings, they tended to go for a good drum track, then they build around that. In the early stages, when they were doing the rhythm tracks, I would be in a booth playing shaker as a rhythm track and Lee would play along to that, because quite often you have electronic clicks and they're not very comfortable to play to, whereas if I'm listening to a click and then playing the shaker and Lee listens to that, it feels more natural.'

To most observers, there seemed to be little sense of band loyalty remaining. In the words of Friese-Greene, Harris was 'dragooned' into the sessions only because neither he nor Hollis could play drums.[5] Otherwise, you feel, he might have been deemed surplus to requirements. According to the demo of 'Eden', Webb wasn't even invited along to the rehearsals prior to recording. 'Paul Webb fell beside the wayside after *Spirit of Eden*,' said Friese-Greene.[6] Or, perhaps more accurately, during it. As on *The Colour of Spring*, he was one of three bass players credited, with Friese-Greene claiming that Hollis also played bass on the album.

For some, Webb had already been cast as something of a whipping boy. 'I remember the first day I worked with them on *Spirit* they were doing bass overdubs,' says Stuart Stawman. 'They set off the smoke machine behind Paul "for a laugh" and the laugh was at Paul's expense, right? It wasn't a joke *with* him. It was *at* him. I didn't feel comfortable from the get-go, watching that. I thought, *Oh no, this is cruel.* They didn't respect him, or his playing, from what I could make out. Paul was the guy to take the piss out of by the time I got there.'

The dissolution of the band, which began during the later stages of the last album, continued apace during these sessions. 'I think the thing that made it marginal as an outfit was the fact that Mark decided after *The Colour of Spring* that he didn't want to tour anymore,' said Friese-Greene. 'That made it very difficult for the other members. After *The Colour of Spring*, we dispensed with other keyboard players totally, because Mark and I thought between us that we could cover that base, and we did. Mark and I had such a good understanding that it was a source of continual frustration to us that we had to constantly explain to other musicians what we wanted. In the end, we would just shrug and say, "We will do it then." We started to play more and more of the stuff ourselves and to cut out the middle man. We didn't have to verbalise so much that way to get people to understand where we wanted to go with it, and to some extent that became the case with the other instruments as well.'[7]

One wonders whether the 'genius' of the Hollis/Friese-Greene method actually masks a deficiency. An almost heroic refusal, or inability, to engage in even the most basic discourse about their music now looks prescient, but it could simply have been their social limitations masquerading as strategy. Neither man, it seems, was able to explain or intuit to anyone other than each other what the task at hand actually required.

For Lee Harris, meanwhile, life in the 'Mark and Tim show' would only get more taxing. 'I think Lee enjoyed himself on *Spirit of Eden*. There was a good vibe, although it was mad,' says Phill Brown. '[But] once we had the drums down, Mark didn't really want Lee hanging around – which is pretty tough if you're in a band and you're not really welcome. Lee would come in each day. He hovered around, playing pool or just popping in occasionally, but he certainly wasn't welcome to sit [in the control room] and follow the procedure. It was really Tim, Mark and myself and the tape assistant that were there all the time.' Often, the tape assistant, Shaun Lambdin, was sent out to play pool with Harris.

Making these records was no bucolic idyll. The control room out-takes from the *Spirit of Eden* sessions give a flavour of the caustic, sarcastic demotic which was a core part of Hollis's nature. Like many people who met him for the first time, Warne Livesey, a fellow 'Essex boy' who co-wrote and recorded with Hollis on his 1998 solo album, was struck by the dissonance between the man and his work. 'He was almost the antithesis of who I would imagine him to be from his music,' says Livesey. 'He was a very down to earth, north London lad. We would exchange incredibly crude stories and have a great laugh together … We got along well on that front, from that mixture of both being a little bit yobbish with quite crass senses of humour, but also really into the arts and multiculturalism.'

Falling into the benign surrealistic duologues of Peter Cook and Dudley Moore's Pete & Dud characters was a favourite way for David Bowie and Tony Visconti to pass time in the studio. During *Spirit of Eden*, Hollis and his cohorts were closer to their wincingly crude alter egos, Derek & Clive: silly, sneery nasal voices, sweary riffs, in-jokes and wordplay; the usual 'fucks' and 'cunts'; some off-colour barely double entendre about 'queens'. Just a bunch of blokes filling the air – they could be on a building site, in a private members' club or a locker room. You want feet of clay? They should release these snippets of badinage to knock Hollis from the po-faced pedestal he has been placed on.

'They could be foul-mouthed bastards for sure, and they enjoyed it,' says Stuart Stawman. 'Like Derek & Clive, they could make it hysterically funny, and at other times it wasn't. Mark went after me once. Unfortunately, I can't remember what it was about, but I just thought, *Oh, here we go. I'm getting the Hollis.* Essentially, he was gunning for me and I thought, *Fuck this.* So I mentioned to Mark that I had seen Talk Talk play [a famously disastrous gig supporting Genesis] at Milton Keynes Bowl in 1982. Straight face. His eyes sparkled. He said something like, "Oh, *well played*" and that was it. I had won the round. I knew I was in a game and I knew I had just played the ace. But I thought, *What the fuck are we doing?*'

'Mark had that kind of London rough streak,' Stawman continues. 'If we were playing table tennis, it's not just for a bit of a laugh. He is playing to fucking win. He could spot when his opponent stopped having a killer instinct. It's that thing of reading the schoolyard, picking the strengths and the weaknesses – which Paul exuded. Paul didn't exude standing up to you. I don't know if Mark went for Phill. He went for me that time. He would have gone for Richard, the technician. It's weird. There was a violence to it. It was unspoken, but you could feel it. It could be hysterically funny at times. And at other times people's feelings got hurt.'

This is true. Dietmar Schillinger, the engineer at Wessex who worked on *The Colour of Spring*, believed at the time that he may have been picked on because he was German. He confessed to being relieved, some forty years later, to learn that almost everyone in the band's orbit received the same treatment, regardless of nationality, creed or colour. 'I was sometimes at the end of the stick,' he says. 'I always thought that it was just me because I'm German. I didn't know how they were with other people, but "grating" is probably the right word. From Mark, yes, but Lee and Paul were quite good, too!'

Until quite close to the start of recording *Spirit of Eden*, Schillinger believed he would be the chief engineer on the record. 'I loved working on *The Colour of Spring* and I was supposed to engineer the whole [of the next] album. Then they went for Phill Brown – who is a really good engineer and a nice bloke. Tim wanted me, but I guess then Mark had other ideas. I left Wessex afterwards, maybe because I was bypassed. I was devastated. I was broken.' Phill Brown, of course, held the trump card called 'Traffic', date-stamped 1967.

Meanwhile, the repartee rolled on.

'I was a bit late to one session,' recalls Robbie McIntosh. 'You know that old joke where you would say: "Ken Dodd died!" "Diddy?" "No, Doddy!" Anyway, I was late and I tried it on Mark. "Did you know Ken Dodd died?" He instantly said, "What, did you get stuck behind his hearse?" That sums him up, really. When I was working with Lee quite recently, he reminded me of it. You couldn't get anything by Mark. I was trying to catch him out and it didn't work. Made me feel about a couple of inches tall.'

In some ways, it was simply the laddish cut and thrust of tour life brought into the studio. It was also a way of testing people's character. 'After shows on tour, we would be in the dressing room having a drink,' recalls David Rhodes. 'If there was anybody [outside the inner circle] there, particularly record company people, Mark would pretend to take a big swig out of a bottle of wine and then pass it to them. I didn't get what was going on the first couple of times. What he would do is just blow a couple of bubbles into it to make it look as though he was really drinking it … There were these kinds of tests that he would throw at people. How are you going to react? Are you gonna keep up? Yeah? *Good luck!* Will you be part of this or are you going to fall at the first bite?'

As for Hollis and Friese-Greene, 'I don't think I ever saw it being abrasive between them,' says Stawman. 'I'm not saying it wasn't, but I never saw any of that harshness between them. It was always going outwards – and close by.'

'There was a lot of humour, dry to the point of arid at times,' says Richard Hill. 'I do remember laughing quite a bit and getting the piss taken out of me. They were all quite good at that. I think if I had been easily affected, I'd probably have been pissed off, but I couldn't take them that seriously. To be honest, I spent most of the '80s stoned. That makes you bulletproof in certain cases.'

Spirit of Eden has an understandable reputation as an album possessing certain narcotic qualities: blissed out; music for skinning up to and surrendering to the drift. Its slumbering pace is not marginal; it 'is of the essence,' said Friese-Greene, 'even if it is a pace that approaches vanishing point at times'.[8] My friend Dave's entry point, I'm sure, would have been Pink Floyd. He would have been alerted to the fact that this, too, was the music of hazy late nights, torn Rizla packets and five-paper joints built on the back of the album cover. It's almost certainly how I first heard it, but *Spirit of Eden* has a lot more going on than that. It has sharp elbows, harsh sonic shifts, precipitous falls and apparently becalmed passages that suddenly fizz like speed psychosis. One tunes *in* to it, surely, rather than drifts *out*.

Despite many of the rumours which swirl around that record – and, on occasion, the band – it wasn't recorded in a chemical blur. It is so bent that it had to be made pretty much straight. Talk Talk were no strangers to weed or alcohol, but Phill Brown says that *Spirit of Eden* – and later *Laughing Stock* – 'was actually made in a very straight head-wise situation. Mark would get stoned, but it would be after hours rather than during the session. I was still smoking spliff, so I would roll up the odd spliff and some nights Mark would say, "Got a little taster?" He would take it home and he would smoke at home, get stoned, come back the next day. He didn't take drugs on the sessions at all. By then, Tim was pretty straight. He was a pretty heavy [cigarette] smoker back then. Lee and I tended to have the odd spliff [in the studio], but Mark didn't.'

Interpretations vary regarding what constituted 'the odd spliff'. For a short period during the making of *Spirit of Eden*, British band the Bible were in Wessex working on their second album, *Eureka*. 'Every time we walked past [Studio 1] and the door opened, you actually couldn't see the interior,' says their guitarist at the time, Neill MacColl, son of folk nobility Ewan MacColl and Peggy Seeger and the half-brother of the late Kirsty MacColl. 'It was like the witches' conference, because there were clouds of dope smoke coming out. You'd get stoned just passing the door. We didn't really see them, to be honest. They seemed to be locked into some drug-hazed underworld. We were stoned too, of course, just not as stoned as them…'

'Phill was an inveterate smoker, same as me,' says Richard Hill. 'He would come up to the workshop. There was a case of little component drawers on the wall and, at the back of the 100-ohm drawer, there was always a wee stash. He knew that and I knew that. I'd keep it stocked and he put a bit in if he used it. Generally, it worked.'

'I think marijuana is a great drug in the studio because it just gives you that bit of calm,' says Brown, leaving unspoken the fact that if you are listening to the same drum pattern for weeks on end while disco lights flash continually, calm is a quality worth more than gold. 'It makes me focus better. It always has. When I was at Olympic, right from when I was sixteen years old, in the studio there was always a bit of dope around. [With Talk Talk] there were no heavy drugs. With the lighting and all the rest of it, and being in the dark, there was enough psychedelic stuff going on without anyone really having to get that wrecked.'

'No one was on coke, grinning and yammering away: "*Great, great!*"' adds Stuart Stawman. 'None of that.'

Instead, like a group of middle-rank office workers, the core trio of Brown, Hollis and Friese-Greene would knock off at six o'clock to go to the pub. Sometimes on a Friday night, Richard Hill was asked along, 'if they remembered to give me a shout. Mark was always first at the door, but last [to] the bar, I noticed. [Even that] was a game for him.'

•

You could fill a book – but not this one – with the technical specifications on *Spirit of Eden*. The music was recorded through a mixture of witch-doctoring, applied science and expert studio know-how. Once again emphasising Phill Brown's counter-cultural credentials, they limited themselves mostly to microphones available prior to

1967 – the Neumann U67, Neumann U48, Shure 57 and AKG C12a – recording mostly in mono and to analogue. The exceptions to this timeframe were some modern microphones used to record the drums and a Mitsubishi 32-track digital tape machine, which they linked up to several Studer 24-track recorders which were used as 'slave' machines.*

The digital tape machine was new and could be glitchy. 'The Mitsubishi did go wrong,' says Richard Hill, whose job it was to put it right. 'It put clicks all over the first eight tracks at one point. I spent the whole night getting rid of those clicks, bouncing tracks, switching off error correction, doing all sorts of things. It was a nightmare of a machine, but we did it.' He laughs. 'Then I had to clear the loo in the back corridor. Oh, it was fun at Wessex…' They added a track of analogue tape noise to the digital machine, just to roughen up some of its clean, bright edges.

They all disliked the sound of the Solid State Logic (SSL) mixing console and tried bypassing it whenever possible, liberating an old Neve valve spring reverb from a cupboard at Wessex where it had lain unloved for a decade. 'We just got all this junk out, basically,' says Brown. 'We had Richard fixing things and making them work.'

---

* To carry out a recording of forty-eight tracks, or indeed more, involved the concept of 'master' and 'slave' reels. When the basic tracks of a song were built up, they went onto one reel of 24-track tape. When this reel was full, the entirety of the music recorded so far was mixed down onto two tracks of a second reel on another machine. This was the 'slave' reel. The original 'master' reel was put away and all further overdubs were done using the temporary stereo mix of the basic tracks as a guide. When the recording was complete, the master reel was brought back, and master and slave reels would be synchronised together ready for final mixdown. In theory, dependent on how many machines you have at your disposal, this can give limitless tracks.

All the musical elements were recorded individually. Acoustic instruments were mic'ed up from a distance of six feet and amplifiers from twelve feet, after several different mics had been tested. 'We would put up, say, five different microphones on an instrument,' says Brown. 'Tim would pick his favourite kind of mic that he thought might work for this [particular part]. I'd pick mine. Then we would get the musician to play and in the control room we would listen and narrow it down to two, then one. Once we had that, we would then fine-tune the sounds in the room, or fine-tune where the mic was.'

The technology enabled them to deploy the cut-and-paste method much more freely without the rigidity of the Fairlight; to capture the 'feel' of the first take, or the fleeting best thought, and then plant it anywhere on the album. 'What we were doing on analogue back then is how people now work with digital. You can cut, paste and move things around,' says Brown. 'Say something interesting happened at 1:30. Mark would say, "It's in the wrong place." We'd play the track and then we'd get to, say, 4:22 and Mark would say, "That's where we want it." It was Mark, I think, most of the time, who was the one saying that. We'd do all the maths, then these machines would all slew off and we would then fine-tune it. We had control over literally getting something down to a millisecond early or later. It was wonderful to watch all these machines, if you have got the maths right, whirring around.'

There is another reason to believe that Steve Winwood did not make the cut on *The Colour of Spring*; he was never invited back. With no assigned keyboard player, Hollis and Friese-Greene would alternate on the studio floor with the various instruments. One of the great attractions of returning to Wessex was the studio's Bösendorfer grand piano, which they had used on *The Colour of Spring*. The live room also had a Hammond organ with a Leslie cabinet, which was joined by two harmoniums for the sessions.

'I became fascinated by the fluid way in which Mark and Tim would take it in turns at the keyboards trying to work out what a particular part should be,' says Stuart Stawman. 'There was no possessiveness at all over who would eventually record the part. Everything was done in the service of the song. In fact, I think there were probably some parts that combined both of their playing. It was the same with guitar parts. Either one might try out ideas and record a part.'

Hollis spent days playing the simple electric guitar lick at the start of 'The Rainbow', returning to it over and over again, trying to strike the (im)perfect balance between rough and proficient, as though a great guitarist – which Hollis, technically speaking, was not – had simply fallen out of bed and started playing it. 'He drove us fucking crazy,' says Stawman, who, while all this was happening, was elsewhere in the building working with the Bible.

'We were in [Wessex] mixing for a week,' says Neill MacColl. 'Talk Talk were in the massive room, doing their thing of moving the microphones an inch to the left or to the right, then trying a take and then moving them back again for fucking days on end. We were up in the games room, which was above their live area. It was me, my brother Calum and the rest of the band, and we heard Mark Hollis doing the main riff from "The Rainbow". I've checked this with Calum. In his memory, they played the same riff for the whole week we were there. In mine, it was three days. Every time he did it, it was *exactly the same* and completely perfect. Calum eventually had enough and called down to the studio. He said, "Look, we've got two really good guitarists upstairs if you're struggling with it. One of us can come and play it if you can't get this right!" Phill Brown doesn't remember that happening, but it wouldn't have been him who answered the phone. It was a magical moment.'

•

By 19 October, five months in, they had six backing tracks completed, with the usual oddball working titles: 'Modell', 'Camel', 'Maureen', 'Norm', 'Snow in Berlin' and 'Eric'.* These were transferred to the Mitsubishi digital 32-track machine in the proposed running order of the record. The first twenty-four minutes ran as one continuous piece, with a minute or so of clean tape left between each song to later record an intro to the record and the instrumental 'link' sections between tracks one and two, and two and three. This became the first side of the record. When they began to build up the backing tracks with multiple overdubs, Brown was able to run the entire twenty-four minutes of side one each time for outside musicians to play over in one continuous sweep, bouncing down any new parts they wanted to keep onto a new track.

The overdubs are where the real fun began, as a parade of inno-cents from the outside were ushered into the inky, hermetic world of Wessex.

Of the few contemporary pop artists Hollis seemed to have any time for, Kate Bush and David Bowie were near the top of the list. We have already seen how there seemed to be a connection with Bush, which would continue intriguingly into the 2000s. Bowie's three 'Berlin' albums, meanwhile, offered a precedent for the way Hollis and Friese-Greene worked with session musicians on *Spirit of*

---

* Two more titles, 'Scarecrow' and 'Rocket Man', were included on a cassette of rough mixes of the album dated 29 January 1988.

Eden in particular. The guitarist Adrian Belew recalled the approach on Bowie's 1979 album, *Lodger*, the working title of which was *Planned Accidents*.

'The original idea with [*Lodger*] was that they said there were about twenty tracks they'd already worked on and they wanted me to go upstairs in the studio, put the headphones on and start playing. I said, "Playing what?" They said, "No, you just start playing. You play what you like." I asked if I could hear the songs first and they said no. I was just given a tempo and time signature. They said they wanted to get my accidental responses. I said, "What key?" And they said, "No … Just go upstairs, put the headphones on and play along to the song." They allowed me to do that twice for each song, no more. And then they'd take their favourite parts of the guitar tracks and cut them up, and string them into a composite guitar track. So all those guitar parts you hear on *Lodger* are things I made up on the spot to a song I'd never heard before. "Boys Keep Swinging", "DJ", "Red Sails" – all made up on the spot. The guitar parts were meant to sound accidental and I think they kind of do. The whole thing took two days.'[9]

Eno, Bowie and Visconti had worked in a similar way with Robert Fripp on *"Heroes"*. The idea of music which is 'meant to sound accidental' is key to how Hollis and Friese-Greene approached these Talk Talk records. There are similarities between both methods, if not the sounds they created, but where Bowie and Hollis diverged significantly was in their patience thresholds. The former threw everything together quickly and moved on. The latter laboured over every brushstroke.

In getting session musicians to play wearing a kind of creative blindfold, the intention was that the results would emerge from instinctive reactions which, though rooted in some form of competence, were not limited by virtuosity; creating a sound or impulse which pre-thought or preparation would not necessarily have accessed or permitted. And with digital editing, the freedom was now available to place that sound anywhere in the musical picture. It did not have to belong to a particular part of a song, or even the initial song itself. It could be moved around the wider canvas and placed anywhere.

On *Spirit of Eden* perhaps more than any other Talk Talk record, the brief for outside musicians was to attempt to bypass the conscious thought, the ingrained reflex, the muscle memory, the active decision. To catch the creative impulse unawares, Hollis and Friese-Greene wore away at each incomer until, ideally, they either stumbled in an interesting way or fell into a subconscious response which made something unusual or unexpected happen. It was a scientific approach to improvisation mixed with the rules of the Colosseum. Harry your adversary into exhaustion and disorientation – and then pounce. The trippy lighting was a literal expression of the intention to ambush players in the dark with music they hadn't heard. Given oblique or opaque instructions – or none at all – each guest was granted a maximum of only eight takes to do their thing.

'For all the musicians that came in, it was completely random because they weren't told much,' says Phill Brown. 'No conversations. They were never allowed in the control room. They were never spoken to on the headphones. There was no, "Hey, great! Let's do another one!" None of that. You just ran the tapes back and then another take would happen. We would only give some musicians the barest track to work to. They might be listening to five or six parts, and they would play to that. Once they got used to that, on maybe the third take, they thought, *I've twigged this one. I know where this is going to go.* On the fourth take, we would take out half of what they had heard and put in stuff that they had never heard before. It almost made the track feel like it was a different thing completely. All the time, Mark was trying to keep everyone spontaneous and on their toes. First takes, first ideas.'

There was a wilful mischief to all this. Hollis and Friese-Greene told Robbie McIntosh that when they had Martin Ditcham in, they had added a strobe to the light show. They were amazed that he was able to play at all.

'*Spirit of Eden* was more of a mystery [than *The Colour of Spring*],' says the guitarist. 'I didn't play any electric guitar. There is just a bit of 12-string and a bit of resonator guitar, which they refer to on the sleeve as a Dobro. It was actually a National Steel. They are slightly different. I remember Mark would say something like, "Do another pass, but don't play anything above the seventh fret." Or he would say, "Just play the bottom four strings" – which sort of makes sense, because the bottom four strings on a guitar are wound, so they would have a more solid sound. He was remarkably clever with textures and dynamics, Mark. He was sometimes more into the sonic space [that] something was taking up rather than what it was actually playing, to a certain extent, although he did have a great harmonic sense as well.'

Other guitarists didn't fare so well. 'I did go in to play on *Spirit of Eden*,' says David Rhodes. 'They had a big chart of what was planned, but I don't remember it being in any way detailed. It was just like a loose map. I don't know how long the piece was at that point, but twenty minutes, maybe longer. I was getting to grips with it, or I thought I was, and on one section, I said, "So are you thinking something a bit like Randy California?" Mark went, "No, he was sat there yesterday. We gave him the *bread line*." Suitably chastised, I carried on. I had them replay a couple of segments for me and when it came time to do a take, they turned off the lights. They had the oil wheel going in the control room and I couldn't see the chart anymore. I spent hours there that day. It was nice. Then we all went to the pub, just up the road from Wessex. And then nothing I did made it onto the album.'

Rhodes was in good company. Stuart Stawman didn't work consistently on *Spirit of Eden*. Phill Brown was engineering the album and, as chief engineer at Wessex, Stawman was overseeing other projects, of which there were many during the ten months it took Talk Talk to complete the album. But every now and then he was called on to stand in for a few days.

During these tenures, he recalls them deploying what he calls the 'Give it Back' principle. If something they were recording started to suggest the influence of another artist, however tangentially, Friese-Greene would adopt a loud, shrill, Pythonesque voice to insist that they should 'give it back' to whichever artist they were reminded of.

'Give it back to Kajagoogoo!'

'Give it back to Miles Davis!'

'Give it back to Aretha Franklin!'

'Give it back to the Andrews Sisters!'

At times, the association was acutely obvious; at others, it was more tenuous or tongue-in-cheek. The list was long and no reputation was safe from being returned to sender.

One of the more high-end musicians who came into Wessex was the bass player Larry Klein (further evidence of Paul Webb's diminished standing). Klein was at the time married to Joni Mitchell and played on, co-produced and occasionally co-wrote songs on her albums throughout the 1980s. 'The conversation was polite,' says Stawman, who had a ringside seat at the back of the control room for this visitation. 'I remember him likening his current home in California to a French vineyard, and then they got down to the business of working out some bass parts. The session was wrapped up and he left.'

Within an hour of Klein leaving, all his contributions had been erased and Friese-Greene was heard to mutter, 'I guess his wife is the creative one.'

'They gave him back to Joni,' says Stawman.

The enfant terrible of the classical violin, Nigel Kennedy, was called in for the day, but his playing was deemed a little busy. They took him to the pub afterwards and ended up using just a single note from his part.

This ruthless process of subtraction is exemplified by the extraordinary 'Wealth', which is in some ways the odd song out on *Spirit of Eden*. There are no drums, though there would have been a drum track when the song was originally conceived. Brown recalls the song 'evolved not in any specific way that was different to our normal approach. This whole process seemed very random. Mark would go out and play a keyboard part or Hammond part. He would do that multiple times, then Tim would go out and play the same part, but with his own approach, and then we would choose what we liked best and what we were going to use and bounce it down and then add something else. "Wealth" was done in a very similar way – doing performances, often using the early takes. Mark had this thing about the first and second takes are often the best. It didn't seem to be treated any differently to everything else other than the fact that there is less on it.'

Brown was learning on the job about Hollis's 'pox' philosophy. A stunning vocal part by the Chelmsford Cathedral choir recorded for 'I Believe in You' sounded positively celestial to him, Stawman and indeed anyone else in the vicinity who heard it drifting through the stairs and corridors of the old, converted church hall. By the following morning, it had been erased for the heinous crime of being 'too good'.

'That was a big saying, which was very much from Mark,' says Brown. 'Somebody is playing, you get the sounds up and Mark would just say, "It sounds too good." And I didn't understand that! It took me probably a couple of months to really grasp what the guy was about. You've got to remember, although I spent thirteen years with Mark, and I kind of understood him during that time, during the first months of *Spirit of Eden*, I knew nothing really about him. When somebody says, "It sounds too good" … *Wait, isn't that what I'm supposed to be doing? Isn't that kind of the point?* But I slowly got what he was about. He wanted things to feel real. He didn't really care about technique or things being technically right. It had to have the right feel and the right vibe. I understood that probably a couple of months in and I think that's why I spent so long with Mark. I think he just trusted me. He felt that I could give him what he wanted, although he never explained himself in those terms.'

Talking about *Spirit of Eden* on its release, Hollis said, 'Generally, we've gone for sounds that, in technical terms, you would say are rubbish, but when you couple that with the way it's played, then it becomes a good sound.' When asked to highlight a specific example, he responded: 'I would say the entire album.'[10]

'I think Mark especially really liked sounds to sing and be very present,' says David Rhodes. 'That when you play something, it is committed, and it has its own life as a sound. I think that is what you hear in the later records, the space that he gives to the instruments.'

He also, I think, desperately wants the listener to hear something of the spirit of the person playing the instrument. 'Mark and I used to talk about Saturday morning *Record Review* on Radio 3, where they look at three or four different versions of the same piece of music,' says Laurence Pendrous. 'We used to enjoy that a great deal, talking about different recordings of music that we both enjoyed – particularly with Messiaen's *Preludes* and his solo piano works. We both loved Peter Hill's recording of those. He actually worked with Messiaen on those interpretations.* Messiaen said the interpretation of each individual pianist is a part of the composition, in direct opposition to what Debussy said, that players shouldn't put any emotion or any part of their own character or personality into music, but simply play it the way it is stated in the score.'

It is an illuminating distinction to make: the player *is part of the composition*. And as such, the character of the player, their demeanour, their approach to the work, to the instrument, to the other people in the room, becomes absolutely critical. 'It's always been very important to me that I have got on with the people we've worked with,' said Hollis. 'People's attitudes have always been really important to me. So much of why someone would exist on one of our albums is what they are like as a person.'[11] Gaynor Sadler, who had played harp on *The Colour of Spring*, understands this approach.

---

* The Piano Music of Olivier Messiaen / Préludes (1929) / Quatre études de Rythme (1949–50) / Cantéyodjayâ (1949); released in 1989 on Unicorn Kanchana.

The attitude of a session player can make a world of difference, she says. 'The worst thing on a session is having anyone come in and being judgemental or dissing it. You can always tell. When somebody is open-minded and willing to try things, that is the period of time when something magical can happen.'

Some musicians didn't respond to the calling. Others rose to the implied challenge and became valued team members. It was not an easy task. 'When I came out of those sessions, I was knackered,' says harmonica player Mark Feltham. 'I couldn't hold my hands up for a week because the muscles in my shoulders were so tense. They were intense, intense sessions. I had my position marked on a square and I wasn't allowed to move outside that square. I had to play from within that. It was very precise. He'd knock all the candles down and you'd have strobe lighting and incense burning and all that. Extremely bohemian and very intense.'

Given this stringent criteria, the process of selection for each and every part was daunting. 'I remember for Danny Thompson, we had the whole of [the first side of *Spirit of Eden*] on the Mitsubishi as a 24-minute piece of music,' says Brown. 'He did eight takes top to bottom. So that took, say, four hours. It then took us more than a day to listen through everything and make a note of what we were going to use and then bounce it and offset machines to move it somewhere else. With some of those things, it might take two to four hours to record something, but then it might take a day or two to actually bounce down what you were going to use. That's why it was a slow process. It feels like five guys in a room, but it is so involved technically. Often note by note, things were placed.'

Even Talk Talk loyalists such as Thompson were not immune to occasional moments of exasperation during this attritional working process. 'Danny once told me about those sessions,' says Neill MacColl. 'He told me he had been playing the same thing over and over – and he just isn't that kind of musician. At one point, Tim or Mark came in and uttered the immortal phrase: "Those two notes in the middle – could you just give them a tiny bit more pressure?" Danny said, "Look, mate, they've measured the pressure I give my notes. It's about 56lbs per square inch. I'm not doing any more fucking pressure."'

For whatever reason, the double-bassist wouldn't return to the fray on *Laughing Stock*. Emailing me in the immediate aftermath of Hollis's death, Thompson, who died in September 2025, wrote that he always felt 'privileged and flattered to have been asked to work with Mark. I did not know what was expected from me at the time, but it quickly became obvious that Mark was an innovative and free-thinking musician with "No Rules". He was very sure of his creations and gave me many ideas to pursue within his musical portraits. He was a free spirit and a pure joy to be able to work with.'

•

Following a break for Christmas, they all reconvened at Wessex on 4 January 1988. The album was coming together. Mark Feltham was usually one of the last musicians to add parts to a Talk Talk record. He was the exception to the rule, in the sense that he was played the full tracks and given specific direction; he was being asked to complete the picture, rather than simply add to it. On *Spirit of Eden*, his blues harp is the first really clear, distinctive sound that we hear, acclimatising the listener to this new world through his astonishing rough-hewn playing on the opening track, 'The Rainbow'.

'Most of the track would be down before I went in,' says Feltham. 'On *Spirit*, I used a Fender Champ and a Mesa Boogie. It was Mark's idea to link the two amps up. I said, "Cor, why do you want to do that?" He said, "Can I just try this? Can I?" This was a guy who didn't play my instrument but knew how he wanted me to sound for him. I had a nice big, wide sound, spread out, and they mic'ed up both amps. He just had that ability to hear sounds and sometimes to hear no sound.'

By this point, several months into the project, Hollis was beginning to address lyrics and vocals. In some cases, this required changes to the tracks. He would request that Brown make a verse or a section of a song a few bars shorter or longer to fit the words and melodies he was now writing.

For the engineer, 'this again enforced the idea that there weren't any demos and we were doing it all from scratch, and now that he was getting the lyrics together, he needed things to be different. He might have had the idea of what [the songs] were going to be about, in his own head, but as far as actually having lyrics, I don't think he had the finished lyrics until seven or eight months into the record. Mark came in and said, "Okay, we'll get some vocals together this week." That was probably just a week or two before we actually mixed. It was very much the last thing that went on. We probably didn't even do eight takes – more like five or six. Then we mixed down and picked the best lines. It wasn't [edited] word by word, like you do now with Pro Tools, and even syllable by syllable. It was a line at a time. It was a fast process – fast for him to record the vocals and a fairly fast process deciding what we were going to use.'

•

On *Spirit of Eden*, says Phill Brown, 'it's an illusion, what you're hearing'; an aural illusion, compiled from odd scraps and snatches of sound that seem familiar, but have been stitched together in ways that defy easy identification. In many ways, Talk Talk wore their influences openly. All these records are studies in applied listening, accumulating techniques the band – primarily Hollis, aided by Friese-Greene and Phill Brown – had heard being used by other artists they admired and which they wanted to test out in the practical arena.

We know Brown was hired principally because of his association with Traffic. I wondered whether his work with John Martyn on his 1977 album *One World* was also noted – given the way that record sounds, the ambient invention on tracks such as 'Small Hours' and the title song, and that Martyn's frequent foil, Danny Thompson, was a Hollis favourite. But apparently not. Hollis was 'aware of the vibe' of both Martyn and Nick Drake, but didn't know much about their work.[12] There were these intriguing gaps in his knowledge, blank spaces where you feel there was likely to have been a full page.

Van Morrison was certainly on his radar. Paul Webb recalls Hollis turning him onto *Astral Weeks* and in that album and others at the deeper end of Morrison's canon, we hear echoes of Hollis's attempts to find space and rapture in his music. The end of 'April 5th' feels most obviously indebted to Morrison's extended incantations on songs such as 'Listen to the Lion', 'You Know What They're Writing About' and 'When Heart is Open'. Hollis put 'Snow in San Anselmo' on compilation tapes for friends and its stunning choral arrangement may well have been in his mind as a reference point for 'Time it's Time' and 'I Believe in You'. And what could be a better summation of Hollis's show-don't-tell mentality than Morrison's wild rap on

'Summertime in England'? 'It ain't why, why, why, why, why / It just *is*.'

Hollis's classical tastes had continued to evolve, but he still leaned towards low-key intimacy, such as the small string quartets of Maurice Delage and Igor Stravinsky; not minimalism, as such, but minor-scale, intricate and detailed. He enjoyed the twentieth-century French modernist Darius Milhaud, with his jazz inflections, and Mikhail Gnessin. Soon, at the recommendation of Tim Friese-Greene, he would push forward through the century to engage with modern composers like Karlheinz Stockhausen, György Ligeti and Cage; 'stuff that's free in its composition and performance … just because they seem to have this understated approach where the music is everything.'[13]

And some hardly perennials. Can, Neu!, old blues, soul and gospel records.

Bowie. Bush. Pharoah Sanders. John Coltrane. Miles.

Porgy and Bess and *Sketches of Spain* were Hollis's favourite Miles Davis records. On the former, the lovely, lilting, mysterious fragment, 'Here Comes De Honey Man', has a haunted, out-of-focus emptiness that feels analogous to Talk Talk, as do those high, floating trumpet peals on 'Concierto De Aranjuez (Adagio)' and 'Saeta' on the latter. The strange Variophonal gusts in Talk Talk's music, those disembodied drifts of breath-controlled synthesiser we encounter so often, can be traced fairly directly back to Miles's trumpet, albeit bleached, somehow, of any whiff of his danger, his wicked groove. Talk Talk would never truly swing; theirs is de-bopped jazz, white and stubbornly sexless.

The influence ran deeper than specific textures. These records are also masterclasses in the dynamics of capturing sound as a whole. In his Miles Davis biography *Milestones*, Jack Chambers recalls Davis talking about the recording of *Sketches of Spain*. 'Davis thought the Concierto's "Adagio" melody was "so strong" that "the softer you play it, the stronger it gets, and the stronger you play it, the weaker it gets."'[14] Given Hollis's affiliations, this seems to say something useful about the approaches used on *Spirit of Eden*, *Laughing Stock* and his solo record. The closer one gets to silence, the stronger the effect can be.

'That [idea] of opening the mics up loud and then playing as quietly as you can was a big thing of Mark's,' says Brown. 'He got into that on these albums. There is a track on *Spirit of Eden* where he is playing this quiet guitar part with the mics wide open, and then he catches one note, and it just *explodes*. That was what he was after. It wasn't intentional, but he was after that. For me initially, as an engineer, I thought, *This is tricky, this is weird*. Things weren't going through lots of compressors and EQ, so when something explodes, it really explodes. You are watching levels that go from virtually nothing to plus two.'

The trick was to blend familiar colours in ways that created a new tone. 'Mark was so clever, but without actually saying why he was doing things,' says Brown. '*Spirit of Eden* could have been made thirty years ago, it could have been made in the 1960s, it could have been made a year or two ago. It's very timeless. That was something that he was really [conscious of], without actually saying it directly. Those kinds of discussions never happened. But I was around it for so long that I got it.'

The illusion was mastered into physical form at Abbey Road on 11 March 1988. Just shy of ten months since they rolled up, the four-wheel drives headed home.

ii

I am listening to *Spirit of Eden*. What am I hearing? What are the sounds, the moods and messages transmitted from this mysterious world?

In purely genre-related terms, I hear elements of jazz, electronic music, twentieth-century classical, folk, blues, choral, heavy metal, *Kosmische*, soul, prog rock. I am made hyper-aware throughout of the power of silence and hypnotic rhythm. I am part of something dense and elliptical, a record with a powerful mystique.

Some listening notes-to-self.

There are no individual credits for each song on *Spirit of Eden*. We can't ever be quite sure who is playing what, or indeed what precisely is making the sound we are hearing.

Side one – the first three tracks – is an unbroken suite of music lasting around twenty-three minutes, linked by a recurring instrumental passage. Side two is not. It features three very discrete and defined songs, neatly spaced out by silence. (This partly explains why one side is almost four minutes longer than the other.)

'The Rainbow' is the longest track, at a touch more than nine minutes.

'Inheritance' is the shortest, at a shade more than five.

The four remaining songs fall into the six-minute spectrum.

We have already heard Mark Hollis explain perhaps all he ever needed to regarding his ambitions for this record. He resolved, he said, to make an album that had 'an absolute calm, but for it to have an absolute intensity inside of that'.[1] That's not a bad summation for a man who yearned to let the music do the talking.

On *Spirit of Eden*, there is a continuous, ever-present tension between beauty and ugliness, release and restraint. Hollis's innate impulse for control is continually challenged. The 'absolute calm' and the 'absolute intensity' are never discrete entities; they co-exist throughout, one within the other, no matter which force feels dominant at any particular moment. Indeed, what we are hearing in the opening two and a bit minutes of the album, on 'The Rainbow', before the guitar slides in and the song proper begins, is a kind of group orientation session, an imperious primer for the album's signature blend of abrasive noise and intense beauty: silence, space and squall; its tidal shifts in tone and texture.

It begins as a muzzy fugue, a low-growling blend of Variophon, piano and treated harmonica lowing and keening, like some great leviathan shaking itself from the depths. 'The Rainbow' begins shrouded in something vaporous: sea mist, perhaps, or maybe it's merely the dawn of time. The squeaky noise at around thirty seconds is a rogue clarinet fluff. There is a tensile drone of strings, aural bad weather circling in the form of rolls, creaks, rumbles. The churn, like a helicopter in slow motion, which picks up speed around 1:55 is Martin Ditcham scraping a pestle and mortar with increased intensity ('Mark and Tim got very excited' when they first heard it, recalls Stuart Stawman). In terms of atmosphere, we are in the realms of Kate Bush's 'Hello Earth' or Bowie's 'Station to Station', a world of fleeting shadows, ghostly noises-off.

Then comes the thrillingly fierce electric guitar riff, a blues, which Hollis spent days trying to get... not *right*, as such, but exactly how he imagined it could be. It leads into the distorted shriek of Mark

Feltham's harmonica, wildly overloaded. The harp has all the really dramatic lines on this track, with the guitar playing a supporting role. The deadened, slack-tuned beat pulls the song into focus, forcing it up and up until everything drops away into a peaceful void of hollowed-out drums.

The central rhythm is dominant, but the music is filled with exquisite details. The little piano interlude just after four minutes is a snatch of jazz minimalism. The naked, very beautiful vocal fragment at the end tumbles into the abstract drift of the opening section, calling back to the notion of the first side of the album as an interlinked piece. It's a beautifully coherent, highly orchestrated piece of music.

There is much that remains hidden about 'The Rainbow', nine-tenths below the waterline, but what we must know is that the song concerns a grievous injustice. We would know this, I think, even if there were no words. But there are words and they point the listener further in that direction. At around three and a half minutes, when the vocal first appears, it tells us what we have already discerned from the music: 'Oh yeah, the world's turned upside down.' Nothing will ever be quite the same and yet Hollis never raises his voice in protest. It is a pure, calm and steady meter, even when it tumbles and overlaps on what we might call the chorus, as he sounds 'the victim's song'.

The lyric begins with two quite explicit citations. The opening line pointedly references 'The World Turned Upside Down', a pre-English Civil War ballad dating to around 1640. This popular broadside was written in protest against the banning of the traditional Christmas festivities in favour of a more ascetic, solemn marking of the day.

Perhaps more directly pertinent, and a song Hollis is more likely to have heard, is the track of the same name written by Leon

Rosselson in 1974 and recorded by many folk-adjacent artists, including the great Dick Gaughan, as well as Billy Bragg in 1985.

Rosselson's 'The World Turned Upside Down' reaches back to the same mid-seventeenth-century period as its namesake to tell a heroic story concerning the agrarian radicalism of the Diggers. A group of politicised English Christian dissenters, the Diggers fought to create a utopian, proto-ecological interrelationship between humanity and nature by attempting to farm on common land, only to be harried from county to county by the powers-that-be in their quest to do so. The song is a rousing pledge of solidarity to the heroic poor against the greedy rich, a wish for good to triumph over evil, but it also carries a more universally holistic message: 'This earth divided / We will make whole / So it will be / A common treasury for all.' Or, to put it another way: 'Our nation's wrong', let us heal it. In any case, this seems a fertile country for Hollis to be wandering around in, and well within the ambit of the humanitarian compassion evident in so much of his work.

In the next breath, he gives some context for this upending of the world, singing: 'Jimmy Finn is out / Oh, how can that be fair at all?'

Jimmy Finn?

Ever since I first listened to 'The Rainbow', I couldn't help but be intrigued by this Finn character. Who is he? What is he doing in here?

It has already been established that something terrible has occurred in the song, some great legal and possibly moral transgression. In sounding the victim's song, the lyric appears to cock an eye at the fashionable notion of reform and redemption, that criminals can or, indeed, should be redeemed. There are glimmers of an Old Testament sense of penal reckoning: you did the crime, now serve the time. It reads like a song of judgement, of sorrow and anger in the face of thwarted or paltry penance. More importantly, it *sounds* like that.

Inspired by the Diggers, I did some digging. Going by the name Jimmy Finn, I felt it might have some connection to Ireland, perhaps relating to political prisoners involved in the Troubles being released early as part of the quest for peace. (Or, at a stretch, going back to the beginning of the Irish Republican resistance movement; one newspaper archive carries a report of a young IRA volunteer from Westmeath named James Finn, who was killed during an attack on a Royal Irish Constabulary convoy in 1920.) 'The Rainbow' was written before the Forum for Peace and Reconciliation in Northern Ireland was established in 1994 – and before the Truth and Reconciliation Commission was set up in post-apartheid South Africa in 1995. However, prisoner swaps involving both sides of the conflict, allowing people convicted of serious crimes to be freed early from jail in order to advance the peace process, was a reality that existed throughout much of the span of the Irish conflict. The Good Friday Agreement of 1998 had similarly significant early release ramifications for paramilitary prisoners on both sides, causing great controversy and high feeling.

'The Rainbow' predates all this, of course, but something of the moral ambivalence of these transactions resonates in the song. What price peace? And who is paying?

Later, I remembered that Jimmy Finn is a character from the writings of Mark Twain. He crops up in *Life on the Mississippi*, while 'Pap' Finn in the Huckleberry Finn novels shares his surname and is an extension of the same character. Huck is his son. The chapter concerning Jimmy Finn in *Life on the Mississippi* is called 'A Question of Law'. It would work almost perfectly as a subtitle to 'The Rainbow'.

Beyond that, any specific relation between story and song seems tenuous at best. Jimmy Finn is not the central character in Twain's story. He is the town drunk and, at the beginning of the tale, Finn is misremembered by one local citizen as the bum who burned to death in the local jail. Having been locked up for vagrancy and drunkenness, he starts an accidental fire while trying to light his pipe and dies horribly. Or does he? In fact, the man who dies this grim death in the calaboose is not Finn but another, unnamed, drunk. In the telling of the story, nobody much seems to care who he was, except the young narrator, who is riddled with anxiety and remorse because he had given the dead man the matches for his pipe, the instruments of his demise.

The story raises questions of guilt, blame, the balancing of transgression and justice. 'The Rainbow' does the same, typically obliquely. As to where Hollis started out from, it is impossible to say. As I say, nine-tenths of this beast lies below the waterline.

*

The song ends shrouded in the same murk and drift in which it began. What lies at the end of 'The Rainbow'? 'Eden', of course, the pot of gold.

'Eden' finds structure and form in the shape of the drums, pattering into earshot, rising in intensity, a heartbeat thud, paying very obvious homage to 'Heroin' by the Velvet Underground. There is a stately, soulful gospel feel to the simple piano chords, which map the chord changes as the guitar holds its course on a single chord.

Both 'The Rainbow' and 'Eden' build, build, build then break like waves. In 'Eden', an uncertain sonic cluster gathers pace to a crescendo of raw electric guitar, before crashing, the drums steady and becalmed. Then a precipitous fall, making space for Hollis' vocal. His third pass on 'everybody needs someone to live by' is the first time he really lets loose on the record, and it's magnificent, his voice gathering force and urgency as he repeats the same line, give or take, three times. By the point where he reaches for the strongest words – 'rage on omnipotent' – the storm is spent, dialled back down to a murmur. To hit hard, he goes soft.

'Eden' is highly coherent and formed. Wearing slightly more expensive clothes, it could have feasibly appeared on *The Colour of Spring*. The instrumental passage at 5:30, that signature cloud-blown Variophon glide into the ether, is archetypal. A beautiful string part saws across the landscape. The closing guitar motif feels properly loosed, an unlocking. But still those drums, a pulse that cannot quite be stilled, rise back into the frame, bringing completion, satisfaction, peace.

They are still pattering away as 'Desire' begins. There is some scene-setting on the churchy organ while that slow-creep instrumental circles back once again to 'The Rainbow'. The key texture here is the string bass, played by Danny Thompson; we could almost imagine John Martyn singing 'Bless the Weather' over the top of it. It's a killer groove, symmetrical and metronomic, and it keeps going, on and on, until finally a new note pops out of the bass, like a displaced limb. Hollis enters smoothly with a neat, simple melody and a lyric almost haiku-like in its stripped-back simplicity: 'Desire / Whispered / Spoken'.

Already, the drums are rumbling away in the background, causing mischief in the low end of the mix, giving fair warning of a sharp lurch into bedlam, which arrives in the form of battering guitar and wild organ, a force-nine gale of harmonica and a thuggish clatter of drums. The voice blurs into a shout. Having set up a thesis – however oblique – Hollis then turns on it: 'That ain't me, babe / Ain't got a bed of excuse for myself.' It feels as though he is calling out the too-easy get-out clauses and convenient self-delusions which enable most of us to get through the day. 'I'm just content to relax / Than drown within myself.'

Lee Harris is gold-standard here, particularly during the passage which features his solo drum breakdown followed by what can only be described as an *avalanche* of wild, tremolo guitar. It could be Black Sabbath; it could be Thin White Rope. Compare and contrast with the opening of 'Happiness is Easy'; we are in a different country now. Imagine for a second Talk Talk playing 'Desire' live.

There is a unity, a cohesion, a conscious repetition of sounds, themes and ideas in *Spirit of Eden*, particularly on side one. The interlocking instrumental pieces provide continuity between each song. The play between softness and noise is mapped out strategically and some form of build-and-break, tension-and-release dynamic is used on each of the first three tracks.

The second side of *Spirit of Eden* has a different sense, its own character. It feels as though we have passed through jagged mountain peaks and are now descending into rich green pastures. The connecting instrumental passages are absent, the sense of whirring upheaval hovering over each piece largely gone. Here are three perfect songs, each – like the Diggers' utopian dream – given their own patch of ground, and each so ravishing I struggle to believe anyone could ever find this music in any sense difficult. The beauty is almost ostentatious, a garden over-flowering.

It begins with 'Inheritance'. What beauty. The organ, the pad of a small animal. The vocal so tender, so fragile. All that fuss over microphones, distance, valves, consoles – all entirely vindicated as the singer lands perfectly in the soft belly of his song. The bass and drums are all feel, mindful of the fragility around them. Certain elements, particularly that flappy snare, lean towards the disassociated scat rhythms of *Laughing Stock*. There are a beautiful few seconds at 1:18 where brush and cymbal kiss gently and the piano responds with a playful sequence of notes. In the pre-chorus, the string bass is rubber-legged, remarkable. There is nothing much else there.

The chorus is melodically and chordally sophisticated, while the instrumental passage fleetingly resembles the kind of music Hollis would go on to make on his solo album – a weird, ungainly version of a woodwind ensemble. And what a beautiful resolution, Hollis left alone with a simple benediction: 'Heaven bless you'. The song is called 'Inheritance'. His first son was born in 1987. You do wonder who he is singing to.

The track ends in an afterglow of awed silence before 'I Believe in You' begins with no great preamble, driven by a quietly insistent rhythmic drum pattern. I fancy Massive Attack and Tracey Thorn took a good look at it before writing their song 'Protection'. Two guitars are prominent, one gently brushing out the rhythm, the other louder, closer to us, somehow, clipping out notes.

First the organ creeps in, then Hollis enters with that gut-punch opening line: 'Hear it in my spirit / I've seen heroin for myself.' Ed Hollis had struggled with addiction for a long time in the form of a longstanding heroin habit he was never able to kick. He is recalled wandering around Southend in the mid-'80s dressed in pigtails and a basque, shooting up through his jeans into his thigh. Still liked, still a music man. He died between the release of *Spirit of Eden* and *Laughing Stock*. It's an almost suspiciously obvious impulse to interpret the title and direct lyrics of 'I Believe in You' as a beam of pure love channelled towards Ed, an attempt to reach someone who was already, it seems, out of reach. Loving, bemused, angry, hurt, pleading: 'Is it worth so much when you taste it?' 'I Believe in You' is perhaps Talk Talk's saddest, most straightforwardly beautiful song, wearing lightly a very personal burden of unutterable waste.

Nonetheless, we can hear why it was the record company's choice for a single, even released in unsatisfactorily truncated form. The idea isn't really so outlandish. It is simply and pleasingly structured, with two runs around a verse and bridge before the chorus, if that's not too mundane a word for Hollis muttering 'Spirit, spirit / How long' as a celestial choir whirls around him. The original choral part was perhaps more impressive; the second feels more *correct*. The arrangement could have gone for broke, building in a fashion similar to something like 'Time it's Time', but instead everything is held back. Or mostly everything: the second verse kicks in with some fairly orthodox rock dynamics that bring up the energy levels. The details are constantly engaging. Little dubby touches on melodica, weird burbling bubbles of wah-wah, and always that drum pattern, constant as the sea.

Spirit of Eden is a journey and as such it needs a destination, a fitting sense of an ending. 'Wealth' is special. However it was composed, there was no rhythm left by the time the essence had been distilled, save the pulse of life itself. Voice and organ. Piano. Bass. A heartbreakingly simple flutter of strummed acoustic guitar. The long, slow fade-out is a work of art in itself, a peaceful surrendering, a grateful slipping away.

The song is a true artist's prayer, a celestial bargain. The bend and push in Hollis's voice on the final plea to 'take my freedom' is beyond artifice. Surely, it is very clear what 'Wealth' is about. This is church music, in both sound and intention. A call to a higher power – call it love, God, music, the soul – to be taken, to be used.

interlude 2

(An indulgence; a reverie)

It is the evening of Saturday, 17 September 1988. International Country Music Day, for those who observe.

At the Roundhouse in north London, a group of musicians have assembled, each familiar to the others to varying degrees. Mark Hollis, Lee Harris, Paul Webb – the core of Talk Talk, though not for long. Alongside them, Martin Ditcham, Robbie McIntosh, David Rhodes, Danny Thompson and Mark Feltham. Tim Friese-Greene has been persuaded on stage. Between them, at various times the musicians utilise one piano, one organ, one keyboard, drums, percussion, two guitars, Variophon, electric and string bass, and harmonica. Voice.

It is the launch night of Talk Talk's *Spirit of Eden*, released a few days earlier. Performing in almost total darkness save for the ceaseless swirl of psychedelic oil projections, the ensemble play the album in full, in order, though not with the aim of perfect replication. Alongside are a few choice cuts from the recent past: 'April 5th', 'Living in Another World', 'It's Getting Late in the Evening', 'Give it Up' and a closing 'Renée' for old time's sake.

A recording is made for future release, but it is never spoken of again.

Don't say it never happened. I can hear it.

We already know the reasons why Hollis walked away from performing. *Spirit of Eden* was certainly not going to change his mind. 'He knew he was never going to be able to reproduce this music live,' says his friend and co-writer, the guitarist Dominic Miller. 'That level of control wasn't going to be possible.'

'The reason Mark didn't want to tour it, or play it live, was because he said the whole album was about being spontaneous,' says Phill Brown. 'His attitude was, "Yes, you could do it live, but you would need to have maybe a ten- or twelve-piece band, and then everyone would learn *Spirit of Eden* and we'd go and perform." He was against that. The album was [created] by spontaneity. So, to learn it, and then go out and play it, kind of defeats what we were trying to do. The other side of the coin is, if he just went out and improvised again, it wouldn't be *Spirit of Eden* but a version of it. It wouldn't be the album. So he never had any intention.'

In purely musical terms, *Spirit of Eden* is unrepeatable but far from unplayable. No group of musicians could recreate the album precisely in all its detail, and none worth their salt would want to, but they could *play the songs*. They were, after all, demoed. They have form and structure. Indeed, after all this time, I am struck, oddly, by the album's powerful sense of order. 'There's a French troupe and they go out and play *Spirit of Eden* and some of *Laughing Stock*,' says Brown. 'It's amazing how well it works.' Will anyone dare to reimagine *Spirit of Eden* and *Laughing Stock* in a style similar to Philip Glass's trio of symphonies based on David Bowie's revered albums, *Low*, *"Heroes"* and *Lodger*? The idea that these are sacred texts does them few favours. They should be played, mussed up, messed around with.

But, still, there is a sense of rightness in the fact that Talk Talk never performed these songs. *Spirit of Eden* was 'certainly not reproducible,' says Mark Feltham, 'because it was just one moment captured.' And there is the truth of the matter. What surer way to spoil the beauty of 'one moment captured' than to try to capture it all over again?

There is something complete, pure and perfect about the Platonic ideal of the final dozen Talk Talk songs never being touched again by the people who created them. The impulse feels charitable, too. It allows the listener to play her part. In one sense, each time we put on these records, we are re-engaging with the music in a way which feels almost to be an analogue of the live experience. Because every time, somehow, it feels new.

Kenny Anderson, aka King Creosote, a key figure among the vibrant group of Fife-based artists known as the Fence Collective, once named *Spirit of Eden* as his all-time favourite album. Yet after all these years, he recognises that the music retains an uncanny ability to surprise and confound. 'There are still bits in those records where you think, *Have I heard this before?*'

iii

(Rivers/Oceans)

'Out of all things I've done in the past fifty years,' says Phill Brown, 'I will probably be remembered for *Spirit of Eden*, which is kind of weird when it was this huge flop.'

The record's commercial performance was certainly disappointing, coming at a time when even established album artists still relied on a statement single to launch their new record. *Spirit of Eden* limped into the UK Top 20 at number nineteen; the afterglow of the success of *The Colour of Spring* would have had quite a lot to do with those first week sales. It was all downhill from there. It spent three weeks in total in the Top 40. An uncomfortable edit of 'I Believe in You' was released as the sole single shortly after the album, not before, and reached only number eighty-five. Parts of Europe were more engaged, but in the United States, where the band had once had some semblance of a profile, the album went more or less unnoticed.

Wikipedia – the go-to resource for so many online researchers nowadays – states that '*Spirit of Eden* has been both acclaimed and panned by numerous music critics'. It certainly wasn't panned when it came out. It's been almost forty years, so perhaps some lack of contemporary perspective or even an element of revisionism is understandable. Anyone discovering the album in recent times might be forgiven for believing either extreme to be true: that *Spirit of Eden* has always been regarded as a classic album, or that it was shamefully overlooked and unheralded in its own time. Neither is quite correct.

Certainly, the notion that *Spirit of Eden* was universally misunderstood or dismissed is not really the case. I have always felt that its forbidding reputation has tended to be slightly over-played, certainly to anyone who has ever been acquainted with records by Can, or Radiohead, or Eno, or Pink Floyd, or Lee Perry, or any number of other artists who have screwed around with structure and form, played with dynamics and dissonance, atmosphere and attack. This is not inaccessible music in the great spectrum of experimental recordings. Strip away the passages linking the opening three tracks and the songs aren't so long or, indeed, so strange. 'Structurally it is built on verses and choruses, just like every other Talk Talk record before it,' said Paul Webb.[1] There are beautiful melodies and graspable song structures. Yes, they are broken up, stretched, interrupted, but there is not a song on *Spirit of Eden* that couldn't be sung in the shower. It is melodically ripe.

In support of this thesis, the album met with a generally extremely positive critical reaction on its release. It was widely reviewed and widely praised; in fact, not only praised but often recognised as something quite special. *Melody Maker* ranked it at number fourteen in their 1988 albums of the year list. *Record Mirror* raved about it, albeit quietly, in a review that absolutely understood the enduring qualities of the music off the bat. *Sounds* called it 'uncommonly beautiful' and gave it four-and-a-half stars out of five.[2] The reviewer from *NME* knew it was remarkable, you suspect, but couldn't quite bring himself to say the quiet part out loud: 'Talk Talk straddle the thin line between painful and pathetic, between attempted comprehension and sneering dismissiveness. Yet they're resolute and determined, flaunting commercial rules with fascinating disregard for understanding or acceptance.'[3] By now, the broadsheets had started paying attention to 'pop' music and there were respectful write-ups. The *Times* enjoyed it as an 'engrossing modern "Head" album', but thought the lyrics 'pretentious'.[4]

Talk Talk had never remotely been the critics' darlings. With *Spirit of Eden*, they received very possibly the best notices of their entire career. Even spiky new *Q* liked it – 'a quite remarkable, possibly even significant work'[5] – comparing it to *Astral Weeks*. Notably, however, the tenor of the review and an accompanying feature fixated on how fiendishly odd the album was, not to mention the people who made it, and how impossible it would be to sell.

A narrative, it seems, was established very early on: this was difficult, uncommercial music. It became a self-fulfilling prophecy – one, perhaps, even encouraged by the band themselves. Intended or otherwise, it was possible to detect a slightly off-putting aura of lofty superiority emanating from the two men who made *Spirit of Eden* as they were prodded into the public arena to explain and sell their wares. 'We're not being naïve about it,' Tim Friese-Greene told *Q*. 'Some people could definitely be put off by the pace of it or the level of intensity and if people are uncomfortable with that maybe, with respect, they should listen to something else.'[6]

Mostly, that is what happened. With no hit single, no live dates, no radio play and nothing creeping over 60bpms, people did indeed listen to something else. *Spirit of Eden* slipped out of sight quickly.

Be careful what you wish for.

•

Fast-forward almost four decades and *Spirit of Eden* has become a staple on those endless All-Time Greatest Album lists. It is routinely praised by a diverse crowd of cultural heavyweights. I have seen Bon Iver perform a beautiful and faithful version of 'I Believe in You' at the Queen's Hall in Edinburgh. Elbow's Guy Garvey has become almost an ambassador for not just *Spirit of Eden* but *Laughing Stock*; thanks to him and his 6Music show, 'New Grass' finally gets played on the radio. Graham Coxon of Blur said: 'If I ever make an album as good as [*Spirit of Eden*], I'll be happy for the rest of my life.'[7]

Steven Wilson, whose music both as a solo act and in Porcupine Tree contains echoes of Talk Talk, described the album as 'the most beautiful pop music ever made … where every musical gesture seems somehow sacred'.[8] Karl Hyde of Underworld recalls being sent a cassette of *Spirit of Eden* by their manager while on tour in Australia. The note attached read: *If you want to know what brave is, this is it.* 'We listened to it on the stereo of a rented car as we drove from Sydney to Brisbane, neither of us able to say a word because we knew the bar had been set higher than we would ever be able to reach.'[9] When I spoke to Alan Wilder, formerly of Depeche Mode, he called it 'one of my all-time favourite albums. Mind-blowingly brilliant in its diversity, atmospherics, eclectic sophistication, and topped off with "that" voice again which found its true position floating painfully over the top in the best possible way.'

The *Spirit of Talk Talk* coffee table book devotes some thirty-two of its glossy large-format pages to mostly short pieces in which an array of musicians, artists, writers, filmmakers, broadcasters and poets rave about the band. In the majority of cases, *Spirit of Eden* gets the greatest amount of attention and love. There have been entire radio programmes devoted to it, numerous magazine features, newspaper articles, online pieces, tribute concerts and cover versions. Prints of James Marsh's *Fruit Tree* painting used on the cover still do a brisk trade. Groups such as Shearwater, Lo Moon and Held By Trees pay explicit homage to this era of the band. The latter, led by David Joseph, includes several alumni from Talk Talk recording history, as well as contributions on piano from Hollis's youngest son, Charlie – now a thirtysomething husband and father.

Make no mistake. *Spirit of Eden* has become a *beloved* record.

A key element in this transformation is that, over time, it has become an album that musicians recommend to other musicians. Artists I spoke to who appeared on the *Spirit of Talk Talk* tribute album discovered the record by word of mouth, as though it were a special kind of secret, a key or a code, passed between like-minded souls. That's how I first heard the record in 1989 and it is faintly touching to know that that process has continued.

An American singer, writer, musician and sometime member of the Danish dream-pop group Efterklang, Peter Broderick recalled having his version of my Dave-in-Montpelier epiphany in the mid-2000s. 'One night, a couple of the Efterklang guys sat me down and played me *Spirit of Eden* and told me how much of an influence it had been to them,' he said. 'It took a while to grab me – but that was the one for me. There is this dynamic in his voice and in his music, it's really something amazing. Mark Hollis's voice, the way it breaks sometimes…'

'A lot of friends of mine have got into them under the same circumstances,' said Charlie Cave from White Lies. 'Someone has recommended *Spirit of Eden* and they've got straight into it.' Wild Beasts made a point of foisting the album onto friends and fellow artists. Good taste likes to travel.

Meanwhile, anyone with a more than passing interest in how records are made, how sound can be used and manipulated, tends to have a fascination with the record once they have heard it and an enthusiasm to share. *Spirit of Eden* straddles the old and new worlds of music making, the big-room studio ambience and the intimate home-studio accretion of tiny sounds. It is a prescient coming-together of the warm world of analogue and the glitchy, cutting-edge world of sampling.

Elements of Dave Fridmann's work with Mercury Rev and Flaming Lips are obviously attuned to *Spirit of Eden*. Musician, producer and composer Brian Reitzell, who has worked with Air and extensively with Sofia Coppola on her film soundtracks, has a framed print of the cover of *Spirit of Eden* hanging in his studio. 'That record for-ever changed my life,' he says. 'I am certain I would not be a film composer without the practices I learned from that record.' Paul Epworth, who has produced and written with Adele, Rihanna and Paul McCartney, is a signed-up devotee.

For Nigel Godrich, who is not so much Radiohead's long-term producer as their sixth member in the studio, 'I heard people talk about [*Spirit of Eden*] and I went and found that record … I was at a point in my life where I was starting to question how things were done, so it made me re-imagine what things could be.'[10]

Radiohead took some moves and cues from *Spirit of Eden*, no doubt, and applied them in their own remarkably imaginative and innovative ways. 'I remember Mark Hollis as an artist searching for honesty in his music, quietly uncompromising, intelligent and human,' says Tony Wadsworth, who had just started as general manager at Parlophone in 1988 when *Spirit of Eden* landed in his lap. 'He was a huge talent. In subsequent years when we worked with bands like

Radiohead, Blur and Sigur Rós, I was reminded, at different times, of just how influential that album had been.'

As those names suggest, *Spirit of Eden* holds near-legendary status today as a pre-'post-rock' landmark, a record that did so much to help break down the many rules and orthodoxies around structure, sound, texture and rhythm in rock music. It is possible to hear echoes not only in Radiohead and Sigur Rós, but Mogwai, Tortoise, Bark Psychosis, Nine Inch Nails and Godspeed You! Black Emperor. It is not just the use of space and silence that compels, nor the commitment to an unhurried tempo, but the noise, the unsettling lurches into abstraction, the constant promise of surprise and the interplay between all these things. 'It's uncompromising,' said Fyfe Dangerfield, who covered "The Rainbow" in collaboration with Thomas Feiner and Robbie Wilson. 'In one way it's slow and quite laid back, but there's this uncomfortable, abrasive quality. They were doing such poppy stuff before, but this was obviously what was inside Mark Hollis's heart – and it feels like it. There's no notion of the outside world at all.'

This last line seems to hit upon another clue. In the age of headphone music, where studio-standard sound can be wired directly into our ears as we lie in bed, *Spirit of Eden* makes a lot of sense. It has always been a record that the listener can get lost in, but perhaps now more so than ever. The closer we get, the more we can savour every tiny sonic detail.

Perhaps for this reason, *Spirit of Eden* seemed to gain momentum in the first decade of the new millennium. Dangerfield, talking to me in 2012, suddenly became aware of 'people talking about *Spirit of Eden* – it was one of those records that people seem to have discovered over the past five or ten years'. I wonder whether the advent of online listening helped spread the word. It was now no longer necessary to make a tape for a friend; we simply sent them a link or even texted the title, and the music was already there, just waiting. It should be noted that traditional industry manoeuvres also played their part. EMI have atoned for any perceived misdemeanours committed when *Spirit of Eden* was first released. The album has been reissued, lovingly, several times on both CD and vinyl, most notably in 1997 and again in 2012. A new half-speed vinyl reissue, overseen by Lee Harris and Charlie Hollis, was released in February 2026.

As for how a record as unique as *Spirit of Eden* can influence other artists, that bargain is almost unfathomable. 'A few people have taken it and moved it to somewhere else, or taken it as inspiration,' says Phill Brown. The idea of 'moving it somewhere else' is the key. It is impossible to replicate, but 'it makes its way in somehow,' says Peter Broderick. 'It's difficult to pinpoint how and where. Perhaps just the encouragement to experiment.' To experiment, certainly, and to stand your ground. 'Undoubtedly Talk Talk were underrated at the time,' Alan Wilder told me. 'They didn't seem to court publicity and I guess often fell under the radar. Mark Hollis was obviously not comfortable wearing the cloak of pop stardom and clearly very frustrated working within the confines of the formats expected of him. We can all now see, with hindsight, where his aspirations lay having heard the later, definitive albums. To see any artist shun potential success … in order to pursue a totally purist goal is inspiring to many.'

The depth of that integrity can only really be measured from a certain distance away. 'Here we are [more than] thirty-five years later and it still doesn't fit with anything,' says Phill Brown. The meaning of *Spirit of Eden* lies always just beyond reach. Part of the appeal of this endlessly beautiful record is its stubborn refusal to give up its secrets, which may be why we keep coming back.

However people find it, they are still listening. Perhaps all it really needed was time: time to remove it from any commercial context; time to let it breath; time, perhaps, to let the mythology recede and allow the music to take centre stage.

interlude 3

(Mirror Man)

'You listen to that music and you don't know where it came from,' says Dominic Miller. 'I knew Mark well and I'll never know. But maybe I don't need to know. It's not that important. All I need to know is that I like it.'

'If I had met Mark and not heard *Spirit of Eden* being made, I wouldn't have necessarily believed it was him,' says Richard Hill.

'It's like a painter works on his painting, or a sculptor on a sculpture,' says Dietmar Schillinger. 'There is nothing that interferes. It's very private, very internal. To meet him, he could have been an accountant.'

The art and the artist co-existed, clearly, but at times there seems a compelling but slightly bewildering disconnect between this extraordinary music and the ordinary man who was at the vanguard of making it.

Having no wish to add traction to the personality cult around Mark Hollis, it is nonetheless useful to learn something about his attitudes to life beyond music and the way he carried himself outside of the studio. What follows are some stories, events, observations, character studies, facts and insights, assembled randomly and passed on in the oral tradition.

They are just things that happened.

·

Hollis liked space in his music and he seemed to like it in his life, too. Warne Livesey recalls the writing room at Stanningfield as being 'very, very stark'. Dominic Miller was a regular visitor to his homes in both Suffolk and, later, Wimbledon. 'In any of the places that I have been to, it was eerily tidy. It used to freak me out. I mean, just so tidy that I used to just feel nervous.'

.

Living in Stanningfield after the release of *The Colour of Spring*, according to Mark Feltham, Hollis 'played football with the local works team, with plumbers and sparks, carpenters, and told them he worked in the local factory. Nobody ever knew who he was.'

.

'I remember having dinner with Mark and Flick one night and we got onto something of geography,' says Laurence Pendrous. 'Mark said something about the border between Burma [now Myanmar] and Bangladesh that was geographically incorrect. I said something like, "Isn't the border actually *there*, so that wouldn't come into play?" He said, "Oh, *well!* Fucking hell, shut me the fuck up, why don't you?" He really went off on one. He was very put out. I wasn't coming from any position of superiority; I was saying it very conversationally and very aware that I didn't want just to be correcting him. Flick said, "It's all right, Mark. Laurence was just saying it in a nice way." Then he calmed down.'

.

Warne Livesey's daughter was travelling home one night after a heavy night of partying in London. 'She was quite out of it – and who should she run into on the Tube but Mark Hollis. He'd been out on the town himself that night and had a few pints. He calmed her down and helped her get back home.'

•

Malcolm Hill tells the story of a colleague, Steve Hayes, who worked in TV promotion for EMI. Hayes recalled an occasion when he and Hollis were en route to the house of John Peel, who also lived in Suffolk. They stopped off at a pub and, as they were having a drink, Hollis noticed a sign behind the bar saying: 'Skinheads Not Allowed'. He looked at this for a while and then abruptly left the pub, mid-sentence, while Hayes was still talking to him. Ten minutes later, he came back into the pub and sat down next to Hayes. He had been to the barber along the road and had all his hair shaved off.

•

Hollis and guitar player David Rhodes – a former sculpture student at Goldsmiths – talked about the work of the British sculptor and woodcutter Eric Gill. This was before the revelations, made in Fiona MacCarthy's acclaimed 1989 biography, of Gill's numerous acts of paedophilia, incest, sexual abuse and bestiality. No previous biography of Gill had disclosed this behaviour.

Gill was a sculptor, woodcutter, typographer and draughtsman who brought a quasi-medieval religiosity into his art, which included several war memorials, church pieces and engraved book illustrations of Chaucer and the Gospels. An 'artist-craftsman' who converted to Roman Catholicism in 1913, Gill established a number of craft communities with a chapel at their centre and shunned modern industrial practices for older manual means of labour. 'We talked about craft and carving, in particular Eric Gill,' says Rhodes. 'I had a biography that I lent to him … I never got the book back.' As with their chats about John Lee Hooker, 'the conversations illuminated his interest in form, craft and structure whilst also enjoying the random and unexpected'.

•

Hollis was always clean, sharp and well-turned out. Nothing out of place, nothing wasted. Walking to the pub with friends, he moved at a military clip, practically marching.

•

Several people who knew Hollis reasonably well aren't entirely sure which football team he supported. Was it West Ham? Was it Tottenham, before he changed allegiance to Fulham for some – no doubt highly specific moral – reason? Was it QPR or his local non-league team, Southfields Lions FC? All, or none.

There is a correct answer, but perhaps it is more fun to leave it open to question.

•

After Hollis stopped releasing music, he went to see Nine Below Zero play club shows in London a handful of times, at the invitation of Mark Feltham. 'He sat right at the back of the bar. You could hardly see him. Right out of the way. He didn't like to be recognised.' Dominic Miller extended several offers for Hollis to come and see him play with Sting in concert. Hollis always declined.

•

He played golf.

•

Warne Livesey, who co-wrote five songs on Hollis's solo album, recounts a story which relates to how his creative side played in the quotidian life – or vice versa, perhaps.

Both men enjoyed a pint, particularly a Guinness. Often, after the day's work was done, they would go for a drink. On one occasion, when they had been working at Livesey's studio in London, Livesey suggested that they go to a pub he knew where they brewed their own stout, something of a novelty at the time.

'I bought each of us a pint of stout,' Livesey recalls. 'Mark took one sip and pulled a face of absolute disgust. He pushed it aside and just went, "No, no, no, no."

'I said, "Do you want me to buy you something else? They'll probably change it. They know me in here."

'He said, "No, I don't want anything else." He said, "I've only got my one pint because I'm driving and I'm not going to waste it on this pub. You finish your drink. Don't hurry, just finish yours. We can chat and then we'll just have a drink somewhere else."

'That was it. He didn't like that stout, so he wasn't going to drink any other beer from there. And he didn't have any explanation for it. It was just a straight "no".

'It is a kind of metaphor for him, musically.'

•

After his spell with Talk Talk came to an end, Ian Curnow recalls some accidental meetings with Hollis. 'He moved to a village near to me in Suffolk and our sons ended up going to the same kindergarten, so we met briefly once or twice when picking them up or dropping them off. Once we bumped into each other in Sainsbury's car park, of all places. That did seem rather surreal, I must say, as he was always a larger-than-life character, someone it was hard to imagine doing normal day-to-day things.'

To Laurence Pendrous, Hollis once said: 'Mozart was a cunt.'

'It was spoken purely for rhetorical purposes, of course, but it shows you where Mark was on every level. And it was a brilliant response to a stupid statement by me. I was making the most enormous assumptions about Mozart's music – I had received that from my parents. There is a whole generation that think Mozart is the absolute nuts.

'Mark always surprised me. He always said something different to what I thought he would say.'

He loved to travel. He loved Italy. He enjoyed off-road motorcycling. He rode through the Atacama desert in Chile and across the US on trails from El Paso to Wyoming with a friend. He took railway journeys across the Rockies. He especially loved Colorado: 'it has a softness that eludes other states.' He had a thirst for experience and discovery. When Brian Reitzell told him about Alaska, from where he had recently returned, Hollis said he would like to see all fifty US states.

The acute and unusual sensitivity to sound, and the painstaking attention to detail he displayed when making music, spilled into other areas of his life. 'He was like that with his Ducati [Monster] bike,' says Mark Feltham. 'He liked cars, racing bikes and tracking bikes, and he would always modify. He'd say, "I've had this tweak done, had that tweak done." It would never be right. You know, that was part of his personality. Nothing would ever be right.'

.

Some musicians mate for the night; a rare few mate for life. Hollis met his wife Flick in 1976 and they remained together until his death in 2019. He was regarded by everyone who knew him well as a committed family man. 'He really was very, very devoted to the boys, and he and Flick seemed to have a really close relationship,' says Warne Livesey. 'He got to know my family, my kids, my wife, and I got to know Flick and the kids. I would always eat with them at the end of the day. When we were working, my wife would always cook for him. We had many a family conversation with the kids. I was very fond of him.'

.

'I remember Mark telling me once about some kind of wooden bowl that he had designed that goes on the end of a woodwind instrument,' says Martin Ditcham. 'He said he walked into one of the music stores in London and said to the guy, "Look, I've got this idea …" and the guy said, "You can't do that!" He had one designed and people loved it. This was how his mind used to work. He would always think outside the box.'

•

'Mark was definitely a higher emotional IQ, but he just would not tolerate small talk,' says Dominic Miller. 'If you started talking about the weather or something that he was not interested in, he would just ignore you. We would be sitting in the pub in silence, then out of nowhere, he would say, "Did you see that fucking goal that Hoddle scored last night? It was a fucking blinder!" Then nothing. He wouldn't talk for another ten minutes.

'We are talking about a musical genius and he just sounded like any guy in a pub talking about football – and then not talking about anything at all. He wasn't much for small talk, but when he knew what he wanted to talk about, he did. I love very intelligent people [where] it's not intellectual, you can just feel it. It was in him.'

•

'When we first met in London in 2006, I was living in Paris working on the film *Marie Antoinette*,' says Brian Reitzell. 'Mark loved French literature and suggested I read some Zola. I kept the cafe napkin [on which] he had elegantly scribbled *L'Assommoir* and used it as a bookmark. I recognised his penmanship from the lyric sheets from the Talk Talk records. I loved that book – fell into its spell, felt the nuanced connection between Mark's music and Zola's writing. He gave me recommendations on loads of classical recordings, always providing the catalogue number.'

•

'He was about as unpretentious as you could possibly be considering the sort of music he was into and the music that he made,' says

Robbie McIntosh. 'You would think he would be all sort of airy fairy, but he was undemonstrative and very unpretentious. He was more into football and telling jokes than he was talking about music, really. He was funny as hell. I'd love to see him again.'

iv

(Unnatural Order)

The title of this book resonates on various levels. Talk Talk's fraught interactions with the machinations of the music industry, an environment largely antithetical to the one in which the music exists, feels like two worlds colliding, to the eventual benefit of both but the contentment of neither.

Hollis in particular was no ingenue. He grew up with an awareness of the industry's rules and rituals, not least through the experience of both his brother Ed and Talk Talk manager Keith Aspden. He took the money; he signed the contracts. He knew what was expected in return and he was always determined not to let the transaction get the better of him.

'I remember something that Flick said, which was that when Mark went into the music industry, he was absolutely determined to succeed,' says Laurence Pendrous. 'But he also went into the music industry with a very clear understanding of what that animal is, unlike most musicians who just crave the deal. He went in knowing the pitfalls of finding that deal – and managed himself very well … It allowed him to be the artist that he was and not to be railroaded between the track lines of what the record companies want. That's an analogy that Mark actually used, which is why I'm using it.'

From the start of Talk Talk, he would jump through some of the hoops required in order for the music to gain exposure: the Dadaist collisions with bizarre European music shows; the grindingly

169

superficial interviews on silly TV and radio shows; the cooler-than-thou impertinence of the British music press in its pomp. Hollis approached these trials without bothering to hide the fact that he thought they were all a bit of joke – and very probably beneath him – but he did not tend to hold the personalities in contempt. Everyone had a job to do.

'Whenever we met, he was friendly, he was approachable,' says Malcolm Hill, who, up until *The Colour of Spring*, was tasked with promoting the music of Talk Talk. 'He wasn't a bastard to me, I think probably because I read him. You have to put it to the artist that if you want to sell loads of records, you have to do stuff you don't want to do – and if you don't want to do it, fair enough, but don't fucking beat me up [when you don't sell lots of records]. As a promotion man, you need a bit of help. You do need the artist to come to the party and do the stuff they would rather not do, like Radio One Roadshows and things like that. But Mark would never do that. I respected him for it, but it wasn't making my job any easier.'

You were unlikely to ever hear Hollis complaining about record sales, or lack of. 'He didn't care much for pop music at all,' says Robbie McIntosh. 'He was never really scornful about anything. He was pretty open-minded. But he knew what he liked and what he didn't care for. He wasn't always going on about the music business being shit and all that stuff. He was a pretty fair-minded, decent bloke.'

•

Between the release of *Spirit of Eden* in September 1988 and the completion of *Laughing Stock* in the late spring of 1991, Talk Talk parted ways with their record label Parlophone, owned by EMI. They did so of their own volition and later signed to Polydor. Their next record would be released via the label's Verve offshoot, perhaps the greatest jazz imprint of them all, which at one time or another had also been home to the Velvet Underground, Frank Zappa's Mothers of Invention and many other legendary artists.

Stating the simple facts of this transition belie a whole host of legal complexities and challenges, none of which it is necessary to go into in great detail, but which in their broader outline are pertinent to the way Talk Talk and Hollis continued to make music – and perhaps, ultimately, why there ended up being no music at all.

It might be logical to assume that EMI dropped Talk Talk like a brick following their dismay at receiving the commercial apocalypse that was *Spirit of Eden*. This is not the case, although the album undoubtedly spooked the label, who were hoping to build on the success of *The Colour of Spring*. Who can blame them? Any right-minded A&R would have backed the version of Talk Talk that recorded and toured *The Colour of Spring* to take on the world. It is not hard to understand why EMI wrote a more or less blank cheque for the next record and let them get on with it, probably expecting something akin to what Tears for Fears delivered with *Sowing the Seeds of Love*: big, intelligent, emotive, slightly tortured, introspective yet commercially viable pop-rock.

They didn't get that, or indeed anything else that really made sense to a major label in 1988. Instead, they saw a cash cow wandering over the hill straight to the abattoir. 'If you go back to the 1980s, and the sound of records in the 1980s, [it's] no wonder that, when *Spirit of Eden* was delivered to EMI, they went, *Wait, what is this?*' says Phill Brown. 'Because it did not fit in with anything else that was around at the time.'

Upon its release, the album was inevitably framed in relation, and in opposition, to a version of the band that no longer existed – not only by fans and critics, but by many people at the record label. 'I'm guessing, after the success of *The Colour of Spring*, the company were expecting the follow-up to have at least a few so-called radio-friendly tracks on it,' said Paul Webb. 'Thankfully we had no interest in making a record like that and the rest is, as they say, history.'[1]

Some of the extreme reaction to *Spirit of Eden* internally was no doubt exacerbated because it felt like a wholesale and possibly very conscious repudiation of the band's momentum and potential. This may have changed the way the music – which is challenging, but hardly unlistenable – landed. There were reports of marketing men weeping at playback meetings. The industry loves a good drama. The prevailing attitude was more like, *What on earth do we do with this?* Had it arrived as a startlingly inventive debut album, you wonder what tricks they might have pulled from their sleeves.

The initial readings were ominous. As soon as he received an early cassette mix of the album – of which nobody at the label had heard a note in advance – Nick Gatfield, head of A&R at EMI, asked for changes to be made, citing 'reservations as to its commercial suitability'.[2] Keith Aspden, who we recall was broadly supportive of the label's efforts when urging the band to write a single for *The Colour of Spring*, reportedly had similar concerns. There was a meeting. It was suggested that they re-record one track (presumably for 'the single') or agree to some make changes. The artists, of course, stood firm and refused to change a note. No Bran Flakes for breakfast this time around. After a few weeks of stand-off, the album was duly accepted by EMI, somewhat reluctantly, and slated to come out in September.

This was happening in the spring of 1988, months before the release of *Spirit of Eden*. Alarmed by the second-guessing of their meticulously crafted creativity and already picking up on a serious lack of enthusiasm from EMI for the record, Aspden began looking for a way out. A fairly complex loophole regarding differing interpretations of the date on which the record had been deemed 'satisfactorily completed' was discovered and exploited. On that basis, Talk Talk claimed EMI had missed the deadline by which to extend their contract and they were now free to go elsewhere. EMI, furious, disputed this interpretation.

The row rumbled on over the summer in the lead-up to the release of *Spirit of Eden*. Not everyone at EMI felt so jaded about the record. Tony Wadsworth, at Parlophone, claims internal hostility at the label to the album has been exaggerated. 'I know the legend is that "EMI" was horrified by the album when they heard it, but all I can say from my point of view and my team who worked closely with me is that we honestly loved it – and I do to this day,' he told me. 'The album sounded like nothing else around at the time and, like all great albums, occupied a space all of its own. It sounds as fresh and powerful today as it did in 1988. It is timeless. We all felt like we were working on something special – not obvious, and maybe not easy for a record label – but I feel it made us raise our game and get creative.' Wadsworth, it should be noted, attended the meeting in March to discuss making changes to the album.

In any case, the band didn't quite see things his way. Paul Webb later recalled that they felt EMI had lacked enthusiasm when it came to promoting *Spirit of Eden*, in contrast to the Dutch wing of the label, who at least put their imagination to good use. Talk Talk had always done well in the Netherlands. At the launch party for the record in The Hague, which the band attended, the Dutch record company hired an IMAX cinema with, Webb recalled, 'a rare, large, wrap-around 180-degree screen and the album was played in conjunction with the visuals of a "Koyaanisqatsi"-type film [*The Genesis*] depicting a travelling bird's-eye view over vast natural landscapes. The experience was nicely immersive, simulating the physical feeling of going on a rollercoaster ride through nature's beauty. We were grateful that the Dutch record company had made the effort and come up with this fitting idea to promote our new record.'[3]

'Cosmic!' said Hollis, who had briefly considered a plan to make a film to accompany *Spirit of Eden*.[4]

Back in the UK, however, EMI were stumped. Their tagline for the record – 'An album for 1988' – reeked of desperation, but some efforts *were* made to promote it. Although Hollis's refusal to play any live shows did not help the album, he did acquiesce to doing the rounds of press interviews – and for the band to appear in Tim Pope's video for the single, 'I Believe in You', on which the singer lip-synched balefully to perhaps the most heartfelt words he had ever written (and afterwards felt utterly sick that he had 'degraded' himself to do so). The press pack was a pleasing custom box set with a flyer, a CD of sample tracks and more than a dozen pages of information sheets, including a thoughtful Q&A with Hollis. It was, perhaps, the bare minimum. The band weren't impressed. EMI 'struggled with ideas to introduce *Spirit of Eden* to the world,' said Webb. 'They were generally very disappointed with the album and didn't know what to do with it apart from printing a handful of album-cover posters.'[5]

It was within this testy context that the legal case between EMI and Talk Talk came to court in November 1988. The judge ruled in EMI's favour, although in the circumstances one might wonder why they were so desperate to hold on to the group. An appeal heard in May 1989, which involved a more detailed examination of all the historical paperwork, ruled for the band. They were no longer signed to EMI and free to pursue a new record deal. Tony Wadsworth always regretted that Talk Talk left EMI, blaming it on 'contractual bullshit' among the higher echelons of the company.

Despite the court case and sluggish sales of the new album, they were not short of offers. There was a sense that Hollis was an elusive and somewhat exotic beast, a great prize to be captured and, perhaps, tamed. From California, David Geffen pursued Aspden with the firm insistence of a wealthy suitor. Aspden knew it would never work and told him so. As usual, in the end they went with character. Their former point man at EMI, David Munns, was now MD of Polydor. They had known him for the best part of a decade. In the spring of 1990, Talk Talk signed a deal with Polydor worth £2 million; £1 million per album for a minimum of two albums. They were granted full creative control.

How on earth Polydor envisaged recouping this extravagant outlay was not explained, although there was perhaps a feeling that now Hollis had worked *Spirit of Eden* out of his system, he might get back to the business of writing more accessible music. Hollis, it is likely, gave the financial ramifications of the deal, or the idea that it came with certain expectations, short shrift. 'If I ever talked about trying to make income from music,' says Laurence Pendrous, 'Mark would say, "Well, you're never gonna do anything worthwhile if you do that. You only get success if you do what you want to do." That was a huge lesson for me.'

David Munns, it has been suggested, enjoyed getting one over on his former charges at EMI by signing Talk Talk. EMI, in turn, exercised their right to use the catalogue as they saw fit. In short order, they did what most record labels do once a band has scarpered: cashed in on the catalogue by putting together a fairly unimaginative 'best of' compilation.

Natural History: The Very Best of Talk Talk was released in May 1990, hot on the heels of the announcement of the band's new record deal. Although it was compiled without Hollis's input, the move was above board, even if the timing was pointed. A large chunk of record company income relies on making money off – and, lest we forget, *for* – their former charges by repackaging the catalogue. It is standard practice. Hollis wasn't happy, but conceded that they 'had every right to do it'.[6]

The real problem was what followed. To promote the *Natural History* project, in 1990 EMI began re-releasing old Talk Talk material as singles. Reissues of 'It's My Life' and 'Life's What You Make It' put the band back in the charts and rejuvenated their public profile considerably. The B-sides of the singles, across various formats, included a number of newly commissioned dance remixes of old material. Piggybacking onto the 'Madchester' phenomenon spearheaded by bands such as Happy Mondays, the Stone Roses and James, the label spied a gap in the market for accessible, on-trend, dance-oriented remixes of already well-loved material. It was not always an edifying listen. Two of the brains behind Jive Bunny – Andy Pickles and Ian Morgan – were involved.*

---

* Jive Bunny and the Mastermixers was a novelty dance act created by several British DJs and producers and fronted by a cartoon rabbit. Jive Bunny had several UK hit singles in the late 1980s and early 1990s thanks to the brutally effective formula of blending medleys of early rock and roll songs with high energy sampled beats.

Hollis didn't have to hear a note to loathe the idea. When management had first got wind of the remixes, a cease-and-desist letter was despatched asking EMI to stop. It was ignored. Hollis became even more animated when Talk Talk were nominated for a Brit Award at the beginning of 1991 on the strength of a song from 1984. Shortly afterwards, EMI released a new remix, 'Living in Another World '91'. It was followed in March by a full album, *History Revisited*, which gathered up the remixed B-sides and added some new ones for good measure.

EMI believed they owned this material and had carte blanche to do whatever they wanted. Hollis disagreed, insisting the label's alterations were unauthorised and tantamount to artistic theft and vandalism. Talk Talk sued in November 1991 and won the case the following year. One condition of the settlement was that all existing copies of *History Remixed* be destroyed and the album deleted. 'The fierceness of that music, Mark had a lot of that in him, although to meet him you might never think that,' says Martin Ditcham. 'He was a mild-mannered man, but he had fire in his belly.'

•

These legal machinations dragged on throughout 1990 and 1991, during the entire period Talk Talk were recording *Laughing Stock*. They hurt Hollis deeply. When talking about it with a journalist shortly after the album had been released, he was visibly shaking and had tears in his eyes. He felt he had been violated. The impulse behind the remix album ran counter to everything he had ever stood for artistically. And all this while trying to talk seriously about his new music, which felt sullied by association, somehow.

'I have never heard any of this stuff and I don't want to hear it,' he said. 'But to have people putting this stuff out under your name which is not you, I want no part of it … To find you've got people you've never given the time of day to going out as though it's you … It's disgusting.'[7]

There is a powerful sense of goodness permeating the music of Talk Talk, a sense that good exists and can prevail, but it is forever competing against a very present and active oppositional force – as perhaps it must. That oppositional force can be personified in many different ways. Maybe this episode illustrated one of them. Did Hollis's dealings with the record industry and the perceived indignities he had to deal with in order to get his music released with some integrity intact become a form of negative inspiration, something which he drew upon in his work in order to place virtue in greater relief?

I find myself wondering whether it's possible, given the battles he faced between 1988 and 1991 in particular, that Hollis purposely created a kind of music on *Laughing Stock* which he knew was going to be of the least possible use to his (new) record company. In 1991, speaking about his arrangement with Polydor, Hollis said: 'Basically, the deal is that I promise to give them the best album I can … What more can you say?'[8] – 'best' being a subjective notion when it comes to artists and the recording industry. A dinner thrown by Polydor for British record retailers at the Serpentine Gallery in London to convince them to stock and support *Laughing Stock* was a predictable disaster. Hollis attended. One journalist present recalled the discomfort as the album was played over canapés. 'Nobody knew where to look as Hollis's muted blues confessional purposely disintegrated into shivering feedback.'[9]

'That album is so far from what the record company would have wanted him to make,' says Laurence Pendrous. 'Maybe it was completely subconscious, [but] was that deliberate? Could it possibly be? Surely he wasn't sullying his work with that negative shit. To even suspect that of somebody who on every other level shows the utmost integrity – how can you conceive of the idea that he is going to do that? But, I mean, does anyone know why the album is called *Laughing Stock*?' Clive Black thought he did. He told Hollis biographer Ben Wardle that Hollis had 'laughed in their face'.[10]

Did this period impact upon the lowering mood of *Laughing Stock*? Was it, along with similar skirmishes in 1997, significant in Hollis's later reluctance to release any new music in the last two decades of his life?

These are ruminations. No answers.

If there was 'disgust', it was more likely to be directed towards personal decisions made, a perceived lack of character, a certain sense of betrayal, perhaps, rather than at the entire industry. One of the figures at EMI prominently involved in the compilation and remix projects was Clive Black, whom Hollis had known since the Island days of the late 1970s. Likewise, Hollis recognised when good people were doing good things on his behalf. Nigel Reeve, a former director of repertoire at Parlophone, later worked closely with Hollis to curate the Talk Talk catalogue in a more empathetic fashion. They became friends and their interactions suggest that Hollis was unlikely to have harboured huge animus against the industry as a whole, certainly not to the extent that it would impact his most intimate creative decisions.

'After he wasn't an active artist any more, he felt he could engage with people he liked in a social manner,' says Reeve. 'I think that freed him up to be more social, and industry things came up as part of the conversation. He drove the agenda, we didn't. He was curious about the industry. People say he hated it … [but] particularly because he was an EMI artist, he wanted to know how that [controversial acquisition in 2007 of the label by private equity firm Terra Firma] went down, partly because it had a knock-on effect to his catalogue.'

The excellent Hollis-curated 'rest of' compilation *Natural Order*, released by EMI in January 2013, was a product of their amiable social interaction. 'He was always slightly troubled by the coverage of *Natural History* and he really liked an album I had put together [in 2003] called *Introducing…Talk Talk*, which was the other side of Talk Talk. He thought that was a great album. *Natural Order* was intended as a companion piece to *Natural History* – you've got the more commercial side and now the other side. It was housekeeping, as much as anything else. We went through the CDs and put out the vinyl again. It was making sure [everything] was in order. Although he was very private and didn't want to talk [to the press], the thing that carried the message was the music. Between us, we hatched plots to keep the music out there.'

And the only way to keep the music 'out there' to any significant degree, certainly then and still today, despite all the changes in an industry which continues to thrive while so many artists struggle, is to dance with the devil.

AUTUMN

Laughing Stock

i

Late September 1991.

I am in my first week studying English at the University of Glasgow and already warming to the task of making myself as thoroughly unhealthy and unhappy as possible. In that pursuit, at least, I graduate first class with honours. During freshers' week, I buy the new Talk Talk record, *Laughing Stock,* from FOPP on Byres Road, praying thanks to a freshly cleared grant cheque. I buy *Hymns to the Silence* on the same day, which turns out to be the last Van Morrison album I bother with for a very long time. It is released on 23 September 1991, a week after *Laughing Stock.* In a pleasing twist, its title is a decent all encompassing classification for Talk Talk's later work.

I can remember finding a spot on a wall past the scruffy Bar Brel end of Ashton Lane in Glasgow's student quarter, sitting down and taking *Laughing Stock* out of the FOPP bag. I read the lyrics on the inner sleeve scratched in Hollis's by-now-familiar spidery hand and can make little sense. I had bought the weekly music papers and noted that *NME* had called the album 'horrible' and 'unutterably pretentious'.[1] Four-out-of-ten indie points, musos, for that year spent disappearing up your own behinds. Dismissed. As a confirmed *Melody Maker* man, this merely strengthened my resolve. Still, I look at the album title and wonder about self-fulfilling prophecies.

At first, I found *Laughing Stock* not horrible but hard-going, more than a tad forbidding. Texturally speaking, *Spirit of Eden* slides neatly into the compact disc player. It's not exactly *Brothers in Arms,* but in places it just *glides*. Some of the plushness of *The Colour of Spring* was, in retrospect, held over. That was not the case three years later. *Laughing Stock* was built for vinyl, with its imperfect buzzes, skips and crackles, deep, prickly unease scattered over silence. *Laughing Stock* – it took me a long time to understand, although it becomes more blindingly apparent with each listen – is the blues.

I could have comfortably lived in *Spirit of Eden*. I'm not sure I wanted to live in *Laughing Stock* – although, as it happens, I did anyway. Polydor MD David Munns famously, and perhaps apocryphally, responded to an initial hearing of the album by saying he couldn't be in the same room as it. Lee Harris left the band after the ordeal of making it was over. Engineer Phill Brown was unable to listen to most of it for twenty years. Hollis and Friese-Greene never worked together again. That's the price of crafting such blasted brilliance, right there. Even as listeners, *Laughing Stock* can feel like hostile terrain. From the verdant if challenging pastures of *Spirit of Eden*, it beckons us higher still, up into the rocky outcrops until there is nothing but thin air.

There's beauty, still, but this time there is no honey.

•

Almost exactly a year to the day before I would lay down my hardly earned £8.99 at FOPP, on the early afternoon of 22 September 1990, Talk Talk returned to Studio 1 at Wessex to begin making their fifth album. They were done by the end of April 1991. Done in more ways than one. 'Laughing Stock was the end,' says Phill Brown. 'It just felt as if there was nowhere else to go.'

Everything was the same, and everything was different. 'When we came into *Laughing Stock*, the only thing that [Mark and Tim] said was, "We cannot repeat ourselves",' says Brown. 'Mark had this big thing of never wanting to repeat himself. We couldn't use any of the microphones and things that we had used on *Spirit of Eden*. We had to come up with a whole new approach.'

'I see *Laughing Stock* as being a refinement of the whole of the *Spirit of Eden* aesthetic, really,' said Friese-Greene in 2006. 'Phill Brown and I sat down before we did *Laughing Stock* and we discussed some of the things that we didn't like about *Spirit of Eden* and in what way we would like to rectify them on the *Laughing Stock* album. We saw it very much as an evolutionary thing, rather than a revolutionary thing, which is what we had been looking at before that … *Spirit of Eden* is a bit too clean for me. It gets on my nerves. It sounds a bit over-earnest to me now. It could do with a bit of humour on it somewhere as far as I am concerned.'[2]

He did not elucidate on whereabouts the humour might be found on *Laughing Stock*, except in the hollow death rattle of its title, but at a stretch we might identify a vandal spirit of rebellious irreverence absent on its predecessor. '*Spirit of Eden* was only intermittingly rough,' Friese-Greene added. 'I do like a lot of noise, really, which is why *Laughing Stock* is a bit noisier. It is because I wanted it noisier … *Laughing Stock* is abstract and difficult to kind of get a grip on and I rather like that about it. It was recorded in a much more lo-fi way, which was a very deliberate policy on my behalf, and I like it much better for that.'[3]

Were there any doubt that Mark Hollis was not by any means the sole visionary force guiding the sound and direction of these records, here is clear evidence. Indeed, it is not entirely reductive to suggest that Hollis's solo album is a logical if extreme extension of the quivering emptiness evident in parts of *Laughing Stock*, while the more abrasive work that Friese-Greene undertook as a producer and musician after he stopped working with Talk Talk illustrates his love of the record's rawer, rougher textures.

After all, although both men were determined to shuck off their origins in shiny pop music, Friese-Greene arguably had further to travel than Hollis. From the Wombles to *Laughing Stock* in a little more than a decade is quite some safari. 'Tim did come from that clean production background,' says Phill Brown. 'I wasn't really as keen on the first two Talk Talk albums – I hated that whole keyboard brass and drum sounds that were huge in the '80s – but *The Colour of Spring* just blew me away because it went into a whole other area. I thought that was a classy record, but it was all done on a Fairlight. It was very, very slick and very controlled, although it may not sound like it. I don't really see *Spirit of Eden* as being super-clean. I just think it's very beautiful. The dynamics are fantastic.'

Certain fundamentals had not changed. 'There are no demos,' Friese-Greene told Brown before they began recording, 'so I can't play you anything.'[4] Not that he ever had. Again, considerable time was spent establishing a hermetic culture in which the recording would take place, ensuring that the studio became a self-contained world and crossing its threshold forced an immediate connection to the work being made. Oil bubbles breaking on the walls, candles, incense and not even a sliver of daylight; if anything, the atmospherics were even more intensely applied than on *Spirit of Eden*. A truer, deeper, darker psychedelia. 'You'd get to the studio and within an hour be totally unable to remember what time it was or how long you'd been in there,' said Phill Brown. 'Very subdued, very strange.'[5]

'The studio was oppressive to the point of unreality – an all-day, every-day existence,' Hollis recalled. 'I wanted to be totally immersed in the environment to the point where all normal everyday concerns were wiped out. For seven months, it was the case that we only left the studio to sleep. Nothing else existed except the recording, the studio and the nucleus of me, Friese-Greene, Phill and Lee Harris. That sort of intensity helps the thing develop.'[6]

This isn't quite true. They worked Fridays through Tuesdays, then had two days off. Everyone had relationships. Hollis had a wife and two very young children, and presumably wanted to see them at least now and then. But it was the case that, in the studio, nothing else seemed to exist but the music. The Gulf War was ongoing during the sessions; Phill Brown would occasionally mention it, conversationally, to be met with blank stares. Sometimes hours would go by without anyone saying a word.

The earliest stages of recording were once more preoccupied with getting six drum tracks finished and mastered (in the end, they only managed five). If *Laughing Stock* was to be the end, it was doubly the case for the drummer. But what a swansong.

An argument could be made that Lee Harris deserves a co-writer credit for all of this record, such is the foundational importance of the drum patterns he contributed. They are not incidental to the writing of the songs. On this album, the drums are the frame, the scaffolding, *the point*. *Laughing Stock* is a rhythm record and everything else sprung up and out from that source. Nothing can grow without them. The drum takes were played, selected and mastered before anything else. Hollis and Friese-Greene marked the parameters of the frame inside which they would paint – and they did so with a beat.

'We started with drum patterns that came from Lee playing them in the rehearsal room,' said Friese-Greene. 'We then wrote the songs around the drum patterns that he came up with.'[7] Composed on a drum machine, *Spirit of Eden* favoured the deadened snare sound; *Laughing Stock* uses space, air, the splash of ride cymbal and a dazzling range of polyrhythms and circling dynamics to emit a kind of sensory light. It undulates. The influence of Jaki Liebezeit of Can, in particular his playing on *Tago Mago* and *Ege Bamyasi*, is at times overt; Harris has the same uncanny ability to combine the thrust and drive of Krautrock with an innate feel, an organic sense of ebb and flow. There are Ghanaian 3/4 time signatures, 7/8 prog beats, echoes of John Coltrane's genius drummer Elvin Jones – numerous and diverse touchstones but all lightly worn. This is Harris's show, and a magnificent individual achievement in itself.

If 'recording the drums' sounded fairly straightforward, we surely know by now that it proved to be anything but. It took many weeks and a punishing regime. On *Spirit of Eden*, let's remind ourselves, Harris had been squeezed into an old storage cupboard, barely big enough to hold him and a set of drums. His kit had several microphones recording it. The default rhythm sound of that record, a kind of dampened subterranean tattoo, seemed somehow to creep from under its door entirely of its own volition.

On *Laughing Stock*, Harris was brought out from the darkness and into the main room at Wessex, which could hold eighty musicians. That was the easy part. The process of finding the best, or most desirable, drum sound began by working out the best place to put him.

'We spent the first days just setting up the kit and then playing it back,' says Phill Brown. 'Lee is a genius, he's such a great drummer. He plays a certain way and his kit was [made up of] all different kinds of drums from different kits, all there to balance the sounds and the levels. We would walk around the room: "It sounds pretty good here." "OK, try the drums there…" Then Lee would move.'

It took four days for them to find the optimum position: two-thirds of the way along the far wall opposite the control-room window, towards the exit doors.

Cue symbolism klaxon.

'Tim, me and Mark would be walking around [listening], and we got to this position, which was twenty-eight feet away from Lee,' Brown continues. 'I said, "Wow, sounds really good here. Let's make [the mic position] here." Because it was so far away, we had this hybrid of a Neumann 47 and the Telefunken II 48, which is basically the same kind of mic. The Neumann is a beautiful 1950s microphone, the nearest thing you can get to reality in a way. It's warm, very open, has lots of air and space in it. I think the Neumann we had had was broken and the maintenance guy there, Richard, had paired it with the innards of this Telefunken. It was a kind of hybrid, but it is basically a 47, an old valve. We just literally slung the lead over a beam at our head height – and that was it. Once we'd gone into the control room and got Lee to play, we thought, *Brilliant, it's great. That's our drum sound.*'

The standard arrangement in rock music when mic'ing up drums consists of using around ten microphones close to the kit, recording the bass drum, snare, hi-hat, cymbals, tom-toms, overheads and ambient sound. Here, there was just one, the best part of thirty feet away. The other instruments were also subjected to similar distant mic'ing techniques as on *Spirit of Eden*. Everything on the album is travelling through air.

'If we had been in Abbey Road, it wouldn't have worked,' says Brown. 'Wessex held eighty people. It was a big room and it was really dead, so it worked. Nothing sounds like it's in a gymnasium, but you can feel this feeling of space in there. Also, when *everything* is recorded like that, everything seems to have [the same] kind of position. The drums, especially on "After the Flood", don't feel like they are twenty-eight feet away. That's the whole thing about what we ended up with as a drum sound – it doesn't feel like what it actually is because the room and all the brightness and everything [else] travelled really well. It feels pretty crisp and sharp.'

In the control room, they would choose a drum pattern for Harris and he would play it repeatedly for at least half the day. Martin Ditcham was once again involved during the early parts of the process. 'We had Martin in a cupboard,' says Brown. 'We used Martin as a kind of human click track. He is a phenomenal drummer and percussionist. He would be there with a shaker, sixty beats a minute, which he could keep up for hours and could even change hands. Because obviously, it's pretty hard to do that for hours. Lee would play to that.' At the end of the day's session, they kept the best take and erased all the others.

While recording, Harris wanted to listen to what he was playing through headphones. This required the drum kit to be mic'ed up with several close-up microphones; nothing picked up by these microphones was used in the recording, aside from the bass drum. They were purely for Harris's benefit to enable him to hear the entire kit clearly while playing. What we hear on the finished record is Harris's drums recorded from twenty-eight feet away, along with a small amount of the bass drum on the close-up microphone.

At this point, they realised that placing the primary drum microphone twenty-eight feet away from the kit created a delay of around twenty-eight milliseconds, which varied depending on the temperature of the room. Brown used the drum mic and the more distant ambient mic to measure the length of the delay. This was not a fixed point.

'It changed if the room was cold,' says Brown. 'If the air conditioner had been on all night and the room was cold and dry, it would be a twenty-five-millisecond delay. But if the room had got humid and hot, it might be a thirty-millisecond delay. We had to basically work out what our delay was to get the phasing right. We ended up using a very small amount of the bass drum. That was the only thing we recorded – those two mics, nothing else. At one point, Mark said, "I'm going to go out and play with Lee." He went into a cupboard with his guitar and we fed him [the sound from] Lee's close mics, but everything that Mark played was obviously [arriving] before our drum mics. We then delayed Mark to be in time with the drums to actually record it.

'This whole thing of just having one mic [for the drums] became incredibly involved. We noted the humidity and temperatures of the room, because Mark was always into this thing of doing recalls.'

Hollis would come back to revisit a track, say, two or three months after he had put down an initial guitar or piano track. He would want to add or replace perhaps a single note. Fine. Easy. A simple overdub or re-do is standard practice. But the unique ambience in the room would have changed since the day that original part had been recorded. This is where the tape assistant, Shaun, saved the day.

'I thought he was over the top at first,' says Brown. 'He was measuring everything – the temperature, the humidity, taking down the serial numbers of the mic. But thank God he did because so much of the time, when Mark came back and wanted to add something, we would have to get the very same mic in exactly the same position and have the room the same for it to work … If we hadn't had reams of recalls, if we hadn't known what the temperature was in the

room and what the humidity was, [it would have been impossible] …
We might measure the mic from three different points so you could
pinpoint exactly where it was and then we would wait for the room
to heat up or cool down or whatever we had to do. Then he would
play that one note. And you can't tell [that it was done at a different
time]. It sounds like it was done at the time.'

If this sounds overly technical, as though we are squeezing the
music dry of all its magic, mystery and wonder, think again. None
of this, remember, had anything to with writing a song, or a lyric, or
composing an instrumental part. This was about what comes after, and
before, and during all of that: sound, feel, texture, atmosphere. The
reason these records sound so extraordinary is because the people
involved went to mind-boggling lengths to make it so. The illusion of
casualness required months of elbow grease. Pursuing the off-the-cuff
as a creative concept involved the endless accrual of tiny decisions
and a painstaking attention to detail.

·

There was, according to Phill Brown, a shift in mood on this album.
Spirit of Eden had been hard but a weird kind of fun. *Laughing Stock*
was more of a grind. Paul Webb had departed before the album sessions began. He had read the mood music and realised that he was
no longer part of the band in any meaningful sense. Webb and Lee
Harris had been friends and musical partners since their early teens.
On *Laughing Stock*, perhaps as a consequence, the drummer seems
to have been a more isolated figure and treated poorly. He was
worked into a state of exasperated and sometimes aimless exhaustion, worn down by Hollis and Friese-Greene in the hope that the
process of playing the same parts over and over again would yield

some microcosmic nuance between one take and the next that would feel somehow unique.

'Mark didn't really speak a lot on *Laughing Stock*,' says Brown. 'He was in a pretty dark place himself. His brother Ed had died [in May 1989], various things happened. He wasn't giving any real direction. "It's great, but what I'm looking for is …" There was nothing like that. Initially, when we started, Tim would be playing along with the keyboards or Mark on guitar, but they got bored with that. So they ended up just coming into the control room and it was just Lee and Martin.

'We'd do a day of drums and there would always be the one take that seemed the best of the day. The best take would be set aside, the rest would be erased – and then the next day they would do it all again. [Eventually], we had about twenty-eight of the best drum takes [for each song]. Then there was a day when we listened through to all twenty-eight individual takes to try and narrow down which one it was going to be. Eventually, it got down to two. Then Mark decided that one of them was *the* take. So we thought that was the master. Mark went out and started playing guitar to it. After an hour or two, he went, "It's just not right." Then, suddenly, the [drum] take wasn't right, either – and off we went again. It was tough on us all, but it must have been [especially] tough for Lee. He wasn't really given much direction or support.'

The image forms of a pit pony shackled to a coal cart. Picture Harris out there on the studio floor for hours every day, every day for weeks. Alone, playing more or less the same six drum patterns to nothing but the maddening whisperings of a shaker. Strapped to the wheel, splashing away. Being called a cunt for his efforts. Being excluded from any meaningful creative decisions. He would be roped in to play foursomes at ping-pong, but his presence was required for little else. It was not an admirable way to make music, or to treat any human being, far less an original and gifted member of your band.

'*Laughing Stock* was more complex' is the only public comment Harris has ever made about the sessions.[8] To Phill Brown, who worked with both him and Webb relatively shortly afterwards on the pair's 'O'rang project, he confided that making the album 'was like World War III. Lee [had] got pushed out slightly on *Spirit of Eden*, and on *Laughing Stock* I always felt that he got treated incredibly badly. We would do take after take after take and they were all so similar. It was Mark most of the time just saying, "Yeah, well, let's just try one more…"'

The caustic humour, jousting and jibing that had characterised the *Spirit of Eden* sessions, and indeed was in some ways the lingua franca throughout the history of Talk Talk, also seemed to have curdled into something crueller.

'There was this thing that started out as a joke,' says Brown. 'It sounded funny when we first started doing *Spirit of Eden*. Mark's comment was, "You really are…" Basically, saying, "You really are a *cunt*." Initially, it was kind of funny. But when that goes on for nine or ten months, and then there's a two-year break and you start another album, and he's *still* there with, "You really are…", it became very sinister, in a way. It became a bullying situation. I don't think Tim naturally had that sarcastic kind of humour, but Tim picked up on it and he would chime in as well. When Lee did a take and said, "What was it like?", Tim would put the button down and say, "Ah, you really are…" It just did Lee's head in. It did *my* head in and I wasn't even the drummer. Just sitting there going, *Wow, this is really unpleasant.*'

In any other working environment, at least nowadays, Hollis and Friese-Greene would have been hauled up in front of Human Resources to explain themselves. 'It was quite cruel as far as I could make out,' says Stuart Stawman, who by then had left Wessex but was still in touch with his former colleagues and friends there. 'I checked in and the guys said what they were doing to Lee was not nice. It just went on for weeks. "No, do it again." That was torture. Phill had a tape op right through *Laughing Stock*, Shaun. He quit the business after that. He was fried, because he would have sat through all of those drum sessions. Jesus.'

The way Hollis saw it, the entire process – the enforced claustrophobia, the bewildering jump cuts between harrying 'humour' and oppressive silence, the punishing work ethic – were all in the service of wiping out any trace of pre-programming or pre-conditioning. In his view, what this way of working built up was an abnormal sense of commitment to the most fundamental aspects of creating something pure. It was a test of character, entirely on his terms. Not many passed.

'The hard core of Tim Friese-Greene, myself, Lee Harris and Phill Brown were all aware of this commitment and essentially it was this body that created the album,' he said. 'There were people who came down to play who just didn't have the right feel or who we didn't like as people. They were got rid of pretty quickly.'[9] He added something quite illuminating – and rather poignant. 'When you work in this way, you work to please yourself, but at the very back of your mind, you feel this desire to have others understand the attitude and the sense behind what you're creating.'[10] To get it wrong, or not take it sufficiently seriously, was to also get Hollis wrong, or to not appreciate or acknowledge his own character. It was personal.

For the first time since the first album, Robbie McIntosh didn't play on a Talk Talk record. 'I would happily have been on it,' he says. 'I think I did get a call, but I wasn't available.' As it turns out, no professional guitar player got the call – or at least, if they did, they contributed nothing deemed worthy of making the final cut. Hollis plays all the guitar parts on *Laughing Stock*, in itself a marked shift from *Spirit of Eden*. By no means a virtuoso, clearly he had a particular sound in mind – rough, resonant, spectral, profoundly human – and had reached the point where he realised that the only person who could deliver what he wanted was himself. The guitar was a foundational part of the songs this time around and he was again capable of complete and obsessive absorption, playing the same two chords relentlessly for five days, trying to capture the sound in his head.

'What we did on this album is what we call rehearsed spontaneity,' said Hollis. 'There are no demos, no plans at all. I go in and put down a basic outline of something using my Country Gent guitar and then we fly other stuff in to build up the dynamics, the space. That's the key – space. It helps to build and resolve the tensions. Silence is the most powerful instrument I have.'[11]

The final line is good for a pull-quote, but when you dig into the meaning in its application, it might even be true. The impact of silence on *Laughing Stock* is both profound and profoundly intentional. Dead air is never dead. There is a touch of the Japanese concept of 'ma' in later Talk Talk work – the notion of negative space as an active agent; the importance of a pause, an interval, an idea seeking completion. For all its sharp edges and daunting terrain, there is a generosity at the heart of this music that can easily be overlooked. For Hollis, for whom each participating musician became a part of the composition, the final act of creative collaboration was to leave enough space in a track for the listener to be able to complete it.

'When I'm trying to think of arrangements in music,' says Dominic Miller, 'I think, *What would Mark do?* And what would he *not do?* What would he leave out? And that's about his use of space. He does it in a way that Miles Davis did it, using space in an incredibly intelligent way – and in an incredibly generous way. Because the thing about using space is that it allows the musician, the composer, to have a kind of a dialogue with the listener. It's generous. It's not throwing all your intellect, or all your ways of describing a musical scenario, at the listener. It is allowing the listener to get involved. That's what Mark did.'

And nowhere more courageously than on *Laughing Stock*.

•

Overdubs began after Christmas once the backing tracks were ready, a process which had been, according to Brown, 'really just getting the drums and a certain amount of guided percussion down. Then we would start replacing the shaker to Lee's playing and build up percussion, and then do guitars and keyboards. It took months to do because of the way we were working.'

On *Laughing Stock*, the musical palette is leaner than ever and the supporting cast smaller than on *Spirit of Eden*; though many were called, few were chosen. Most of the outside players whose parts were retained contributed strings, brass and woodwind, instruments the three principals could not play. In the absence of Paul Webb, the bass was played by Simon Edwards and the South African jazz musician Ernest Mothle. Only Mark Feltham and Martin Ditcham were present from the regular crew. 'It was extremely free,' says Ditcham. 'I recall, again, being given a free rein and coming back on two or three occasions to do more. Again, I was really concentrating on trying to come up with some originality. That's what they were always looking for – alternative ideas, as opposed to the standard offerings. It really was far, far, far away from any commerciality.'

Beyond Harris's essential contribution to create the rhythm tracks, *Laughing Stock* is principally the sound of Hollis and Friese-Greene working mostly alone, and completely obsessively, alongside Phill Brown for many months. Continuing the process of using multiple 24-track 'slave' tapes meant they now had access to more than 120 tracks on which to record ideas. 'Quite a lot of it was playing on instruments we weren't familiar with,' said Friese-Greene. 'Playing in the wrong key or coming in at the wrong place. But inevitably they were the best bits, so that album is made up of things that are unrepeatable.'[12]

As well as traditional musical instruments, they taped the sounds of a water heater, hissing kettles, electric fans, backwards FX. And yet these songs are not in any sense *full*. There are perhaps only half a dozen instruments on 'After the Flood', for instance, although we are often hearing multiple performances. The Hammond organ is not one Hammond organ, but up to ten separate parts, selected and then blended into the mix.

By February 1991, it was time to record the vocals, which were addressed last, as per usual, once Hollis had gone away to write the words and the melodies. The process had become more piecemeal, the final vocal assembled not line by line but word by word. The session sheet for 'After the Flood' references twenty-two separate vocal takes comped together. The line 'Shake my head' uses a different one for each word. There is a sense of a circle contracting.

Because they had spent so long with the tracks, staring at the faders for months on end, it was hoped that the mixing process would be relatively straightforward. It began promisingly. 'After the Flood' was completed in a matter of hours. Phill Brown started counting his chickens. Then 'New Grass' took two full working weeks to mix and almost drove him to a breakdown.

The last day of recording was 10 April 1991 and final mixing was completed by 30 April. It hadn't taken *that* long. They were in the studio for around seven months, a shorter sentence than *Spirit of Eden*. The album was released twelve months after they started. There have been more laborious births, that's for sure. But the intensity of the sessions is what left its mark. There were no long breaks. It was a more gruelling, deeper immersion into other worlds even than *Spirit of Eden*, with a less convivial working atmosphere. The unyielding, obsessive process brought forth extraordinary results, but took its toll on everyone. Well, almost everyone.

'*Laughing Stock* was an interesting and intriguing and challenging record to make, but I had never had this massive psychological overload that the others did,' said Tim Friese-Greene. 'I don't think that Mark did either. I can understand why Phill in particular did, though. It took a long time to record. He was in a darkened room for a year listening to the same six tracks … It must have been a particularly intensive experience and probably what forced him to have a period of readjustment afterwards.'[13]

At the end, they simply packed up and parted ways without ceremony.

Was it all worth it?

Maybe.

Probably.

Yes.

ii

I am listening to *Laughing Stock*. The same vinyl record I bought in Glasgow in September 1991. It would be worth a few bob now if it hadn't been played into a state of near disintegration.

I know it so well, but I'm trying to hear it afresh. I want to be clear what all that madness-inducing attention to detail adds up to. Six tracks. Forty-three minutes. Well, yes. But what else? Not a hit record, that's for sure. Hilariously, Wikipedia records for posterity that three songs from *Laughing Stock* were released as singles – half the album, almost as though this was the 1990s version of *Purple Rain* or *Thriller*, ripe for strip-mining to maximum commercial gain. More likely, Polydor were motivated by sheer desperation to find some other revenue stream for a record that spent precisely one week in the Top 40 and two weeks in the Top 100 before disappearing from sight. It was deleted within three months.

The singles? They reached 107, 108 and 111 respectively.

'After I had left Wessex, I remember calling into the studio to say hello to everybody,' says Richard Hill. 'They were doing safety copies of the mix for *Laughing Stock*. Tim played it for me and asked me what I thought. I said I thought it was incredibly clever music, but how the hell was the record company going to market it? It was interesting, because he laughed. He knew.' Not only did he know; Hill was hearing his letter of resignation.

'I knew from halfway through *Laughing Stock* that it would be the last album that I would make with Talk Talk,' he later said. 'Nothing happened after *Laughing Stock* to make me think again … I felt that four albums was enough.'[1]

According to Phill Brown, they erased 96 per cent of what was recorded. You get the sense they were aiming for 100 per cent. It is a skeleton of a record. Yet, on *Laughing Stock,* even the silence is undercut with some undefinable quality of unease, like the thrumming crackle on the lines strung between electricity pylons in the most isolated outposts of the countryside. It is a silence with eyes and ears; the quick, thrilling shudder of voltage when a guitar is plugged in and something connects deep in the electronics, the sound before the sound, as the player somehow becomes part of the instrument. 'For things to endure, they need to be in their most pure form,' said Hollis on the album's release. 'I mean, it wears on you if you're hearing all this echo or something all the time. You just think, *Let me hear this thing for what it is.*'[2]

On *Laughing Stock,* we are hearing the thing for what it is. This is not music so much as *sound.*

Though it contains less of everything – fewer words, fewer musicians, less information in general – *Laughing Stock* is a more sonically turbulent album than *Spirit of Eden,* with more confrontational textures. It is a record of razored edges, dissonant interference, blues distortions; a deeper, unmapped immersion into experimentation, sense, mood and texture. The two albums are siblings in so many ways: at Hollis's insistence, the cover art consciously connects one to the other. There are six lengthy tracks on each and several of the same musicians. They were made in the same studio using similarly exacting methods and released almost exactly three years apart.

They are undeniably connected and yet, like many siblings, they are at heart markedly different. Although Friese-Greene has stated that 'to some extent I see the leap between the last two [Talk Talk albums] as being smaller and them having some similarities',[3] if we removed any song from *Spirit of Eden* and placed it on *Laughing Stock*, or vice versa, it would sound jarringly out of place. I have heard *Laughing Stock* called 'an innovative remake of *Spirit of Eden*',[4] as though it were simply more of the same, but somehow less. Nope. Not to these ears.

The two records seem to me to stand back to back, facing in opposing directions. If they are one, then they are Janus. The former was released in the afterglow of the summer, the warmth and promise of that season still blowing through the music like wind-strewn honeysuckle. The cover image depicts the elements in full spate, an ocean overblown and a veritable riot of nature festooned precariously on the tree of life. The second side unravels like shadows slowly chasing evening sunlight down a hillside.

The latter, on the other hand, looks balefully towards a future of straitened days. The branches on the *Laughing Stock* tree are blown bare. The ground is hard – the sole song of real uplift prays for 'new grass' – the sea reduced to a trickle, a cold blue sky shading into icy pink. The flood has done its work. Winter is coming. *Laughing Stock* was recorded in a mostly unbroken spell between late September and April – clocks-back season. Interesting, too, that this is the one album where Mark Hollis told artist James Marsh exactly what he wanted on the cover.

The mood is not post-apocalyptic so much as pre-industrial. We can imagine the creator of this music walking through plague towns with a sturdy staff, seeking to scourge, cleanse, usher in a harsh kind of enlightenment. Domesday Book stuff. The work here is punishing and any respite hard-won: when it is glimpsed, it seems to come from above, in the vaguely medieval promise of heavenly reward after earthly toil. *Laughing Stock* yearns nakedly for relief and redemption, more in hope than expectation. 'Bet I'll be damned', indeed.

At least, that's how I hear it. The difference in the way I perceive these two albums may just be a personal matter of place, or displacement. In the late 1980s, I was still living in Bristol, happily melancholic and open to the world to come. Perhaps for that reason *Spirit of Eden* always feels like a safe harbour from which to contemplate setting sail into the world; it is womb-like, amniotic. Whereas by the time I first heard *Laughing Stock*, a week or so after its release, I could already feel a thread inside me loosening. My grip on optimism was less firm. Something about the world was already breaking my heart. For that reason, perhaps, the album has always sounded to me brutally exposed. The framework of something very vulnerable is revealed, stripped to the barest bones.

We fill in the spaces in all music with the clay of our own experience, of course, and few albums have more space to fill than *Laughing Stock* – but still I think I can hear a blasted quality in the marrow of the music. It somehow lies beyond the point where we can hope to hold on to anything solid. It is a wilderness record. Lear on the Heath.

Phill Brown, for one, agrees. But then he has plenty of personal experience to play with when it comes to his feelings on *Laughing Stock*, too. The intensity of making these records contributed to problems in his marriage and for him the process became 'very dark and really disturbing. I don't really play *Laughing Stock*. For me, it's quite a dark record, and quite difficult to make, whereas *Spirit of Eden*, for all its madness, was very positive and uplifting. And quite beautiful. *Laughing Stock* I just find a bit too extreme at times. When we finished, Tim [said], "Well, where do you go from here? We've erased ninety-odd per cent of what we recorded, this is the bare bones of a record. We've come to the end." And obviously he was proved right.'

'Dark' has become a too-easy descriptive shorthand for music that has any sense of challenge or complexity to it. Where is this sense of 'darkness' manifest?

As we know, between completing *Spirit of Eden* and finishing *Laughing Stock*, there had been a considerable amount of turmoil regarding Talk Talk's relations with the music industry. It's hard to think of two albums as perfectly and appositely named as *The Colour of Spring* and *Spirit of Eden*. The album titles, clearly, were a carefully considered matter. *Laughing Stock* feels ominously loaded.

There had also been more personal upheavals. Ed Hollis had died, aged thirty-seven, in May 1989. Paul Webb was gone, although he later insisted that he and Hollis parted on good terms. Harris was going. Any semblance of Talk Talk as a band was over.

No doubt some of these feelings, and many more privately endured personal and professional challenges, spilled over onto the record. But, still, I would be wary of projecting too much personal angst – mine, yours, the band's, Hollis's or Friese-Greene's – onto *Laughing Stock*. It is a consciously fucked-up record. The darkness and aggression were clear aesthetic choices. Remember, Friese-Greene told Phill Brown that he felt *Spirit of Eden* has been too slick, a little too polite and polished. It's all relative, but the point feels valid. Parts of *Spirit of Eden* are country proud; not exactly bucolic but heart-bustlingly beautiful in ways that only nature can be. In a sense, it strives to sound non-man-made, a work delivered complete by the hand of some omnipotent unseen force.

In contrast, *Laughing Stock* brings the blood and guts of human frailty into the room. We can hear the pulse, the ragged breath, the sheer messiness of it all. It has a serrated edge. The infamous distorted one-note Variophon solo on 'After the Flood' is a kind of scar, the sound of a nervous system gone haywire, of unattended car alarms ringing forever across waste ground. It is the sound of humanity loosed from reason. But it doesn't mean everyone – or even anyone – making this music felt that way. It is, first and foremost, an interesting creative exercise.

There is little evidence of Hollis keeping a close eye or ear on new developments in contemporary music. He confessed he had not heard any of the indie bands *du jour*, such as Ride, My Bloody Valentine or Chapterhouse. 'I'm really not familiar with what is happening,' he said. 'I haven't heard any of them, but it's not because I'm in any way dismissive of what is currently happening. It's just that I'm basically uninformed. That's all it is.'[5]

Friese-Greene, however, continued his career as a jobbing record producer between Talk Talk albums. In the gap between finishing *Spirit of Eden* and starting *Laughing Stock*, he had worked with two young English guitar bands, Lush and Catherine Wheel – and also with winsomely inoffensive Irish singer Brian Kennedy, just to keep things weird and confusing. 'After *Spirit of Eden*, I found it really difficult to find anything that I found challenging enough,' said Friese-Greene. 'Talk Talk records were quite fulfilling. I didn't really feel that I was desperate to go off and do something else. The one thing I did try and do was go back to doing guitar bands again, just to kind of keep myself a bit roughed up.'[6]

I think we can hear in the more abrasive parts of *Laughing Stock* his attempts to bring into play some of what was happening at the outer edges of the indie music landscape in the late '80s and early '90s: the phased sonic assault of the Jesus and Mary Chain, My Bloody

Valentine and their ilk, the strange, off-kilter pop adventurism of A.R. Kane, the first stirrings of grunge. Noise as art, as beauty.

Then again, if *Laughing Stock* is anything at all definable – and it might not be – it is a primal blues album. When I spoke some time ago about Talk Talk with the American artist Joan Wasser, who performs as Joan As Police Woman, she caught me off guard with her reference points. For Wasser, who covered 'Myrrhman' on the tribute album *Spirit of Talk Talk*, the track 'has a blues thing that makes me think of New Orleans. Like a big, old house full of ghosts and swirling memories. A spectre-y vibe.'

At the time, this was at odds with my own received sense of Talk Talk as a terribly English proposition. I heard something in these records that echoed Vaughan Williams's notion that music is 'the expression of the soul of the nation'; the nation in question was some drowned-world version of pastoral England. I realised I hadn't really been listening properly – or, at least, fully. I listened again, sliding the coordinates from Highbury to Tremé, and it was apparent that Wasser was on to something. *Laughing Stock* is quite obviously singing the blues. The real blues: the ancient, primitive pulse of existential reckoning, ghosts on the bayou, blood in the soil. Heaven and Hell.

Hollis loved all that. 'As far as my guitar-playing goes, I only really listen to John Lee Hooker and Robert Johnson, the late ['30s], '40s and early '50s sound,' he said. 'There's no tangible beat to that stuff and you can't predict when they're going to change chords or go off into something else. I like that.'[7] He gifted Dominic Miller a handmade CD compilation of 'early blues' music, to which Miller admits he never got around to paying much attention. David Rhodes recalls talking to him about John Lee Hooker, after which Hollis made the guitarist a cassette compilation. 'He really enjoyed the fact that what was ostensibly a twelve-bar might be thirteen or whatever felt right, and that the sound of Hooker's stomping foot had been recorded.' So, blues, but the twisted variety. The cracked, impulsive incantation of Hooker – which also so enchanted Van Morrison – is where the blues meets the mystic; blues as a channel, a conduit for pure emotion, memory, invocation, to the soul. The sheer *beyondness* of the metaphysical blues, where extreme simplicity bends into extreme complexity, where time and rhythm have their own logic and compulsion, following an internal pulse and impulse. You can understand why Hollis was so attuned to it.

Lyrically, he had been here already, notably on 'Desire' on *Spirit of Eden*. The insistent 'That ain't me, babe' is a direct echo of Bob Dylan, the 'babe' sounding oddly incongruous, no doubt deliberately. It is also a blues intonation, as is the key line: 'Ain't got a bed of excuse for myself.' Hollis here is working, lyrically at least, firmly in the blues vernacular; all those 'babes', the 'ain'ts'. There were other intimations. 'John Cope', recorded during the same sessions and released on the B-side of 'I Believe in You', is the sound of the band inching towards *Laughing Stock*. It is loose, guitar-heavy, appealingly rough and built on a rolling electric guitar riff. On *Spirit of Eden*, the harmonica of Mark Feltham, whose day job was with British blues-rock group Nine Below Zero, became a critical texture in the sound picture.

But *Laughing Stock* takes that connection much further. Here, the blues touches aren't an augmentation; they are the first colour on the mood board. Once we tune in, it's striking how often the record echoes the vocabulary, the feeling, the form. The opening line of 'Myrrhman' – 'Place my chair at the back-room door' – is a direct blues connotation in line with the music, an agglomeration of numerous tropes: back-room blues, back-door blues, back-door man.

Then there is the odd closing line, another borrowing: 'Step right up, something's happening here.' The second part is another echo of Dylan, in this case, 'Ballad of a Thin Man', yet it also seems strangely quotidian, banal even, in contrast to the rest of the lyrics – which is another way of saying it sounds timeless, universal.

'Ascension Day' follows a blues structure, however pushed about and deconstructed: B flat minor, E flat minor, A flat. You can play the bones of it on an acoustic guitar easily enough. Elsewhere, everywhere, we find the rawness of the blues. In the isolated, individually picked out notes on the electric guitar, left in the air to hang and hum. In the exquisite worm-like lines that twist through 'After the Flood' and 'New Grass', which are hooks in themselves. There are even *riffs*. On 'Taphead' and 'Runeii', the vocal melody walks along the crooked path laid out by the guitar part, just like John Lee Hooker murmuring to the contours of his picking. We hear the slide and squeak of the strings. Has any electric guitar sounded more like an electric guitar than in the opening few moments of 'Taphead'? It is the purest essence of the form.

'There's a real feeling in those records of just a guitar on its own,' said Radiohead producer Nigel Godrich. 'Just noise through a tremolo and a guitar and it's that feeling that you get when you plug in a guitar and you just play one chord. You just sit there and listen to it resonate. And these people appreciated this, understood it and were managing to frame it in the context of a … pop record, essentially.'[8]

•

Some pop record.

'Myrrhman' begins with twenty seconds of not-quite silence – already there is a scuzz of tape noise and a scurrying rhythm worrying away in some malevolent corner of the mix. Then the sound of an acoustic guitar in a minor key and disassociated rumblings. We are back in the same atmospheric space as *Spirit of Eden*, but the weather has worsened. Disembodied drums, wandering piano. The guitar cuts around like a rusty old knife. Hollis sounds hollowed-out, wearied.

At 1:56, the quick hiss of a random atrocity arrives then rapidly departs. *What was that awful thing? A boiled kettle or the death knock?*

The drums, having taken so long to capture, are almost entirely deconstructed, odd splashes of ride cymbal rising and falling on the tide of the music. A passage of instrumental chamber music sounds a little like something from *Porgy & Bess* heard via a clapped-out stereo in a room two walls away. The final ninety seconds detach completely. A beautiful half-folk melody enters the piece, played on viola, heard only twice but instantly and utterly unforgettable. This is contemporary classical music; Talk Talk are making their own version of the form. The last cuckoo of summer. It's a landscape, a tapestry, with distinct movements.

Between those shifting frames, from blues to Miles to Delius, lies a short poem, sung by Hollis with tremulous conviction, about death and perhaps ascending to heaven, 'stair by idle stair', half in faith and half in fear. 'Blessed love, the love I've seen.' Glimpses, again, of a better world.

'Ascension Day' arrives with a tip-tapping ride cymbal and the thwack of snare. The shuffling, off-beat drum pattern resembles that of Can's 'One More Night'. The 7/8 rhythm gives the song its spring and bounce, which all parties seem keen to preserve. You can see how the stop-and-go surge of the beat would have suggested the lovely liquid guitar line, vaguely African, vaguely Middle Eastern, wiry and wobbly, constantly threatening to unhook from its moorings.

It is the first of the song's two outstanding guitar parts. The second is a battering-ram burst of electric on a single chord, reminiscent of 'Desire'. The drums rouse themselves, before a jump-cut back to a scene of fervent agitation.

Hollis sings over the restless rhythm and the sound of the room breathing – 'Bet I'll be damned.' His voice is getting better, richer, looser. The way the organ – in reality, many organs – slide into the chord change at the word 'farewell' is a wonderful production touch. Mark Feltham's cut-throat harmonica ripples underneath the wild stabs of fuzz-toned guitar that hammer away during the final minute. This glorious racket yields to sudden, shocking silence, cutting the song dead at the knees. What a performance. What a construct. Again, imagine it live.

●

'Ascension Day' is a terrific title. Hollis borrowed it, which was not uncommon for him. He didn't go in for referencing specific artists, albums or songs in the studio when it came to providing guidance for what he might be looking for, but there were clues to be found for those paying attention.

'Ascension Day' is the title of a 1971 single by an obscure English hooligan garage band called Third World War. It appeared as the opening track on their self-titled debut album. The engineer on the album was Phill Brown. One day in Wessex, in the early stages of working on *Laughing Stock*, Hollis arrived with a copy of it under his arm.

'Third World War was a band I had worked with in 1970,' says Brown. 'They were like the first punk band, completely out of sync with the times – a really violent, aggressive band. Mark came in right at the start [of *Laughing Stock*] with this album that had a track called "Ascension Day". He said, "I want you to have this copy of this album. I love it." I thought, *How has he ever heard of this album?* Nothing was discussed or really referenced in that way, but there were these little things that, if you pieced it all together, you could kind of go, *Right, now I see.* "I have brought you a record …" It's interesting. There were these influences in the background. He worked in mysterious ways.'

Buried beneath the barbarian roar and blues-rock scuzz of Third World War's 'Ascension Day', which flails about thrillingly like a drunkard's punch, it is indeed possible to hear a connecting thread between the melody of both songs.

Hollis was a borrower. Someone who ingested culture at such a rate and in a very alert way was bound to reflect that in his work. That he borrowed from himself, smudging any sense of a fixed legacy, is evident from the amount of cross-fertilisation there is between songs in the Talk Talk catalogue, most obviously with *The Colour of Spring* and 'The Colour of Spring', one an LP, the other a solo track, released four albums apart. There is also 'I Don't Believe in You' and 'I Believe in You', 'Renée' and 'Runeii', 'Mirror Man' and 'Myrrhman'; the last pair of examples is an almost literal representation of the blurring of the past into the present, like a finger rubbing over the still-wet ink of a fountain pen. There are a preponderance of 'Life' songs.

He frequently borrowed or referenced from outside sources, too; we have already noted some lyrics which lean close to Bob Dylan. The trait is especially prevalent when it came to song titles. The connection with 'Laughing Stock', a song by American Music Club on their superb 1988 album *California*, is very probably coincidental, though not necessarily. The connection to the Love song of the same name most certainly isn't. Love also had a song called 'The Daily Planet'. Hollis liked that one, too.

The title of 'It's Getting Late in the Evening' came from an old gospel number, with a message Hollis may have savoured: 'Where do you stand, who is on the Lord's side / Oh sinner, I wonder what will you do? / You better choose today, tomorrow's not promised to you.' 'New Grass' is the title of an album by Albert Ayler. 'For What It's Worth' is a classic song by Buffalo Springfield. Bob Dylan wrote 'I Believe in You' a decade before Hollis and released *Desire* a few years before that. Everything But the Girl's 1984 album is called *Eden*. 'Dum Dum Boys' by Iggy Pop clearly inspired 'Dum Dum Girls'. The positively bouncy B-side 'Pictures of Bernadette', with a hint of a Motown beat, nods to the Four Tops' 'Bernadette'. There are more. Many of these connections, if not most, would have been made with a conscious awareness. But with what intent or to what effect, it is hard to say. It is interesting, that's all: that a man so obsessed with not repeating himself or leaning on past glories, and one who laboured long and hard over his lyrics, should be so unconcerned about casually borrowing song titlcs.

•

'Ascension Day' is abruptly guillotined, making way for the unhurried drift into 'After the Flood', one of the two centrepiece recordings on *Laughing Stock*. It comes into view like a seed falling slowly from the high canopy of a sycamore, twirling in the breeze. The first thirty seconds is a beautiful miniature song in itself. There is a guileless piano motif, a circling whirring sound, harmonica in a holding pattern and some scratchy sundries, before the drums rise up in the mix like vapour, a ghost army on the march.

The song is beautifully constructed, split into three parts, each of which goes round twice. Hollis's voice here has the same cruel undertone as on 'I Don't Believe in You', leaning into lines which by now have become terse, abstract fragments, communicating a hovering dread: 'Thirsting / Within without / Sighted / Weeded / How they run / Slain in number.' 'Shake my head,' he sings as hard as he ever would, and the music becomes a great wave, perhaps the mightiest Talk Talk ever summoned. The song rises up through the melodic gears in a way that feels comparable to the super-charged thrust of 'Living in Another World', with which it shares an impossibly serpentine structure – and a definable chorus. In another world, 'After the Flood' could have fitted on *The Colour of Spring*.

There is another go-round of the first section, this time instru-mentally, before that furious buzz of atonal treated Variophon. It's the pinnacle of Hollis's abdication from the mainstream, an eighty-three-second professional suicide note. He would not have been human, surely, had he not pictured the faces of the Polydor executives who had paid out £2 million to sign Talk Talk when they first heard this. 'Dissonance is important' might have been his response to any dis-sent. 'Where your ear bends.'[9] Here, the ear does not so much bend as twist clean off.

'After the Flood' may be the apotheosis of late-period Talk Talk. It is avant-garde soul music, moving from abrasive stirrings of post-rock through neo-classical ambience to hymn-like calm, all held together and gently pushed onwards by Harris's rustling drum figure. It is a masterpiece, wildly satisfying. A skittering guitar motif raises its head as the song begins to fade, before leaving the way it arrived. The drums retreat as slowly as they advanced. If you told me that they are still playing now, I would believe you.

I have always found 'Taphead' slightly terrifying and awfully sad. The first sound we hear is the distant flurry of music in its preparatory state, a brief muffled concerto before the guitar enters. It begins as a spectral blues – electric guitar and voice, Hooker-style. We can hear the fretboard and the very bones of the rhythm. Then comes a disturbance in the ether. On the Talk Talk song perhaps most obviously in thrall to Miles Davis, midway a spiralling high trumpet peal, played by Henry Lowther, makes its claim. There is a kind of creak and a growl, and the track falls into a strange, loping half-rhythm, some corrupted funk. It returns to the sonic terroir of 'The Rainbow', that rough-beast harmonica slouching out, the trumpets and Variophon performing a sad duet. And, always, that oscillating sound in the background, a kind of madness, never ceases.

Hollis finally returns, high and heartsick, with a quavering litany, near-indecipherable without the lyric sheet, and even then doggedly oblique. The tension on 'Taphead' threatens to become insufferable until – finally – it breaks. The opening, blues-based guitar riff returns into the unsettling silence. Hollis murmurs some form of consolation. A strange spell, indeed.

Nobody shouted, 'Send it back to Miles!'

'Runeii' sounds like, what? An old blues, but in space. As the murmured vocal melody follows the guitar line, it appears almost as though Hollis is picking up this song for the first time, playing a freshly coined riff that has caught his fancy, loosely improvising a vocal while he does so. The lovely, liquid sliding sound as the fingers move up and down the strings becomes an instrument in itself – we will hear this kind of oceanic texture, or something like it, with increasing frequency as post-rock starts to find its feet later in the decade. For most of the song, there is almost nothing there. The drums are more a rumour than a fact. Guitar, voice, piano. Finally organ and drums enter, and it becomes an off-kilter gospel-blues.

It's a feeling as much as a song, and a love affair with instrumentation. The final elegant shift upward to a point of grace is magical. Hollis finds the exact right words to fit and with which to end the record. They could almost be a bookend to 'The Rainbow' in its revocation of some misdemeanour: 'Slow to bleed, fair son.' It beggars belief, in a way, that a song as empty as 'Runeii' could have been the result of such a long and attritional recording process. There were no shortcuts when it came to the art of subtraction.

I wonder whether Hollis was particularly proud of *Laughing Stock*. When Dominic Miller first visited him at his home in Suffolk, Hollis gave him a cassette of it to take home. It may simply have been because it was the most recent music he had made, but I like to think that perhaps it was because he thought of it as his best work. Miller certainly thinks it is (I would agree). He listened to it nonstop during the car journey back to London and ever after.

'I became addicted to that album and I still am,' he says. 'I think it is his best album. I think that it is the *ultimate* album. *Mark Hollis* is great, of course it is, but I think his real moment was *Laughing Stock* – which I'm not on. I was incredibly seduced by the album and I still am. I was very moved by it. The more I listen to it, the more I realise that it really sets the ground for bands like Radiohead and even Nine Inch Nails. I can't imagine Trent Reznor didn't hear that record. But especially Radiohead, and the early Coldplay. Mark has been an incredibly influential guy.'

I haven't mentioned 'New Grass'? That's because 'New Grass' gets its own chapter.

iii

(Heaven Waits)
((A short meditation on 'New Grass'))

In 2022, I spoke to Green Gartside of Scritti Politti about Nick Drake, specifically his love of Drake's third and final album, the luminous, lowering *Pink Moon*. 'I have to ration listening to Nick,' said Green, 'because it can take as much as it gives. I have to be careful.'

I think of these sage words while listening to 'New Grass', the fifth track on *Laughing Stock*, the penultimate song Talk Talk ever released. It feels like the strongest medicine. You should only take so much. You wouldn't want to abuse its potency or somehow take its power for granted.

'New Grass' is both a dream and an awakening. We might call it a post-rock 'Madame George'. We can identify splashes of Coltrane, King Sunny Adé and Robert Wyatt, but it is all Talk Talk, and somehow seems to capture the essence of what Hollis, Harris and Friese-Greene were painstakingly reaching for throughout this period. It sounds like nobody and nothing else.

With its simple, gently circular chord sequence, mesmeric drum pattern and bobbing guitar lines, 'New Grass' is the spiritual centre-piece of *Laughing Stock*. It begins like the first lick of daylight breaking through the reeds and rising over the hill on an early sum-mer's day, and sets ten minutes later with the 'evening sun recedent'. 'They'll come, they come,' sings Hollis, lost in some reverie of a better world which, for once, seems within reach.

At once ecstatic and profoundly sad, it is a song that seems to be fading out even as it begins and yet, conversely, seems only to be beginning as it drifts away. It seems to have always existed and yet still be in the process of being written.

.

Such beauty was hard won. First, of course, was the customary war of attrition to get a perfect drum take. In this case, it was time well spent. If we as listeners feel that 'New Grass' is borne upon something precious, and it is, then Lee Harris must take the plaudits. A spirit buoys it, light and lithe, but the kick drum is propulsive, circling around the waltz time signature to give the track its constant sense of surge and motion. The soft susurration of snare and ride cymbal practically demands the unspeakably beautiful guitar line, the sound of light rippling on water, which in turn demands Hollis's most gentle vocal, which in turn can hardly do anything other than sing of rebirth. The song is a chain reaction, each connection spiralling into the other until the beginning and end simply become one and the same.

There's nothing to it, really. Those drums, that guitar line, some double bass, glistening notes of piano. Hollis finds a melody that rolls over it all with exquisite grace and guile, up and down, the same and different, like an ancient folk ballad heard from across a lake, familiar but the source never quite catching. It doesn't deviate from its course, the current is too strong, but there are moments where a kind of hush descends, a breath stilled to pause and reflect. The final few minutes simply *settle*, everything riding along on the drums. No rush, no hurry. They'll come. They'll come.

Imagine sending this level of beauty out into the world to be summarily graded: four marks out of ten.

Laughing Stock, indeed.

*

For a period while writing this book, every time I listened to 'New Grass' I would post those two words on what I still insist on calling Twitter. New Grass. Nothing more. It always elicited some small but heartfelt response. Sometimes there was a jokey reference to weed. Now and then – appropriately – it would land into a great silence, spun away on the never-ceasing scrolling tide.

Occasionally, a tweeter would ask to clarify whether I was referring to the Talk Talk track or the album by Albert Ayler.

'New Grass' seems hermetically sealed, a thing entirely in and of itself. Like every track on *Laughing Stock* aside from 'Ascension Day', the title phrase is never mentioned in the lyrics to the song. Instead, the title acts as a signpost, a way in and out, a means of somehow shepherding all the words beneath it towards a unified destination.

As a jazz aficionado, Hollis would certainly have known Ayler's 1968 album and there is an intriguing intentionality in his naming his own song after it, even if the association travelled no further than that.

Ayler was a tenor saxophonist at the vanguard of free jazz experimentation in the 1960s, who on *New Grass* shifted to a more accessible tack. It was the first album he made for Impulse Records without his brother Donald, who played trumpet in his band, and who had recently suffered a mental breakdown. *New Grass* is an odd record which, in trying just a little too hard to appear joyful and carefree, often just sounds sad. It features manic vocals, knocked-off hippie platitudes, rousing funk and soul rhythms; pop songs, even.

Hollis may well have been aware that the album was for a long time widely regarded as one of Ayler's weakest. It was made in testing personal circumstances and offered up, in part, as a sop to his record company to appease their aspirations to sell the artist to a hipper, more mainstream and considerably whiter audience. Ayler was not in good health when he made the record and, indeed, it can be viewed as the beginning of his descent into psychic disrepair and artistic decline. He would be dead, aged thirty-four, by the end of the 1970s.

It is tempting, but no doubt fanciful, to suggest that Hollis discerned a morality parable in the story of a gifted artist attempting to negotiate the record industry's most commercial appetites – and not just failing but receiving critical derision for a work that, in hindsight, was misunderstood and in some ways ahead of its time. It can be all too easy, after all, to allow the beauty of Talk Talk's music to steer solid common sense deep into the weeds. More likely the phrase 'New Grass' resonated with something more allusive. With its intimations of drug use, natural regeneration, rebirth and redemption, the title has an obvious appeal. Perhaps it was a coded ode to the hidden charms of New Cross. Maybe it was about Phill Brown sneaking off to the maintenance room at Wessex for a toke. Anything is possible. But I like the idea that poor Albert Ayler is being given his due somewhere among it all.

The wheel of influence continued to turn. Ólafur Arnalds later used the same title for an instrumental track on his 2020 album *Some Kind of Peace*. The melodic lines were distinct yet not entirely dissimilar to the Talk Talk song; you could feasibly sing one over the other.

●

'New Grass' sounds like a dream but it became a nightmare. The mix took eleven days to get right. There are entire legendary albums that took considerably less time to record and mix in full. In the end, the results justified the means, although Phill Brown might disagree. He is only now just about recovering from the experience.

'Drums, bass and guitar was the basis of it,' says Brown. 'Everything is in mono, so it's not like we were dealing with lots of tracks. I'd set up a balance and Tim would say, "It doesn't really sound right to me." So, he would come in and balance it – and it's still not right. We did that for about six days, twelve-hour days, just trying to get the basis of the mix then build it up.

'After that, Mark says, "Well, obviously something is wrong with the bass. We have to redo stuff." We were mixing in Studio 2 at Wessex, having recorded it all in Studio 1. So, we had to wait until Studio 1 was free and then go back in, set up all our recalls, and then redo the bass, having finished it and been happy with it. When they finally decided they had the mix, it meant very little to me other than the fact that I never really wanted to hear it [again].'

Many years later, there were bands that wanted to work with Brown simply because they loved *Spirit of Eden* and *Laughing Stock*. Some thought he might appreciate a demonstration of the depth of their devotion.

'Sometimes in the studio, late at night, when we had finished work, somebody would put on *Laughing Stock* – and I would immediately leave!' he says. 'I might get through "After the Flood", but when it got to "New Grass", I would leave because I didn't want to go there. I didn't really listen to that track for twenty years. Then, about ten years ago, I was in a studio and they put on *Laughing Stock*. I thought I would stick with it and see what this is all about. On came "New Grass" and I could finally hear it. So beautiful, so uplifting and light. But for me, that's not how it felt after ten days' mixing. It completely freaked me out. I got into a really weird space by the end. I couldn't really hear things anymore.'

The story is illustrative not only of the more challenging emotions that came to characterise the making of *Laughing Stock*, but also the almost stupefying precision and labour behind the art.

There is certainly a sense of exhaustion in the song, but it is a peaceful kind of enervation, rather than the freaked-out burnout Brown experienced. 'New Grass' is a long, slow relinquishing of anxiety, a surrendering. Where Hollis often seems to be singing in some or other shade of anguish, here is a resolution. The release he is so audibly searching for throughout so much of this music is finally palpable. The serenity of virtue, for once, simply scrubbing away the dirt and disgust. Heaven waits.

Hollis had a fairly narrow bandwidth as a lyricist, and it became increasingly squeezed as the albums progressed. You sense that really he had *one thing* that he desperately ached to say and kept struggling to find the best means of articulating it or, at least, communicating its essence. A song for the life – and ever after.

On 'New Grass', somehow, he perhaps came closest to touching the Grail.

iv

(Sacred Love)

It is probably for the best that Talk Talk more or less stopped talking.

Interviews were often a painful process for everyone involved: artists, journalists, broadcasters, the publicity staff at the record company. 'Mark was a lovely, lovely guy, but if you didn't love him, he was a pain in the arse,' says Malcolm Hill, succinctly.

One representative encounter with a Dutch radio DJ in late 1985 found Hollis in plainly obnoxious form, jibing away at the journalist in that sneering estuary drawl which implied the entire world was stupid apart from him. Most people who knew Hollis would concede that this chippiness was an active part of his personality, but it was also armour when it came to adopting a public persona. 'He wanted to give this geezer image,' says Peter Woolliscroft. 'A journalist came to do an interview and Mark said, "Quick, give me an empty beer can and sunglasses. Gotta keep up the image."'

The interviews up to 1986, and occasionally those beyond, usually find Hollis, often spurred on by Webb and Harris, either playing faux-dumb and mocking, or being suspicious and consciously, performatively surly. Sometimes there are displays of superiority and acute sensitivity. Occasionally, he simply bolted. The sense of pious prickliness often on view was not arrogance (or not only). These edgy, awkward exercises in mutual distrust can be illuminating. They reveal something very present in Hollis: a deeply moral worldview. He stood staunch not only against the belittling of his own music and

223

art in general, but also against what he felt was the venality of the world as a whole. In 1986, he made a quietly revelatory statement during an interview. 'I see so much lack of morality around me,' he said, going on to explain that this directly influenced the way that he approached songwriting.[1] And it's true. There is often a moral, sometimes censorious tone in many of the lyrics of Talk Talk.

'Mark was unquestionably a very morally guided person,' says Laurence Pendrous. 'That whole integrity permeates every aspect of his personality because it is absolutely pure. Whatever his thoughts may have been, there was a kind of purity, because he had no agenda other than being honest, and other than finding the truth, other than doing the right thing, whatever avenue you might go down in that regard.'

In attempting to find a through line, a thread, in Hollis's admittedly opaque lyrical view, I keep coming back to one word. It is, perhaps, the least rock 'n' roll word there is.

Virtue.

It is present from the title track of the very first Talk Talk album – 'Take this punishment away, Lord / Name the crime I'm guilty of / Too much hope I've seen as virtue' – and it is still there in more or less Hollis's final interview, conducted late in 1997. Speaking to the *Wire* magazine about some of his favourite films, a list that included *The Bicycle Thieves* and *Les Enfants du Paradis*, he said: 'What they deal with is character and virtue. They don't deal with narrative. That's a very secondary thing.'[2] Hollis didn't deal much with narrative, either, certainly from *The Colour of Spring* onwards, but the character so evident in his voice and his words brings its own understanding of meaning. It was also the quality that he looked for above all others in his collaborators.

Years earlier, in another print interview, he had used precisely the same vocabulary. 'It's just about virtue, really, just about character. That's all it is. I can't think of any other way of being able to sing a lyric and actually sing it and feel it unless I believe in what I'm singing about. That goes back to the gospel thing. I'm not saying all lyrics have to be about religion but, in a way, there must be that kind of thing in it.'[3]

Hollis could hardly have been clearer about his lyrical preoccupations. He handed it to us. Character and virtue. Strength of will and moral certitude versus failure, humiliation, resilience. Disgust, despair. The space between what could be, what was promised, and what is, is at the heart of many Talk Talk songs. Among these confusions and frustrations lies a path to what Hollis wrote about for the greatest part of his creative life. Goodness glimpsed, goodness attempted, goodness promised, goodness soured, goodness mocked – just occasionally, goodness prevailing. Goodness and its opposite are what these records wrestle with.

'In my lyrics is my life,' he said on the release of *Laughing Stock*. 'They say a lot more about me than any interview. They are the result of my observations and represent the values I believe, on the humanitarian level ... For the people who recognise values in life, they need no further explanation of this record, they will intuitively understand. For the rest I will never explain.'[4]

To access these feelings, to explore character, values and virtue, he turns to the language of religion over and over again. Not 'spirituality' – that wafting, wishy-washy handrail for rock lyricists since time immemorial – but Christianity: Jesus, Christ, Babel, Galilee, Heaven, Hell, Christendom, the Sacraments, Jerusalem, Sacred Love. *Laughing Stock* in particular returns again and again to matters of eschatology:

the science of last things – death, judgement and the final destiny of the soul. The nature of damnation, salvation, rebirth and resurrection all adds up to a kind of medieval reckoning of one's character. Meanwhile, as the writer Rob Young observed, 'the confession box on *Mark Hollis* is thick with purification, repentance, atonement and redemption'.[5]

Although many of Hollis's lyric choices were seemingly influenced by the sounds of words, not simply their meaning, these themes emerge too frequently to be random, or without significance. In a thoughtful and passionate essay, the American academic and writer Bradley J. Birzer wrote: 'If Hollis had sung about Christianity on only a song or two, I wouldn't disagree [that it might be coincidence]. But there's a huge continuity of Christian lyrics in what he sings. He might not mean them. He might not have lived them out in his own life. But he clearly strove for something greater than himself.'[6]

There is a prevalence of Christian language and imagery. The final lines of 'Wealth', a devastating slow dissolve into spiritual surrender, explicitly echo the Suscipe Prayer by St Ignatius of Loyola, the founder of the Jesuits: 'Take Lord, and receive all my liberty' is, after all, simply another way of saying 'Take my freedom for giving me a sacred love.'

It goes on: '[Take] my memory, my understanding, and my entire will / All that I have and possess, thou hast given all to me, to thee, O lord, I return it / All is thine, dispose of it wholly according to thy will / Give me thy love and thy grace, for this is sufficient for me.'

In both, the person writing is offering unconditional submittance to a higher power.

'Religion is a good thing and I see no reason why it should be linked to things that are wrong,' said Hollis, whose wife, Flick, was the daughter of a vicar and therefore presumably grew up in a highly religious home environment. Discussing 'Happiness is Easy', Hollis was asked if he believed that religion was a positive force for humanity. 'Absolutely! There's no doubt about that. I think it is absurd, for example, as happens in Ireland, Catholics warring with Protestants. Just the idea is utterly ridiculous. How can you wage war on the basis of religion, as religion is about love?' Asked if he would describe himself as religious, Hollis replied. 'I know what I think is good and what is bad. And I think you have to live accordingly.'[7]

Religion, therefore, for Hollis is a means of denoting love, decency and virtue, of parsing right and wrong. 'Happiness is Easy' is not an attack on organised religion, but a comment on the way religious belief can be perverted. If religion is to deliver on its promise, its reward must be granted in the present, not in some jaded bargain that 'after death [it's] so much fun'. The faith expressed in the chorus is genuine, the words heartfelt. 'Joy be written on the Earth / And the sky above / Jesus, star that shines so bright / Gather us in love.' It's a hymn. The children's voices are used to negate any sense of ironic detachment rather than accentuate it. They are exactly what they appear to be. To take the opposing cynical view of the song would only prove Hollis's point that, to borrow from Nick Cave, people just ain't no good.

Many more Talk Talk songs feel like bible stories, the simple Sunday-school parables of Easter, Eden, Jerusalem, Noah's Ark; moral trials and tests made opaque and shadowy. Nature appears as balm and tormentor, rainbow and flood. Both 'The Rainbow' and 'After the Flood' connect explicitly to the early chapters of Genesis. Ten generations on from the creation of Adam, the flood is God's way of returning an already corrupted earth to its factory settings. It's a moral reset, a great cleansing: 'To eliminate everywhere all flesh in which there is the breath of life.' God spares Noah and his family, and instructs him to build the ark to preserve two of every animal species. Following forty days and forty nights of relentless rain, the flood subsided after 150 days and leaves the ark resting atop the mountain of Ararat.

After the flood, Noah and his family were instructed by God to multiply and given animals to eat. A covenant between God and man is established, and God sends a rainbow as a sign of hope and restoration, promising not to flood again.

James Marsh's cover art for *Spirit of Eden* and *Laughing Stock* reference the flood first in full fury and then its aftermath, portraits both of abandonment and preservation. The resonance for Hollis, meanwhile, would be obvious: the reversion and renewal not just of humanity but for the animal kingdom, earth's rightful heirs, symbolised in the destruction of an imperfect amoral world and the rebuilding of it in God's image.

Scattered among the intimations of Biblical apocalypse and rebirth, the evocations of a prelapsarian Eden, there are, in Hollis's later lyrics, throwbacks to established folk and blues tropes, opiate songs, laments for youth and war. But as he progressed, he seemed increasingly to be eyeing up some great prize, heralding the imminent arrival of a new world. 'Someday, Christendom will come,' he sings on 'New Grass', where he imagines 'seven Sacraments to song'. 'Time it's Time' has a whiff of the crucifixion about it, with its kiss 'in a grey garden' and the overpowering sense of sacrifice, redemption and resurrection: 'The wicked and the weeping … Now that it's over, rest your head.' The final song on his final album is called 'A New Jerusalem'.

This was not a subliminal preoccupation. 'What is there to sing about? God, sex and death – that's all,' suggested one interviewer. 'Yeah, well, I've certainly picked up on two of the three,' Hollis replied, meaning the first and last of those themes.[8]

As a great lover of soul and gospel music, it could be that the language of religion was simply a vehicle he felt worked well for him as a writer, a means by which he could best express sentiments that mirrored the mood of the music – which is to say, it was not something that appeared to play an active role in his personal life. It seems that Hollis had no formal faith, did not worship by any creed. 'I'm not a born-again Christian, no,' he stated plainly in 1997. Yet he returned repeatedly to its lexicon.[9]

Hollis is at once geezer and seeker. 'I never thought of Mark as being religious,' says Phill Brown. 'Spiritual, yes, but I never thought of him as being connected to any kind of religion. But when you start to listen to some of the lyrics, *Wow, maybe he was much more religious than I imagined*. But with his sense of humour, and with the fact that he was very derogatory about stuff, I never thought of him as being a God botherer. *Spirit of Eden* has almost taken on much more of a spiritual thing for me than I felt at the time we were making it. Lyrics aside, there wasn't that kind of vibe in the studio, making something that was spiritual or religious. There was a lot of dark humour, a lot of sarcasm. Now, when I listen to it, it does feel like a spiritual record. But it certainly didn't at the time.'

For our purposes, it hardly matters whether Hollis used religion only as a writing tool rather than as a lifestyle. The effect is what endures.

He appears to enter a deeply private spiritual space in his work; it does not seem to have been a physically 'lived' part of him so much as a place he inhabited in a kind of heightened parallel to the quotidian life. Nick Cave spoke about this process to Seán O'Hagan in their book, *Faith, Hope and Carnage.* He evoked the priest and religious writer Cynthia Bourgeault and her concept of the 'imaginal realm'.

'There is another place that can be summoned through practice that is not the imagination, but more a secondary positioning of your mind with regard to spiritual matters,' Cave said. 'It's complex and I'm not sure I can really articulate it. [It] seems to be another place you can inhabit briefly that separates itself from the rational world and is independent of the imagination. It is a kind of liminal state of awareness, before dreaming, before imagining, that is connected to the spirit itself. It is an "impossible realm" where glimpses of the preternatural essence of things find their voice … Inside that space, it feels a relief to trust in certain glimpses of something else, something other, something beyond.'[10]

This is not precisely the process Hollis undertook perhaps – in truth, we will never know – but it does go some way to explaining where the music in him lived, and the sometimes jarring disconnect with the sweary bloke ranting about Sol Campbell in the pub. The art serviced a part of him that could not be accessed via any other means. He could rarely articulate it in common speech, nor to his collaborators, and he did not appear to live it in his everyday existence. With most artists, we can see where the art rubs shoulders with the life. It's harder with Hollis. The music is all we have of this part of him, which is presumably why it was so hard for him to talk about it. Interviewed in 1997, Hollis became awkward and amusingly shifty when it was suggested that his recurring theme as a lyricist is to examine 'dejection' and 'compassion'. 'You might have got me there!' he said.[11]

One thing is for sure: whatever was going on died with him. It was deeply personal and mysterious, and it lived in a place far beyond the reach of posthumous biography. But it is a very present part of those songs.

.

Hollis spent a considerable amount of time – three months, typically – writing the lyrics, a process he only undertook once the music and melodies were completed.

This tells us two things, I think.

First, that the words mattered. These are not incidental daubs thrown over the music. He sweated over each word – and, by the end, we were indeed down to individual words – to chisel out the bare essentials of what he wanted to express. A significant amount of subtraction and deletion went on to arrive at the final lyrics.

And, second, that the music and mood and the shape of the melody had a direct influence on the words that he wrote. He was fitting into its orbit, submitting to its demands, rather than vice versa.

'On the solo album, all the [working] song titles from the studio were different,' recalls Hollis's final close collaborator, Warne Livesey. 'Because Mark – and he said that he had been doing this for a while – didn't write the lyrics until after we had recorded. We wrote the melodies, but he was insistent that he wanted to write everything, record it all and then take three months off, and that's when he would write the lyrics. He didn't even have a concept for what the song was going to be about. He said he wanted it all to be informed by how the music sounded. I believe he did say that that was the way that he did the previous two albums as well.'

It's an intriguing idea: that the elevated quality of the music brought the religiosity out of him; that it was the only language he could turn to that could do justice to what he was hearing. Because it is not only the words that evoke religion; somehow the music does, too – as well as the spaces between the notes, which became increasingly elongated as Talk Talk and Hollis evolved. The quest for silence is a sacred thing, connected to very old and established ideas concerning the divinity of music.

'The notion that silence is present as a mystical or metaphysical "substance" is one that has many musical analogies,' wrote the composer and conductor James MacMillan in 2025. 'Music itself grows out of silence, the emptiness and solitude of the composer. Silence is nevertheless pregnant with promise, the promise of possibility and potency. Since music is not a physical reality that one can see, touch or taste, but is a presence, the composer must start with an encounter with a mysterious silence to bring the music into being. This encounter sparks compositional possibilities. Composers seek new music from deep in our creative imaginations and, if you like, from our souls.'[12]

As ever, Hollis was contrary, tricky to pin down. 'I lent him copies of choral music, which is pretty much all religious, and he just couldn't do it,' says Laurence Pendrous. 'I think just the association of that sound of the choir … with the church was something that he just couldn't do. He was absolutely eclectic in his listening to music, but he wouldn't do choral music. I guess that you might deduce from that that his morality was a personal morality and not drawn from religion.' For supporting evidence, perhaps, see the brutal dismissal of the too-perfect cathedral choir on 'I Believe in You' – send it back to God, perhaps – while on 'Time it's Time', the choir is operatic rather than choral.

Then again, 'Wealth' is absolutely the music of the church. Those thick washes of organ are positively hymn-like. Goodness, Hollis loved the sound of the organ. Might his somewhat eccentric insistence that Pendrous should play on the *Mark Hollis* solo album stem from seeing him not only play piano, but the church organ during school performances?

And then there is Hollis's voice. When Dave played me and my brother *Spirit of Eden* back in 1989, before a word became clear I'm sure that it struck me instantly as sacred music. When the singer sang, I immediately knew that it hurt. For all that Talk Talk were a band, with valued members and collaborators, and for all their much-vaunted evolution from glistening synth-poppers to post-rock pioneers, their music contains one clear through-line: Hollis's voice, and what that voice communicated.

Whether backed by a Roland MC4 or a woodwind ensemble, he sang the English gospel. A soul singer in the same way that Robert Wyatt, Sandy Denny and Nick Drake are soul singers, his voice contained no trace of bombast or affectation. It is a voice which sometimes seems, in a very English way, to surprise itself with the intensity of its passions, as on 'Renée' or the surging chorus of 'Living in Another World'. At its lower register – on 'Westward Bound' or 'Chameleon Day' – it is the murmur of a confessional.

These are collaborative pieces, but Hollis created the final vision. The words, the way they land on his tongue, are highly consequential. Often we intuit such things, rather than decode them. His voice was a powerful conduit to other realms. The lyrics for the last three Talk Talk albums are written on the inner sleeve, reproduced in a facsimile of Hollis's own handwriting, but they sit uncomfortably on the page as terse, disjointed thoughts and phrases. It's awkward poetry. It is not until you hear the way he sings 'Wealth' that the overwhelming catharsis floods through.

'There is an effortlessly devastating and passionate tone to it,' says White Lies bass player Charlie Cave. 'It sounds like he's always struggling and I love to hear that.' When Hollis sang, it was the pure expression of a form of a feeling which it seems had no other outlet. On stage, he tried to reverse-disappear by hiding behind dark glasses, like a child who thinks when they cover their eyes nobody can see them. In the studio, he turned the lights down to sing and arrived back in the control room with his shirt drenched in sweat. What happened in between was almost beyond meaning. The voice was given unfettered rein, and the voice is the vessel through which we believe. 'There was a passion there,' says Peter Woolliscroft. I am tempted to write it as Passion.

Through his voice, Hollis is our guide into this world – and we feel the specialness of the music so acutely because something in his voice, his intonation, his words, make clear that it is a matter of great existential urgency.

If there has been a tendency to attach somewhat ludicrously elevated personal qualities to Hollis and furthermore hand him more or less sole credit for music that was by nature intrinsically collaborative, it's partly because of what he sings and the way he sings it. He personalises this material with such intensity – in the modern parlance, he *owns it*. The literal meaning is elusive, but the soul meaning is acute. *We know what he is trying to tell us.*

If Hollis was a genius, and there is no shortage of people calling him that, it may have been in his ability to not only painstakingly help shape the music, but to then complete it so perfectly. Perhaps it is the voice, after all, and not the words, that is sacred.

Not everyone wants to hear this. Belief is the great vibe-killer of rock 'n' roll, yet rock 'n' roll happens to provide a perfect playground for the great showdown between the spirit and mammon. It is tempting to regard Hollis's use of explicitly religious language as a means of addressing a subject he knew well: the more or less constant battle between the (virtuous) pursuit of art and the (venal) demands of the music industry. This would bolster the idea that *Laughing Stock* was conceived in some ways as a calculated kiss-off. If so, he pulled it off with more grace than Van Morrison, whose tussles with the music industry left him disgusted and who allowed that disgust to pollute his writing with screeds of scornful reproach and cynicism.

Hollis preferred to seek the higher ground. It is tempting to see something of William Blake in him; another ordinary London boy struck by the divine. Yet Blake passionately, not to say wildly, lived out his visions in his daily life, as well as in his work. Hollis reserved any sniff of religiosity for his music. He was more doughty ploughman than ecstatic half-mad angel seer. There was a whiff of the exiled prophet about him. A hint of martyrdom, even. He was far from immune to ridicule; in fact, you sense he rather invited it, in order that he could stand steadfast in the face of scorn.

'I remember I gave him a copy of George Eliot, *Silas Marner*,' says Laurence Pendrous. 'He really loved that book.' What did Hollis find to love, I wonder, in the tale of the poor weaver, cast out and maligned for a crime he didn't commit, robbed of both love and gold, yet finding succour and solace in the simplest manifestations of a pure love and moral goodness.

interlude 4

(Natural History:
A conversation with James Marsh)

After graduating with a National Diploma in Art & Design from Batley College in his native Yorkshire, James Marsh (born in 1946), began his artistic career creating posters, adverts and cover artwork for Pye Records, then Decca, in the mid-'60s. He worked with artists such as the Moody Blues and the Rolling Stones, as well as overseeing the design of catalogue releases for the estate of Buddy Holly. When he joined Ink Studios in 1967, he worked on book projects involving the Beatles and a poster series for Andy Warhol.

In 1968, he set up his own highly successful design studio, Head Office, in partnership with James Farman. In 1976, he became a freelance artist. Since that period, Marsh has combined his work in the commercial world – creating designs for advertising, book covers, magazines, albums – with his work in fine art and illustration. It was this early state of independence that inspired his painting *Fruit Tree*, created in 1975, which later became the cover of *Spirit of Eden*.

Marsh has designed album covers for, among others, Kirsty MacColl, Gerry Rafferty, Jamiroquai and Erasure. But it's his career-spanning and remarkably simpatico relationship with the music of Talk Talk for which he remains best known within the world of popular culture. He started working with the band in 1981 and created the distinctive and eclectic artwork for all five of their albums, as well as all their singles and compilations such as *Natural History* and *Asides Besides*.

He lives by the sea in south-east Kent.

•

How did your connection with Talk Talk begin?

It was a roundabout commission, because I knew their manager, Keith Aspden, socially. Me and my partner at the time were visiting him and his wife and family to see their new place in Surrey. During the course of the afternoon, he brought up that he had left Island Records and decided that he was going to try his hand at managing, and he had found this band who he wasn't sure how to represent. That was his introduction to me about what he was doing with Talk Talk.

He asked me if I'd like to think about [doing their artwork]. He didn't really tell me what he wanted, per se, but he did say what they *didn't* want, and that was not to be represented in the typical style of the day, which was photographic. Pin-up boys on the cover. This was coming from Mark, but I think everyone was in agreement with it. The main motivation behind that was what turned out to be their nemesis, Duran Duran, being aligned with them in the media. There was slight resentment about that.

I went away to think about it. I didn't have anything to go on apart from the name. That's why I came up with the image [on *The Party's Over*] of the lips for the eyes and the mouth – literally repre-senting Talk Talk. I saw it more as a kind of icon or logo, initially – a way of branding them.

From Keith's friendly invitation it turned out to be a proper job, because they liked what I did and said they wanted to go with it. That led me into the early singles, which were following on using the facial features. That was the theme and it carried on from there.

Can we talk a little about what instructions, if any, you worked from for each of these records. Did you ever work from demos or finished tracks?

I didn't have any music. I did go to see them play live in the early days when they first started performing, so I heard the music then. But mainly everything was done right up to the wire. *It's My Life* looks so different [from the others] because I had a holiday planned and they wanted to bring out the second album fairly soon. I suggested an image I already had, which had the same theme. It was done for a book cover, a life story, so it fitted perfectly in my mind and everyone else agreed. That's how that album cover came about, otherwise I probably would have suggested something quite different for it. Often, they wanted promotion before they had even finished the album. That's why most of the stuff I did was slightly esoteric or symbolic. I didn't want to be too specific in the imagery. I always tried to be metaphorical in some way, so people can read into it – because people do that anyway, whatever you do, so if it's ambiguous, it works better.

For *The Colour of Spring*, *Spirit of Eden* and *Laughing Stock*, the artwork feels so perfectly aligned to the music. And yet you never heard any music beforehand! How do you explain that?

People have talked about this. 'How did you manage to do something that is so perfect for the albums?' I think it is a two-way thing. Once the work becomes the album cover, and people like the music, the two become synonymous, whatever it is. It's almost an automatic thing. One listen to the music and you see the album cover. You can't separate the two.

The Colour of Spring was the one time, actually, where I did get a bit more information. I got track listings. In fact, Mark sent me all the lyrics for that album. I think it was going to be called *Chameleon Day* originally. It was all about spring and change [and] I did various visuals for that, based on spring, but no one was jumping up and down about them. I always wanted to refer back to the original concept of the band, so I did various ideas with facial imagery. I wanted this to always be a theme throughout all the albums. If you look at *The Colour of Spring*, it is still a facial image, subliminal within the context of the group of moths.

For some reason, I was looking in my studio at a collection of moths and I thought that could be a good idea. There were three or four singles from that album and, by this time, they were telling me they wanted at least three singles [covers] to go with the album cover. It helps if you know that in advance, because you can do something you think aligns. My idea was to do single moths for the singles, each one representing one of the songs, then they all come together as a collection for the album. That was a simple concept and it worked.

One of those singles, 'Living in Another World', was an existing piece. The others were created for it, but that one was an existing moth I had done for a book project of my own and it just fitted fine. They were quite happy to use that one. Apart from that single and *It's My Life*, the rest of the art I made was commissioned – apart from *Spirit of Eden*, which you could argue is slightly different.

The image on the cover of *Spirit of Eden* fits so perfectly to that record, yet it wasn't created for the album.

It's a very good example, actually, because the artwork was done in 1975, I believe, and it was done as a very personal piece. So there is a kind of synchronicity about it. It wasn't a commissioned piece – it was a personal piece. As I have found over the years, that happens with my work. Somehow they tend to find a home, a purpose. I don't necessarily know why I do things at the time, and eventually they find their final home, their perfect resting place.

It was done at a very transitional time in my career. I had a design studio and I reached a stage where I was a bit jaded with what I was doing. I was in partnership when I had a studio, which was very successful, but I had got myself into a bit of a cul-de-sac. I wanted to get more into illustration, but I also had a yen to go into fine art. I thought that was where my direction was pointing. I started doing a few personal pieces with that in mind and that picture was one of the early ones. It's a transitional piece and a milestone. It marked a turning point in my career. That's when I became completely self-employed. I started experimenting and that sent me in the right direction. I didn't particularly end up doing much fine art work, but it led me into illustration. It is one of the pieces I still have because it wasn't commissioned. That was the agreement I had with Keith at the time on the commissioned pieces. I was paid quite well, but it included giving them the artwork.

Did that piece have a particular meaning and resonance for you when you made it?

It was a very personal piece. It was expressing where I was coming from creatively. It is all about the environment, really, and all about where I was at the time in my head, but not necessarily what I was doing in my work. It is a figurative thing, but the image is really symbolic. It's more about life force and the whole thing of where we come from. Everything springs from the sea. It's a giver and a receiver of life. People read different things into it, but, for me, it was all about trying to paint things that interested me, visually as well as conceptually. I did have an exhibition of that work, along with some other pieces at the time. It was my first one-man show and I had that piece in the show. The limited edition prints sold quite well, but I'm glad they didn't sell the original, because I wouldn't sell it now. I could have sold it lots of times, but just because it is a more personal piece, I suppose, I never wanted to part with it.

With *Spirit of Eden*, was it the case that you were given the album title and you thought, *Okay, I have some pieces that might fit with that* and then showed them to Mark?

I was never given much to go on. But I was told that was going to be the title of the next album, after *The Colour of Spring*. I didn't hear the music. I was completely in the dark. *Spirit of Eden* went on and on. I think they had to draw a line, because it was just going on indefinitely. That continued with *Laughing Stock*. I think that was how he liked to work. It's collage work – take things and play around with it.

I've got visuals in my files which show that I used the title on a prospective idea for *Spirit of Eden*, which must have been shown to them at the time, but nothing came of it. I wasn't personally involved in how it actually happened, but the directive I got from Keith was that Mark really wanted to use that *Fruit Tree* image on the cover. Originally, when we had started working together, Keith had some samples of my work just to show the band what I was doing and who was going to do the work for them. He still had these and Mark had remembered that image and he said he would like to use it for the cover. It was really as simple as that. This is a message I got through Keith, because he and Mark discussed everything. It was pretty much a fait accompli. I didn't have anything actually to do with it, apart from doing the work in the first place.

I think Mark picked up on the vibe in the piece. I think he picked up on the sincerity that I had myself about it. I think he read into it. He was quite intuitive that way, Mark, and I think he picked up on all the things imbued in the picture. There is an ecological aspect, which he aligned with, more than anything else. I'm glad that people get that, because that was the sincerity behind it. It just felt it was right to use it. It was quite a drastic change in direction, *Spirit of Eden*, from what had gone before, though you can see signs of it on *The Colour of Spring*, I suppose.

Did you have to do much to it to make it work as an album cover?
Nothing was changed at all. My only gripe is that it was used much too small on the vinyl. It was pretty much the size of the CD because of the big white border. There is such a lot going on in the image and I think that misses a trick. You need to look into it a bit more. I couldn't really see the reasoning for using it bang in the centre of the album cover. It seemed a bit odd to me. I quite like minimalism, but in that particular case, you could have still had a white border quite easily, but [the image] could have been twice the size, at least. I've done prints of it. It blows up very well. I don't think there was any reason for doing it so small. I didn't want borders on any of the albums, actually, but after the first singles, which I designed,

I didn't really have any autonomy. The art was handed over to the art department and I wasn't consulted. I wasn't commissioned to do the packaging, just the cover.

Spirit of Eden and _Laughing Stock_ seem umbilically linked, musically and visually. Is that how you see it?

Mark said he wanted to have this continuation. _Laughing Stock_ was an original piece – it was created for the cover of the album. I was asked to do that cover and I presented some visuals, one of which was the image [used on the maxi-single] 'After the Flood'. A bird made from many birds, which is very much an environmental ecological image in itself, flying over a barren landscape. I did that visual first for _Laughing Stock_ and I was given the go-ahead to go to artwork stage for that. But when Mark saw it, he felt it ought to align more with _Spirit of Eden_ and he asked me personally if I would do something else that followed on, as it were.

We didn't really have much dialogue about many things. That was the first time he got involved and wanted to discuss it, so he picked up the phone to talk about it. He was never very good at saying directly what he wanted. He would always beat about the bush – a bit like the music. He would know it if he heard it or know it if he saw it, but he couldn't really express what he wanted, particularly. But for the most part, it worked out. That was my job, really, to try and come up with the goods for what suited the project.

He had this thing about the tree. He was keen on the tree image and that's when I suggested what became the _Laughing Stock_ cover, which is a global tree form with birds in the shapes of the continents. That was the best I thought I could do that incorporated the tree to follow on from *Spirit of Eden*. He liked that idea, so I went away and created the artwork for that.

I always thought that the first cover I did was better, personally, but it didn't get wasted. It was used on a three-CD box set for 'After the Flood' – and inside a promo case as well, as a little print. Things have a way of working out, but I still prefer it as an image. I think it's a stronger piece. I've done some prints of *Spirit of Eden* and that print, and I think they work very well together.

There are, to my eye and ear, themes that connect regarding the music and the artwork; ideas around ecology, nature, environmentalism, humanitarianism, a universal spirit yet a sense of peril. It's not overt, perhaps, but it seems to be there. What are your thoughts on that?

I suppose that comes from me. I wasn't really directed in that direction. It is something that I happened to pick up on, certain things to do with that. I did discuss it with Keith and he agreed with me, particularly when we're talking about the later period and the environmental issues imbued in the work. I think they tried to represent that in some of the videos at the time, but it was really coming from me, in terms of imagery.

I like to use images that I find interesting to work with and, also, it's a personal passion of mine to make people aware of environmental issues and so forth. It is just something that resonates with me. I like drawing parallels with nature and the human condition. I like people to engage with the work and see beyond the basic imagery itself, which is sometimes quite obvious. Some people say, 'Oh, that's great, I love moths!' That works in itself. That's okay because people are getting something out of it. At least they like the imagery. But you have to look beyond that with my work. You have to see the double entendre or the metaphor contained within.

Were you ever invited into the studio with Talk Talk?
No, I was never invited. There was never any reason for me to be there, apart from if someone thought I might like to sit in, but I was never invited. I never really thought about it. From the stories I hear, it might have been a bit awkward!

Were you invited to work on Mark Hollis's solo album?
No. I was only aware of it when it came out. I think because there were fewer session musicians, and none of the actual members of the band performed on it, it just transpired that it became a solo album. And since he decided it was a solo album, I think he thought, *I'm going to do something different.* That is why he ended up using a photograph that had some resonance with him. He had no allegiance to people that way, Mark. I think he just felt that was what he wanted to do.

It sounds as though you didn't particularly get to know him on a personal level.
I don't think anybody did! Maybe his wife. Even his manager, they fell out big time, and it seems to be that most people fell out with him along the way. I think a lot of people were walking on eggshells around him. People in the band seemed to be like that. I never had any problems with Mark, actually, apart from in the latter days. For my own book project, I asked him to say something about the work, but he didn't want to do anything like that. In the end, he would only communicate through the solicitor. I couldn't speak to him [directly]

about it. I sent him a missive via the solicitor and got something similar back – just, 'Sorry, wish you well with the book, but I'm not having anything to do with it.' You have to accept these things. Who knows what is going through someone's mind? He will have had his reasons. I don't resent it. It's just a bit disappointing.

How do you look back on having such a strong collaboration and association with the music of Talk Talk?

It's established and people are interested. It has taken on a life of its own and the music is embedded in pop history, really. I am grateful for that. I'm very happy about my work being used on album covers, because most of the time throughout my career, I have worked in a very ephemeral medium. Unlike book covers, album covers don't really get changed – or rarely. They tend to stick with the original covers because the fans relate to it. From that point of view, it is good to have my work still in print, as it were.

Mark had a good ear, but he also had a good eye. I think he recognised that it was a good idea just to let me do my thing, just like he wanted to do his thing. We never discussed that, but I think it was a kind of mutual respect. And it just worked.

WINTER

Mark Hollis

i

Mark Hollis was released on 26 January 1998. The blunt, joyless butt of winter. The eternal 3 a.m. of the night shift, seasonally speaking. And the floor scrapings of the bazaar, from a commercial point of view.

Exactly twenty-five years later in Edinburgh, the January skies are bleached out, coloured the same shade of grey-white-nothing as the record cover.

I have spent the past short while listening to 'Westward Bound', the sixth track on the album – playing it through, then picking up the needle and dropping it carefully back at the start. I'm hovering around the record player, crouching over it every few minutes to replay the song before sitting, stiffly, cross-legged to listen to it once more. The album sleeve is on my lap. I keep looking at it, flipping it from front to back, as though doing so will yield some secrets about the music playing. I'm sure it will, in time. That is its job, after all. For now, the photograph of what looks like a small, squished woodland creature being prepared as a sacrificial offering isn't helping much.

This was how I spent much of my teens, communing with the holy trinity of stylus, vinyl and a square foot of cardboard. Now, as then, I'm looking for clues. I'm trying to hear what Mark Hollis heard, or at least what he was searching for, when he wrote and recorded this song – and, by extension, the album that comprises the last significant musical statement he ever made.

What does the record sound like? There's a question. It's fair to say that we are now fully outside the realms of what could plausibly be classed as popular music. The dynamics lean to minimalist jazz, the instrumentation to deconstructed pan-tonal chamber music. The sound is woody, entirely acoustic and yet rarely comfortable. It clicks and creaks, breaks and flutters, thin as the wind. There is no whump, no clatter. Everything is brushed. We can feel the room, but the microphones bring us even closer than that. I imagine I can hear the musicians holding their breath as they play. When 'Westward Bound' ends, I realise I have been listening in the same way. On the final note comes an exhalation.

On this track, no attempt is made to separate the body of the musician and the body of the guitar. The strings squeak and the belly of the instrument groans. Hollis's voice might be the smallest, least *there* sound I have ever heard, which means, somewhat contradictorily, that it is startlingly present. The force of his quietude is almost shocking. Listen closely and we can track the infinitesimal movements of his head via the minute shifts in the cadence of his voice. We hear his lips part on the word 'child'. Many of the lyrics are often impossible to discern – which seems at least half the point. Throughout much of the album, the vocals are often rendered as simply one more acoustic instrument, his singing a quiver in the grain, a tonal blip, a quavering incantation.

'Westward Bound' is a track which takes time to form. Listen to it once and it sounds as though it is surely the product of improvisation; a first take, an exploration gamely ventured upon without a map. Hesitant. Almost empty. Listen to it a few more times and … well, patterns emerge, yet still it struggles to come into focus. The beautiful opening guitar motif and Hollis's tumbling scrap of melody seem to arrive, only to lose their bearings and scatter shyly out of view.

The finished track might be the scribbled outline of some undefined shape, a beautifully crooked branch in search of its trunk. But no. 'Westward Bound' is an idea which has been pursued fully to its final destination. The music took a year to write, each part scrupulously annotated. The lyrics were sweated over for a further three months. It was recorded with absolute precision. The hesitancy is the point. This can be frustrating until you realise it is actually a gift: a song that sounds new every time you play it.

To help understand, I spoke with Dominic Miller, co-writer of the track, who also plays that gorgeous nylon-string guitar part. A sought-after session guitarist who has recorded and toured extensively with Simply Red and Sting, Miller, it turns out, is almost as baffled as I am.

'When you hear that song, it sort of sounds like we just made it up on the spot,' he tells me. I nod. 'But, actually, it is incredibly detailed and every single detail is considered. It's not a jam. It's very, very carefully constructed. Although it sounds incredibly simple, it wasn't to us. I urge you to listen to it and bear in mind that it took nearly a year to write and it just doesn't sound like it at all. I mean, genius!'

It is tempting to brand anything we can't easily or immediately digest with the stamp of genius, as though inaccessibility or complexity is somehow a grander prize than instant connection. Is the act of taking two years to write and meticulously map out a song that *sounds* improvised evidence of genius? Or of something else?

•

In the autumn of 1991, Hollis went back to the life more ordinary in Stanningfield having taken some time out to promote *Laughing Stock* with a handful of interviews and industry playbacks. These did little to shed light on a record which met with a confused if, once again, largely positive critical reception – although, fittingly for such an extreme album, the people who didn't like it tended to hate it. The man from the *Independent* joined the man from the *NME* in thumbing his nose; he even put the word 'songs' in ironic quote marks. 'The "songs" here, of which there are apparently six, are at best half-glimpsed through the instrumental shrubbery which, despite Talk Talk's obvious desire to make something fluid and organic, remains deathly throughout. As for Mark Hollis's lyrics, heaven only knows what the poor chap is on about. Analysis, one suspects, may have proven cheaper.'[1]

Lee Harris was already out of the picture, having apparently undergone an emotional crisis precipitated by the unpleasant experience of working on *Laughing Stock*. When Phill Brown bumped into the drummer by chance in November 1991, it all spilled out. 'Lee told me of his feelings, his state of mind and general lack of well-being over the previous seven months – his sense of failure and of being inadequate and the spiralling darkness and void that took him over on finishing the album *Laughing Stock*. He described his numbness and anger … From what Lee said, it sounded like he had suffered a mild breakdown four months earlier.'[2] Happily, Harris would shortly embark on a new music project with Paul Webb, also involving Brown, called 'O'rang.

Even so, it seems Hollis at first envisaged continuing with the working practices and steady rate of output established on the last two Talk Talk records. In an interview at the time of the release of *Laughing Stock*, he spoke about the future in terms of the deal with Polydor. 'I think they have options across four albums which, at the pace we work, is the next twelve years,' he said.[3] It sounded like a man intending to go back into the studio in due course with the same core collaborators – 'we', I would suggest, means Tim Friese-Greene, and also Phill Brown – to make another Talk Talk album, which would fulfil the second part of the two-record deal with Polydor.

Friese-Greene, however, had other ideas. 'I felt that Mark and I had simply run our course,' he explained fifteen years later. 'We had had a really good run of making records that constantly pushed things forward. I didn't see any way of moving further beyond that and I wanted to go. Mark wasn't happy with that, but he didn't have any choice. He went away and decided what to do on his own.'[4]

It marked the end of the most longstanding and creatively satisfying collaboration of Hollis's life. It's interesting that Friese-Greene seemed to tire of it before Hollis did. Friese-Greene moved on to form another embedded producer-plus relationship with Catherine Wheel, and later launched his own music project, Heligoland.

Like the handsome hotshot who is always the dumper, never the dumped, Hollis wasn't much acquainted to rejection. Friese-Greene's comments suggest he didn't take it terribly well, even if the parting of ways was perhaps inevitable.

Friese-Greene talked somewhat wearily of ploughing a 'stylistic furrow',[5] of the 'purdah' of recording a Talk Talk album.[6] He had tired of minimalism and he no doubt intuited that Hollis was heading to the point where all paths would converge into silence. Not enough was enough. During the making of *Laughing Stock*, he later said, 'I remember thinking, *This is the end. This is as far as we can go. After one note, there's no notes. This will be the last album we make.*'[7]

Perhaps he saw other issues on the horizon – money matters were not always handled perfectly within the Talk Talk orbit – or simply spied the writing on the wall. After all, Hollis had alienated or exiled every one of his closest collaborators, notably Simon Brenner, Ian Curnow, Paul Webb and Lee Harris, and more would follow. 'Unlike Lee or Paul, I bailed before I had a chance to get into serious acrimony with Keith or Mark,' said Friese-Greene in 2006, implying certain threads were already fraying.[8] 'Mark and Tim seemed to leave a trail of bad blood behind them,' says one confidante. 'Eventually, I think Mark and Tim themselves seemed to exhaust their possibilities as a creative partnership.'

There is a certain poetry in the idea of Hollis as the last man left standing, alone with his virtue. He later suggested the decision to separate was mutual, that both were 'of a like-mind' that they had gone as far they could without repeating themselves.[9] But there was a clear fissure. The two did not remain in contact, although that may simply have been a reflection of the way the relationship had always been. They had come together initially to work, and work brought out the best of both of them. Between albums, they went off to live their own lives. Neither were much minded towards small talk. When the work finally ended, what was left?

I doubt Hollis would have voluntarily ended the partnership. He had built a team of trusted collaborators since *The Colour of Spring* whom he greatly valued. When it came to the solo album, he recruited his favoured group of musicians and proved particularly persistent at trying to persuade a reluctant Phill Brown to take part. With Friese-Greene, a mutual shorthand had been built up over a decade that meant many parts of the creative process could remain unspoken. For a man who forever struggled to adequately express his ideas, Hollis was sure to have realised that such dumb luck rarely strikes twice.

•

During 1994, Hollis set about drumming up a brand-new set of collaborators. Dominic Miller was put in touch via an intermediary – A&R consultant Mark Fox, once of Haircut 100. Miller was perhaps an unusual choice for a blind date: an A-list, grand-a-track session man who looked more like a rock star than Hollis ever had or would. A date was nonetheless set for him to visit the Old Rectory for a chemistry test. 'I drove to Suffolk, met Mark and we hit it off straight away,' says Miller. 'We went to his loft, he had a studio there, and we got down to writing a little bit. He also had a place in Islington and a few times I met him there. I was living in Wimbledon and sometimes he came to my house. I saw him seven or eight times [in total] and we wrote "Westward Bound", which took us about a year.' Their first session, Miller recalls, yielded a single bar of music. 'This is the thing about Mark. Everything was *so slow*.'

Hollis's principal collaborator on the album was another new face. Warne Livesey was no Friese-Greene *manqué*, but they shared a number of broad similarities. Livesey is another English producer who began his working life as an engineer, who also writes and plays music, and whose CV suggests catholic tastes and a certain fluidity in approach. By the time he first met Hollis, he was in his mid-thirties and had worked extensively with artists as divergent as Julian Cope, Midnight Oil and Paul Young, as well as the House of Love and Deacon Blue. He had also forged a long and close relation-ship with one artist, Matt Johnson of The The, with whom he has now worked for almost forty years, spanning from *Infected* in 1986 to *Ensoulment* in 2024.

The first contact came from Keith Aspden, who approached

Livesey's manager. 'They said that Mark was looking for people to write with, though I ended up co-producing,' he says. 'It took me about two nanoseconds to say yes. I guess we all have dream people that we would love to work with. Mark was certainly on that list. I was shocked and surprised. It was not a gig I thought would ever come up because Tim and he had been such close partners for such a long time – and successful ones. Why would he ever bother to look for anybody else to work with? Tim was basically another member of the band.' Livesey did ask Hollis what had happened to end their association but 'he didn't divulge. They had decided to move on.'

Livesey was under the impression he would be working on the next Talk Talk album. 'Looking through my old tapes [and notes], they all say Talk Talk on them,' he says. This confusion lasted until very close to the album's release. In many ways it proved academic. Although it ended up being released as a solo record, this was another collaborative project, one that shared many of the personnel who worked on the previous three records.

Hollis had a clear and precise plan from the start. His creative process was now well-established: to allow an extended period of open-ended exploration and the intense interrogation of possibilities of sound, tone and placement to guide the form and direction of the music. This time, however, all flights of fancy, spontaneity, improvisations, quests for interesting sonic details and textures would be locked in at the writing stage. When it came to recording, every second of every song would be mapped out in advance. The recording would be an exact representation of where the writing process had led. Everyone would play designated parts. No alarms, no surprises. It was, in fact, the inverse of what he and Friese-Greene had done while making *Laughing Stock*. He had tried Messiaen. This was Debussy.

This idea was so traditional – it is, essentially, the way classical music works in both composition and recording – that it felt positively radical: a mix of open-to-the-elements creative adventurism in the writing and inordinately strict absolutism in the execution. There was also a practical subtext. It's likely that Hollis realised that, without Friese-Greene's enormous 360-degree input, relying on everything coming together in the studio would be both creatively risky and very expensive.

'In the first meeting that I had with him, he said that he wanted to approach the album very, very differently [from the previous albums],' says Livesey, who ended up writing five of the album's eight tracks with Hollis. 'Those records very much evolved in the process of recording. When he approached me, he said very specifically, "I don't want to do that. I want to write everything [and] all the experimentation I want to do is in the writing."'

Can we even call it songwriting? The approach was closer to classical composition – and to an extent the music sounds that way, too. Livesey and Hollis demoed each track using a blend of organic sounds and digital samples. Livesey scored it all into notation, which was given to a copyist so the players could read the charts in the studio. 'We wanted to have everything mapped out,' says Livesey. The only elements where even a degree of improvisation was permitted were two solos, one on harmonica and the other on trumpet. These were left open. Everything else was written on the page.

And still it took more than a year in the studio, two entire goes at recording and three drummers, to complete the album to Hollis's satisfaction.

●

Working at Hollis's home in Suffolk, the Old Rectory, and also at Livesey's house in London, they quickly established the parameters of the project – or, rather, Hollis told Livesey what he had in mind. Certain fundamentals were laid out early on. 'We talked about the palette for the record and wanting, number one, for it to be acoustic guitar, not electric guitar, and for it to predominantly be an acoustic record.' The watchword was to avoid any sense that the music was the product of a specific time period. 'When you're looking at writing music, the ideal must be, *I'd like to make music that can exist outside the timeframe*,' said Hollis. 'Your biggest chance of doing that, I guess, is working with instruments that by their nature don't exist in a time period.'[10]

He envisaged woodwind being the prevalent instrumental texture, alongside acoustic bass, acoustic guitar, piano, drums and percussion. In the end, only Mark Feltham's harmonica was put through an amplifier.

These acoustic sounds reflected Hollis's dominant musical interests at this time. Though the walls in his writing room were lined with shelves of records and CDs from all eras and genres, Amon Düül sharing space with the Seeds, he had two overriding fixations. 'I'm listening to classical music from the twentieth century or jazz from the second half of the '50s to the end of the '60s,' he told an interviewer.[11]

Debussy, Webern and Ravel remained favourites, but he was also listening intently to Arnold Schoenberg, the Austrian composer who pioneered the influential dodecaphonic compositional method, also known as 'serialism' or the '12-tone method'. In broad terms, this method required composing with an equal emphasis on all twelve notes in the chromatic scale, each to be played once in a preferred sequence before any note is played again. This effect favours an ordered atonality, working against any sense of the music settling on a central or tonic key, and thus using fewer notes on the scale.

The strangely disembodied woodwind parts on some of Hollis's solo songs find their antecedents in works such as Schoenberg's dodecaphonic *Wind Quintet*, composed in the mid-1920s. Laurence Pendrous also recalls him talking admiringly about György Ligeti's use of woodwind. There are moments in *Six Bagatelles*, the half-dozen short piano pieces Ligeti transcribed for a wind quintet in 1953, which seem particularly pertinent to the direction in which Hollis's music was now travelling.

Perhaps most significant was his interest in the modern American composer Morton Feldman, whose ten-minute composition *The Viola in My Life 2*, written in 1970 for viola, flute, clarinet, percussion, celesta, violin and cello, is an obvious touchstone for Hollis's solo album. There are, indeed, a few moments around the two-minute mark that feel almost as though they could belong to the same record. 'That's the closest thing I've ever come across that I feel I identify with, not only for its minimalism but the actual level at which he hits the notes,' said Hollis in 1997. 'He is as much interested in the tonality of the instrument as he is with the note itself, and that's really important to me.'[12]

Tonality would be crucially important to the solo record. His intention was to record the instruments playing very quietly yet intensely and to be heard as closely as possible to how they would be heard were the listener standing in the room with them. Hollis recalled enjoying an informal half-hour performance in the foyer of the Queen Elizabeth Hall at the Southbank Centre in the mid-'90s, when the audience were encouraged to walk amongst the small chamber orchestra as it played, moving towards and away from different instruments to experience how the sound and dynamic changed through proximity. 'It would be great if you could bring that onto disc…'[13]

Hollis was also gravitating towards modern experimental composers such as Tōru Takemitsu – himself a follower of Messiaen and Debussy – and the pioneering Italian Giacinto Scelsi, who died in 1988. Indeed, there is evidence of Hollis testing out some of Scelsi's most avant-garde methods of writing music, such as in his 1959 piece, *Quattro pezzi su una nota sola,* one of several Scelsi scores which explore dynamics and microtonal nuances by using only a single pitch throughout. During this period, 'Mark bought and took lessons in the clarinet,' says Dominic Miller. 'It is a very difficult instrument to play. But he only wanted to play one long note at a time.'

'He took some clarinet lessons with a friend of mine, Ian Stewart,' says Laurence Pendrous. 'I don't think Mark probably ever had any real intention of becoming a virtuoso on the clarinet. Technically he wasn't the strongest. He couldn't sit down and play a piece of music by somebody. I would be very surprised if he was ever going to kid himself that he was going to get to the level that the clarinet players that he would listen to would play to … The business of exploring the potential of the instrument was the thing that Mark was really interested in. He wanted to always find out, *What else can it do?*' Tonality and texture, then, rather than virtuosity.

It is illuminating to view *Mark Hollis* partly as the consequence of him pursuing these interests. Clearly, his fascination with 'small forces, those little groupings of instruments' had only deepened and had begun to influence his writing more directly than ever before. In the period following *Laughing Stock*, he said, he spent 'a couple of years … writing little woodwind quartets and quintets … It was just writing for its own sake.'[14]

The formality of the instrumentation, in turn, suggested a more formal recording environment. The idea of making a record focused on these ideas and these sounds, in a relatively intimate setting, on a minimal scale, made perfect sense in terms of Hollis's own interests. The problem was, neither Morton Feldman nor Giacinto Scelsi had ever been given a million pounds by a major label to make their next record.

•

How does a pop producer write an incredibly quiet, textured, fully scored acoustic woodwind-centric record with Mark Hollis? It's a simple question with a complex set of responses. Thirty years later, Warne Livesey still isn't quite sure how it happened. He found the process left him snow-blind, creatively speaking. 'To be honest with you, I really felt like I lost my ability to tell [what was good or not],' he says. 'To this day, I don't understand how Mark was able to keep his vision. The intricacy of it was insane.'

Like Dominic Miller, he was struck at first by the glacial pace of the compositional process. 'It took a long, long time,' he says. 'I was writing with him over a period of about two years. Not all the time. We tended to work in three-day blocks. In terms of numbers of days, it took ten months over two years to write five songs without lyrics. It was *a lot* of time. I was producing other albums and he co-wrote a couple of things with other people as well when I wasn't available. He was living in Suffolk at the time, I was living in London and we would alternate. I would drive to him and then the next time he would come to my place. To begin with, I would stay at his house, but he didn't live that far from where my mum lived, so later I got into the habit of staying with her.'

Even the relatively tame appetites of the heady 1980s seemed to have ebbed away. Hollis had just turned forty. A post-work pint was about as hedonistic as life got. 'I didn't see him doing any form of drugs, and even when we were drinking, when we were working, it would just be one pint,' says Livesey. 'He had one night a week where he would meet with all his old buddies and have maybe four or five pints. He was a pretty straight-ahead guy by then, I think.'

Hollis's writing/recording room was a converted space above a garage. It was, says Livesey, 'bloody freezing! During the winters, it was really quite cold up there. We had these space heaters blasting away. It was a very beautiful room, with an old beamed ceiling. Quite big, but very, very stark.'

The approach in some ways mirrored the ways in which Hollis and Tim Friese-Greene had written the basic song structures on *The Colour of Spring,* mapping out the synthetic parts on a Fairlight, later to be replaced by real instruments. Once again, Hollis was using the very latest technology in order to access the most pure, organic sounds. He and Livesey were starting work at the point where digital audio workstations, or DAWs, had become viable. They offered the ability to record directly onto computer rather than tape.

Hollis's recording set-up was not complex. He had an early Pro Tools four-track system with computer, and a keyboard to play and control sounds. In his music room, he had an acoustic guitar, his Country Gent electric guitar and a Tremolo amp; the Country Gent was rarely, if ever, reached for. Livesey's home recording set-up was slightly more elaborate. He had an eight-track Pro Tools system and an AKAI sampler, which he would bring to Stanningfield, containing a library of samples including oboes, bassoons, flutes, clarinets and acoustic bass. Hollis's pump organ, or harmonium, was also sampled. All the samples were 'played' via MIDI keyboards; MIDI was no longer a four-letter word, seemingly. On the Pro Tools system, they could digitally record ideas physically played in the room on acoustic guitar or piano. These sounds and instruments provided the 'colour' palette for the record.

'It was informed by the ability Mark had never had before, where we could design woodwind parts,' says Livesey. 'Normally, you would sit around and have a couple of guitars, strumming away, coming up with a song. We weren't doing that. We were composing an orchestration, like a piece of chamber music.'

What follows is a description of how a typical three-day writing session unfolded during the two years that Hollis and Livesey composed together.

They would begin by searching for some hint of a fresh, interesting idea, via any musical medium. Hollis might pick up an acoustic guitar, while Livesey would bring up some woodwind samples. Or it could be a harmonium sound, or the harmonica. Or string bass. Or a rhythm. Using these prompts, they would jam for perhaps an hour. Everything would be recorded while they played around with melodic and harmonic possibilities. They would then take a short break before returning to listen back to everything they had just recorded. Hollis would speak up whenever he heard a part that he felt had some glimmer of potential. Livesey would note the precise time that it occurred.

At the end of that process, they would run through the short list of brief musical moments or sections that they had identified as promising and whittle each one down further. Eventually, Hollis would home in on specifics and say that he wanted now to focus intently on three or four bars that he particularly liked. They would then take those bars and, in the words of Livesey, 'do everything possible that we could imagine to change them. We would push notes. *What would it be like if that note came half a beat later, or that note was a semi-tone higher? Or lower? What would it be like if we changed that part from a clarinet to an oboe?'*

The pair would subject these handful of bars (I'm beginning to feel sorry for them) to this intense process of examination for the remainder of their three-day work session. At the end, Hollis would say, 'Okay, let's come back to this next time.' The next time they met to compose, which might be some weeks in the future, Hollis would reflect on what they had done in the previous session and, almost always, say, 'No, I don't like any of that. Let's start again.'

Livesey laughs ruefully. 'Ninety per cent of the time, that's what it would be. We would spend three days micro-editing and he would just go, "Nah, don't like it." We could have been working on an idea every day for days and days, and he was enthusiastic and everything was great, then he would just go, "No, no, it's not working for me."'

Livesey stopped asking why after the first few times, because the answer was always a variation on the phrase 'I don't know, I just don't like it.'

'Mark just didn't know how to articulate why something wasn't moving him,' says Livesey. 'I think ultimately that's where the decisions were coming from – it was a *feeling* he was after that he wasn't getting. In our process, we tried all the different changes of notes and timings. We'd gone well beyond just making a chord a major or a minor or whatever.' Confident that he had exhausted every possibility, Hollis was then able to conclude with some finality that it just wasn't working. But the *why* was never clear. Livesey was primarily a producer, hired by a range of demanding and idiosyncratic artists. He regarded the ability to tap into the wavelength of the people he was collaborating with as a crucial professional skill, in order to interpret and facilitate their artistic vision. It was something he felt he usually did rather well. With Hollis, however, he was stumped.

'I could never really figure out what his internal process was,' he says. 'Mark was somewhat of a closed book and difficult to read. There was something held back, always. Even though he was a lovely fella, it was quite difficult to get to know him. He was quite a guarded person … In many ways, he was very black and white. No middle ground. Things were either brilliant or rubbish, [although] his expression for "that's brilliant" would often be "that's pretty good" or "Yer, that's all right" … But, creatively, he worked so intricately in the greys between the black and the white. In fact, he saw more subtleties of shades of grey than most of us even knew existed.

'I think that's what we all love about his music – how the emotionality is so subtle and shifts so gracefully. He was after such fine nuance, but he would or could only describe it in black-and-white terms. It was difficult from my perspective to understand what it would take to move something from "that's rubbish" to "that's all right", but I had such high regard for him that I trusted his judgement, even when it didn't make sense to me. I would just keep experimenting and creating with him. It was unlike any project I have ever worked on from that point of view. I just had to go by blind faith. It was a challenge for me to get over my own frustrations from time to time, [but] the fact that I had such a huge respect for him as an artist from before I ever worked with him meant I was able to trust him and think, *Well, it's Mark Hollis. It's his record. I think the part we have here is bloody great, but he doesn't like it so let's find something else.'*

'Mark had such a fine line between something that is great and something that is shit,' says Phill Brown. 'And you and I wouldn't even see the line.'

That was how the album was composed: walking a thin, thin line only one person could really see.

•

By the end of 1995, this intensive writing process was complete. The collaboration with Livesey resulted in five instrumental tracks (as ever, there were some unusual working titles, including 'Ramah' and 'Gonque'). Hollis would again take time away during recording to write the words, but aspects of the melodies and vocals were already sketched out. 'When writing vocal parts, sometimes we would use some form of sample instrument, or Mark or I would hum something with maybe a few nonsense words and filter those down,' says Livesey. 'He evolved them, essentially, [but] we had rough parts of melodies.'

Their five co-writes would become 'The Watershed', 'The Gift', 'A Life (1895–1915)', 'The Daily Planet' and 'A New Jerusalem'. 'Inside Looking Out' was a rare solo composition. 'Westward Bound', aka 'Om', was a fruit of the composing sessions with Dominic Miller, while 'The Colour of Spring' was a co-write with Phil Ramocon, a classically trained keyboard player with an innate jazz and soul feel. Ramocon had briefly played a prominent role in the Talk Talk story during the period between Simon Brenner leaving and Tim Friese-Greene becoming fully established as Hollis's creative partner. He is credited with playing piano on *It's My Life,* but his influence was more significant than that suggests. He rehearsed with the band and helped Hollis considerably with the task of coaxing several of the songs from that era into their final form.

The pair, therefore, already had a positive history when they reunited in 1994 after a chance meeting in a music store in Denmark Street, where Hollis was trying out a Yamaha electric piano. Hollis invited Ramocon to the Old Rectory to collaborate. As the sound and shape of the song perhaps suggests, the methodology for writing 'The Colour of Spring' differed from the rest of the record; this was much closer to a traditional songwriting partnership. They worked on Hollis's grand piano. Ramocon was at the time heavily influenced by Ravel and Debussy, and he combined rich chord progressions suggestive of both composers with those from a 'gospel-music' tradition. All the music came from him, with Hollis acting as a kind of musical spirit guide. 'I'd play him chords and he would say, "Can you take me from *that* chord to *that* chord but without those others in between?",' said Ramocon. 'It became a journey and a musical dialogue between Mark and I.'[15]

Again, elimination and essentialism. The song as it appears on the album is a study in absolute simplicity. It's almost as though Hollis could no longer permit himself to be so elementary; or perhaps it's truer to say that by now he struggled to freely access such things.

The songs were ready and Livesey was signed on as co-producer. There have been suggestions in the past that he believed the home-studio demos he and Hollis had made were going to actually *be* the finished album; this is not the case. The idea of Hollis releasing an album of sampled woodwind sounds and other synthetic instrumentation beggars belief. From the beginning, the intention was to bring the written scores into the studio and have real musicians replicate the parts, and to do so precisely.

Pre-production began late in 1995, with recording scheduled to begin early the following year. If the writing process was exacting, completing a record fit for release required a whole other level of perseverance.

In 1978, the Canadian-American pianist, composer, arranger and bandleader Gil Evans recalled taping his arrangement of a movement (*Il vecchio castello,* or 'The Old Castle') from Modest Mussorgsky's *Pictures at an Exhibition.* Evans's arrangement, titled 'The Troubadour', was written for and recorded by the Claude Thornhill Orchestra in 1947.

During the interview, some three decades later, Evans experiences a kind of epiphany: *Why must all this recording business be so damned complicated?* 'It's a very interesting track, for the simple reason that it was recorded with one microphone,' he said. 'And really, it picks up everything. It's what I'd like to do when I record again now; I'd like to hang a microphone, or two, down over the whole band, so that I can turn one of those channels on sometimes and hear that band with perspective ... Because it's different, nowadays, when you record multi–track. Here we are out in the room playing, and it's sounding great, but that 16- or 24-track machine is scrambling it. It's putting it into 16 tracks, say, each track having something different on it. Then the record date is over, you've got these tapes, and then you must go into the studio and unscramble the whole thing and get it back the way it sounded in the studio, anyway! That's the thing that gets me down.'[1]

Almost twenty years later, and fifty years after 'The Troubadour', Mark Hollis pondered a similar question and came up with a similar answer. He talked of 'taking things back to the most basic level that you can have as a recording technique. Right back to the thing of when you're in a room together and you just want to record it, and you've got one mic and you turn it on, and that's all it is.'[2]

After years spent obsessively 'scrambling' the tracks so the records ultimately sounded nothing like 'the way it sounded in the studio', he was radicalised into contemplating a simpler approach. A single microphone had already been used to record the drums on *Laughing Stock*, of course, but the idea of applying a similar technique across an entire record was another matter. Perhaps predictably, a straightforward-seeming plan ended up giving everyone a sonic migraine.

The notion of using this minimalist recording set-up for the songs they had written originated from Warne Livesey, who had been inspired direct from the source. It was based on the techniques used by Evans while working with Miles Davis on three of the greatest jazz albums ever made. Livesey believes it was this suggestion that convinced Hollis to ask him to help produce the record, rather than simply co-write some of the songs. 'In fact,' he says, 'I think it is probably the reason why he decided to work with me in the first place.

'When we first met and he started talking about what he wanted to do, I immediately told him something that I'd been thinking about for quite a while. I'd planned it in my mind. I'd even mapped it out as drawings that I showed him. It was designed around when Miles Davis worked with Gil Evans on those three albums Evans arranged: *Miles Ahead*, *Sketches of Spain* and *Porgy and Bess*. I'd loved those records for a long, long time and I'd done a lot of research on how they recorded them. There was a particular way that they set the band up in the studio, a particular mic'ing arrangement. Everybody would have played together in the same room, and the drums would be off in the distance and the quieter instruments would be right up front around a central pair of microphones. Essentially, they got to the sound balance [according to] how far away people were from the microphones.'

For the Hollis record, each acoustic instrument would be taped ambiently at a fixed and immovable distance from two valve microphones placed at the front of the studio room. Everything would be recorded using these two mics, without ever changing the EQ or levels on the desk. They would move the musicians around the room to the required location to determine the correct sound balance.

Hollis agreed this would be an excellent and interesting approach. He already knew and loved those Miles Davis records intimately, of course, and was no doubt familiar with the way in which they were made. His one major reservation was that Evans had recorded all of Miles's band playing at the same time; those records are a brilliantly constructed audio rendering of an ensemble live performance. Hollis didn't want that. Of course he didn't. Ever the micro-manager, he wasn't confident that he would be able to get the performances that he wanted by everybody playing together. He intended recording every instrument individually and separately, giving each one his detailed attention.

Livesey suggested they could apply the same methods anyway. 'The musicians will stand where they're going to stand, we'll have all the mics set up in the studio for the entire project and we'll leave all the mics open … so that's what we did. In a way, this was trying to capture that idea of how the whole acoustic space in the studio would respond.'

Hollis was building a ghost ensemble, a virtual group. All records do that, or most do, but here the presence of the other musicians would be tangible even in absentia. Their places would be marked out in the studio for the duration of the sessions, their relationship to the microphones and other instruments pre-determined, but they would never, or rarely, meet on the studio floor.

In November 1995, Livesey, Hollis and Phill Brown tested several different studios in London in order to find one that met their stringent acoustic demands. They finally settled on Master Rock, a former cinema on Kilburn High Road in north London; it would be hard to find a less fitting studio name for the album they were about to make. Hollis had hoped Brown would agree to engineer the sessions and, before recording began, he had invited him to Stanningfield to hear the record in demo form, mapped out with samples. 'He had it on a Logic system, the whole album,' says Brown. 'It was without the lyrics, but he sat and played me the record, basically.'

Following a period of ill health which resulted in a major operation – and mindful of how exacting and exhausting it could be working with Hollis, albeit with the promise of significant creative rewards – Brown declined the offer. Brent Clarke would engineer instead, although Brown agreed to spend a week helping Hollis and Livesey set up the studio at Master Rock.

'We deadened the room with additional acoustic panels and I positioned our chosen [Neumann] M49s [microphones] at the front of the room as a crossed cardioid pair,' he recalled. 'This is a technique developed in the early years of stereo, whereby two identical cardioid mics are rotated about forty-five degrees to the left and right respectively. "I think we should set up some close microphones, just for insurance," I said. "Later, if you want to bring something nearer to you, then you could use them." It wasn't my fault, but this act of caution had unfortunate consequences.'[3]

The romanticised 'one room, two mics' rule was something of an aural sleight of hand from the start. What Brown was suggesting was a deviation from the recording practice as initially envisaged. As well as the pair of central ambient microphones, each instrument would also have the 'insurance' of its own close microphone. This was essentially intended to claw back some of the control ceded to the room during the mixing process, offering the option to mix a more direct sound into the recording if required; for example, to boost the bass or amplify a kick drum. It would also provide further ambience. When the clarinet was being recorded, the clarinettist would stand in their designated spot, but all the other close microphones – for the bass, the drums, the guitar – would remain open and would record the sound in the room from their various positions. '[It] was to try and encapsulate that idea that everything was recorded in the same acoustic space at the same time, even though it wasn't,' says Livesey. 'That was really the basic idea of the production. Of course, it wasn't ever going to be exact because you wouldn't have all the bodies there all the time. But we did do the whole thing like that.'

As Brown implies, the use of these additional close microphones caused trouble down the line.

Once the studio set-up was finalised over the course of several days, many of the musicians who were earmarked to perform on the record were brought into the studio individually. As each played their written part on a test recording, Hollis and Livesey adjusted positions and levels to determine where each musician should stand. Once the optimum point for each instrument was agreed, its position was marked out by tape on the floor. Adjustments between the virtual and real worlds were sometimes required. At one point, the woodwind arranger, when faced with the musical notation, told them that it would be impossible to play the written part on a clarinet. It would need to be a bassoon or an oboe instead.

Recording began in January 1996 and continued for three months. As usual, Martin Ditcham was called in to mark time and a tempo on each track and would return every few weeks to add more parts.

It was the first album that Hollis had made that did not include Lee Harris on drums. To fill the void – and the void was a considerable one – he turned to some of the more revered names in the world of session musicians: not only Dominic Miller, but American drummers Steve Gadd and Vinnie Colaiuta, as well as British bass player Chris Laurence, whose work spanned classical, jazz and rock. These were A-listers, the cream of the session world – and, in the case of the Americans, very much part of the rock establishment.

Robbie McIntosh remembers being in the studio with Gadd on 'The Daily Planet'. It was a relatively rare instance of musicians playing together in the same room, perhaps because the track was such an involved one. 'The first thing I did on that album was just me and Steve Gadd in Master Rock,' says McIntosh, 'going over and over that song. I forget how many times. I don't want it to sound like a bad reflection on Steve, because I know Steve – I did an album with him with Paul Carrack. He is one of my heroes and a lovely fella to boot. But that was quite a long drawn-out affair! There wasn't much to play to, to be fair. There were a few parps and some stuff that Mark had done on the computer, and it was just me and Steve Gadd. Then they replaced the drums with Vinnie Colaiuta, and I went back and redid the guitars for that.'

After Gadd's contributions to the sessions, which did not go entirely to plan, Dominic Miller offered Hollis another A-list option. 'I had been with Sting for years,' he says. 'I was between tours, but we were rehearsing, I think. When Mark wanted a really good ride cymbal player, I said to him, "Look, Vinnie Colaiuta is hanging out with me and would love to do it." So he got Vinnie in, but he didn't like Vinnie's feel. Fucking hell! He had got Steve Gadd to come in and he didn't like Steve Gadd's feel either! I mean, *What the fuck?* I remember at the time thinking. *This is not a normal kind of record…'*

When Miller came in to play on 'Westward Bound', he was placed on a wooden riser and approximately two feet from the M49s. It was just him and Hollis, with Livesey on the desk. They played the track at least thirty times. 'The way that Mark recorded was very meticulous. That album is absolutely inch-perfect in the way that it's choreographed, musically, and the way it's arranged. Very few artists I've worked with are that clear about what they want to do.'

Though the performance features just Hollis and Miller, the details on their co-composition were carefully thought through. 'Westward Bound' was played on a nylon-string guitar, tuned down three steps to D flat, an unusually low key for the instrument. 'If you play at all hard in that key, your intonation is going to go way out,' says Miller. 'The only way to play that tune was to just literally stroke the strings. So, I was *right* on the mic. That's quite eccentric. Not to mention the fact that it was dark in the studio. There was no light. The only light that was coming into the studio was from the control room.'*

The subdued lighting aside, in contrast to the sessions for *Spirit of Eden* and *Laughing Stock*, working life at Master Rock was calm and civilised. There were no psychedelic bubble projections this time around. Instead there were – mostly – 'medium lighting levels,

---

* In part, 'Westward Bound' feels like it was conceived as a love letter to the sound of Miller's classical guitar. 'Mark bought a guitar exactly like the one that I had, which is the Rodriguez guitar,' says Miller. 'I tuned it to [the non-standard open tuning] DADGAD once and he loved that tuning so much he just kept that guitar in DADGAD.'

a wide assortment of food for lunch and dinner, the possibility of a quiet space to work in and a helpful staff. The only downside was an erratic air conditioning unit.'[4]

Miller was initially only supposed to play on 'Westward Bound', but he was asked back by Hollis to contribute to several other tracks. He is a superb guitar player but, perhaps more crucially, they got on. The measuring of some almost indefinable nuance of character and feel continued to determine Hollis's choices when it came to choosing, and losing, musicians. 'You just had to make the right sound rather than overplay,' says Mark Feltham, who again played harmonica. 'He chose players that he got on with personally, as well. He would always surround himself with guys that he liked to work with. I think that was part of the success.'

This became apparent in one of the more eccentric choices he made in terms of the personnel on the record.

•

By the time recording began in January 1996, Hollis and his family had left Stanningfield and relocated to Wimbledon in south London. 'Around the end of when we were writing, he moved,' says Livesey. 'I think there were a lot of things that he really liked about living out in the middle of nowhere, but it was a decision for the kids to give them the education that he wanted them to have.' That meant an education not just in terms of schooling, but in diversity, culture and life experience. The Old Rectory in Stanningfield was sold at the end of November 1995 for £335,000.*

––––––––––––––––––

* The Old Rectory was sold again twenty years later for more than £1.6 million. Some of its outbuildings are now rented out by its current owners as Airbnbs.

'I think that it was a very lonely existence out there,' says Mark Feltham. 'He had a lovely house, but even when I went up there with my wife, he was pretty isolated in the middle of the Suffolk countryside. This is a London boy! I think Flick also missed her friends back in London as well. I think it was just too quiet for them. When he came back to London … I remember him calling me and saying, "Oh, it's just heaven to be back!" You would never see him down the hippest bar in Wimbledon. You would see him in the working men's club with his shirt and tie and badge on. He even got Dominic Miller to get the old badge, shirt and tie on to go down there. That's what he was like.'

Miller lived in Wimbledon – so did Keith Aspden – and Hollis grew enamoured with the area on visits during the writing sessions for 'Westward Bound'. 'We used to hang out,' says Miller. 'He liked it, so he put his kids in the same school as mine.'

This was Hall School Wimbledon, a fee-paying co-educational 'all through' independent school that enrolled pupils between the ages of seven and eighteen. Laurence Pendrous was the music master at Hall, a school that took music seriously.

Pendrous's piano playing is the first sound we hear on the solo record. During the run-up to Christmas 1995, Hollis had heard him play at a series of the school's end-of-term concerts and his antennae had twitched. 'That's how my connection with him all started,' says Pendrous. 'Having heard me play three times in a couple of weeks, at music concerts at school, he asked me to play on that solo album.' Thirty years later, he still sounds gratefully bemused by it all. 'Mark plays the piano and the material that he wrote on the piano he could have played, as per all the previous albums. [Yet] he wanted me.'

'He liked the way Laurence played upright piano,' says Dominic Miller. 'He loved his feel. So he was pianist [on the album]. He is not a session player, not by any stretch. It makes me laugh a bit because all these A-list players didn't make the cut …'

Hollis gave the role to Pendrous as a gift of blossoming friendship, a token of trust. In return, he believed he would get something out of the ordinary. The care taken over the recording of the piano on the first song, 'The Colour of Spring', is a case study for the meticulous way each instrument on the album was approached. As Pendrous suggests, the chords and parts are far from complex, but it required a highly sensitive approach.

'I had the luxury of being shallow-walked into the process of the pressure of studio recording,' he recalls. 'Mark was just so good, managing each individual aspect of what he was doing, meticulously and intricately. With me, that was a slow walk.'

Pendrous had been given a CD of the rough song in advance, along with a print-out of computer notation, which he initially thought was hideously complex until he realised it had transposed anything Hollis played slightly ahead or behind the beat into the score as a 'hemi-demi-semi-quaver'. Because the piano part itself was not technically complicated, 'I expected to just go in and play it, and it would be great. But Mark said, "I just want to start to get into the zone of where it's flowing in a nice way. So if you just play it the way that you would play the track, that would be great." We did that maybe six or eight times.'

On 'The Colour of Spring', it was the manner in which the weight landed on the second chord that Hollis considered in a very particular way. 'He spent a lot of time getting me to play that the way he wanted it,' says Pendrous. 'I was sat at the piano for probably an hour

and a half into the session before we started [recording] tracks …
Before that, when I was thinking I was good to go, Mark wanted to
take me several steps beyond that to a place where I have never been
before in terms of recording and probably will never be. He gave me
a view of what is possible in the studio and how important the way
you record something is. Every single aspect of the recording of that
solo album was [about] time and attention to detail.'

As well as piano, Pendrous also contributed harmonium on the
record, an instrument he played in church on Sunday mornings to
accompany hymns. Traditionally, in such settings, the first and last
verses are pumped out as loudly and rousingly as possible to encourage people to sing. This involves pummelling the pedals to produce
a big sound. Hollis sought the opposite effect. 'He wanted it right
on the tip of where the air is going through the reeds, when it is just
starting to make a sound,' says Pendrous, who could also be describing the way Hollis sings on much of the record. 'So the pedalling was
unbelievably delicate. It has to be so consistent otherwise it just dies
in an instant, or swells, because you've just quickened up a tiny little
bit, especially between the switchover between your feet. It had to
be so well coordinated to get that sound that Mark was looking for.'

The harmonium they were using was an old instrument. The
reeds were worn and each one produced a sound with a different
tone and slightly different level of delay. It meant it was impossible
to play on the beat, as the sounds from each key emerged at slightly
different times. 'I suggested to Mark, because there was only a few
notes involved, that I'd get used to the delays on each individual note
so I could probably get them coming out much closer together,' says
Pendrous. 'He said, "No, I don't want that. I want it just to come out
the way it comes out of the instrument and if it delays, then that's

fine. If it comes in a bit afterwards, that's absolutely fine." It was extraordinary. Most people would say, "Oh, we'll just have to use a keyboard …"'

Pendrous did five days of recording in all, for which he was paid £400 per day, bumping Aspden up from £300. 'Very decent. I'd be happy to work for that today.' But the richness of the experience, he makes clear, could never be measured in money.

By April, the bulk of music for the album had been recorded. As was customary, after three months in the studio, they took a break to allow Hollis to write lyrics. Six weeks of studio time at Master Rock had been scheduled later in the year, between 20 August and the end of September, to add vocals and some final guitar and woodwind parts.

And then, says Robbie McIntosh with a seen-it-all-before laugh, 'everything got shelved'.

In May 1996, during the planned break, Hollis invited Brown to help finish the record with him and Livesey. Brown was tempted. In June, he visited Hollis at his new home in Wimbledon to listen to what they had recorded so far.

'After a quick pint in his local, we settled into his sparsely furnished music room to listen to the mixes,' Brown recalled. 'The floor was carpeted and all along one twenty-foot wall were shelves housing records, CDs and books.' At one end of the room was a new Steinway grand piano that Hollis had recently bought, accompanied to the showroom by Pendrous for a second opinion. At the other end was Hollis's hi-fi system. 'We sat on the floor directly central to the speakers and played the DAT of rough mixes,' said Brown. 'The sound was not at all what I had expected. I tried to remember how it had all sounded back in January and was surprised by the lack of air or room feel, the bright top end and the upfront energy of most of the sounds. This can't be the same as I set it up in January, with just two M49s at the front of the room … We listened to three of the backing tracks and then Mark stopped the DAT. "What do you think?"'[5]

Brown thought something had gone wrong. As per his suggestion during the initial studio set-up, as well as the two principal central room microphones, each individual instrument had also been recorded using a close mic. According to Brown's account, difficulties arose when, after listening to the rough mixes, he pointed out to Hollis that those close-mic recordings had been mixed into the multitracks and could not be removed. To his ears, it meant the ambience of the room was lost. Hollis called Livesey to confirm if this had been the case. He returned, Brown said, looking 'shaken and upset'.[6]

From Livesey's perspective, the clean, simple aesthetic for recording the album had already crumbled. 'What happened during the three months off was Mark would be calling me up every couple of days.

'"Oh, I don't think that's quite right, that part."

'"Well, it seems fine to me, but if you think it needs to be done again, then we'll do it again."

'Then, a couple of days later, something else would be wrong, and then something else would be wrong. It just went on and on, months of that, to the point where I was starting to get a little bit frustrated. The idea had been that we were going to spend all this exacting time writing all the scores and then a lot less time in the studio. The three months that we spent in the studio were supposed to be it [in terms of] recording all the instruments. After a whole bunch of these phone calls, it looked like we were going to be re-recording quite a substantial amount of the stuff that we had already recorded. I guess the relationship started to deteriorate a little bit. I got a little bit frustrated with him and he got frustrated with me.'

Dominic Miller has a more colourful and perhaps not entirely verifiable take. 'I know for a fact that Warne at one point was unhappy with the level of probably one of the clarinets,' he claims, 'so he moved one of the faders. Then what happened is, I think, Mark fired him – because he moved a fader. Said, "You can't do that." He was a fucking loony, you know, but a genius loony ...'

However it went down, by August, Livesey had left the project on which he had spent the best part of two years. Another one bit the dust. 'In the end, Mark decided that he wanted to finish it on his own,' says Livesey. 'It was his call. I didn't want to get into an argument about it. We just left it at that. That's essentially what happened. I'm happy that I still got the credit for writing those songs with him.'

Phill Brown duly came in to, in effect, help Hollis re-make an album on which he estimated he had already spent more than £100,000. Beginning on 20 August 1996, within forty-eight hours, they had erased 40 per cent of the previous recordings, including all the parts played by two of the greatest session drummers in the world. The following day, Martin Ditcham came back in to begin re-recording all the drum parts, as well as shakers and percussion.

Robbie McIntosh, meanwhile, hoped that the third time would be a charm as far as 'The Daily Planet' was concerned. 'We went back in with Phill Brown and I went back and did that track onto Martin Ditcham's drums,' says McIntosh. 'That is the version you hear on the record. I had to do three different versions with three different drummers. That's how much of a perfectionist Mark was.' The drummers may have changed, but the drum parts did not. 'The drums were very organised *indeed*,' says Ditcham. 'The parts were written by Warne, or Mark and Warne … and [they] were very, very organised. I suppose there was more clarity [on this record] because he did seem to know exactly what he wanted.'

It was a bit like redecorating. You begin with one room and then realise the whole damn house needs painting. In the end, Brown estimates they re-recorded 90 per cent of the record – ironically, about the same percentage as was erased on *Laughing Stock* – with the same cast of musicians and using more or less the same techniques. They were still using the additional close microphones, but this time everyone was paying closer attention to what was going onto tape from the control room.

Despite these setbacks, Hollis seemed a more settled, contented person than he had been during the making of *Laughing Stock* – perhaps because he could now go home to his family every night, or perhaps also because the bulk of the high-wire act had been negotiated during the writing period. For the first time in a long time during the recording process, the music was already a clear picture in his head and he seemed consequently more at ease. He talked humorously about the previous album sessions at Wessex and reminisced with some of his established collaborators about their shared experiences touring *The Colour of Spring*. 'The solo album was a very different kind of project,' says Brown. 'He was a breath of fresh air to work with, because he was communicating with the musicians. He knew exactly what he was after, so he would go out and discuss things, especially with the woodwind sections … Although it was all scored out, they were playing his parts.'

The musicians from the classical world found Hollis's approach fresh and energising. 'Even though we went over some parts at length, there was a lovely, friendly atmosphere in the room,' said Margaret Pollock, who played bassoon on the record. 'He wanted one track to sound tentative, so we imagined we were drops of water that had waited thousands of years until, at last, we were to fall from a stalactite. Unusual strategy! … He had a unique gift for blending different sounds to create an entirely new effect and it all flowed together seamlessly.'[7]

By 13 October 1996, they were almost finished. They returned in November for final overdubs and vocals. On the record, Hollis is listed as the sole producer, Brown as engineer and Livesey as the co-writer on five songs. It does not, perhaps, quite reflect the division of labour.

'I felt a bit sad that it ended with us not being on the greatest terms,' says Livesey, 'but ultimately, when I heard the record, finished, I was very happy with the way that it turned out. He did a superb job of finishing it. A lot of it didn't seem significantly different from where I left the project. He took my name off the co-production in the end, [but] I think it still represents exactly what we had always planned to do. It says on the record that he produced it and, in the grand scheme of things, that's fair enough. But I did spend three months with him in the studio.'

In the end, the purity of the Gil Evans method was muddied. The tracks got scrambled more than a little as they were sent back from the studio floor to the control room. On one song, Brown recalls 'dropping' in two bars of a new drum part every six seconds to make it work. We are not quite hearing the room through the aural lens of two microphones, but it sounds that way, which was always the point.

The sound balance and final mix was in theory supposed to be pre-determined by the microphone settings before they began recording. In reality, two weeks were spent mixing in December and some remixing was done again in January to address issues with the bass. Even after the record had been mastered in February 1997, at AIR's Lyndhurst Hall facility, there was still time to recall the songs later in the month at AIR and give the mix 'a last final tweak'.[8]

The album was finally and definitively mastered by the end of February and delivered via CD and DAT to the A&R department at Polydor with the provisional title *Mountains of the Moon*.* It was handed in as a solo record, but Polydor originally listed it for release as the new album by Talk Talk. Although it featured only Hollis from the group's original line-up, given his prominence within the group, using the name would not have been particularly beyond the pale. 'It was slated as a Talk Talk album,' confirms Nigel Reeve. 'I think that came from the record company and not Mark. Contractually he was possibly under a Talk Talk contract at that time.'

The record industry was in a state of flux and would only become more chaotic in the coming few years. Polydor had not been spared. The label was underperforming and had recently been extensively

---

* The Mountains of the Moon are a semi-mythical, white-peaked range in East Africa, clustered around the source of the Nile. The phrase was coined by local tribes and popularised by early Greek and Roman explorers and map-makers. Various modern-day attributions have been made, including Mount Kilimanjaro in Tanzania and the Rwenzori mountains of Uganda and the Democratic Republic of the Congo. It is also a song by the Grateful Dead, appearing on their 1969 album *Aoxomoxoa*. Another conscious borrowing, perhaps.

pruned by its parent company, PolyGram. Key personnel had left since Hollis had signed up in 1990, among them David Munns. Lucian Grainge became managing director of Polydor in 1997. He had inherited Hollis, an artist who now seemed something of an indulgence, perhaps even one symbolic of where the label had lost its way. The album was one of the first records Grainge dealt with in his new position. At the very least he wanted a Talk Talk product, although once he heard the music, he wasn't sure that he wanted it at all.

Through the summer of 1997, Phill Brown recalls, there were various stand-offs with the company. In June, Hollis was apparently informed that the record would be released as Talk Talk, like it or not. Then he was told that Polydor would not release it under any name, but that two other labels owned by PolyGram, A&M and Mo' Wax Records, were both interested in picking it up. Two weeks later, Polydor allegedly told Keith Aspden that they would neither release the new album nor give it back to Hollis to take to another label. A part of Hollis seemed to appreciate the absurdity of it all. In one meeting, he was told that Polydor didn't want his new album, but *did* want him to sign the option for a third album. He told Brown, 'Like I'm likely to sign to someone who is saying, "The first album's crap, the second album's crap, but please sign to us for a third …"'[9]

At the beginning of November, Polydor finally confirmed that the album would be released in January 1998 under the title *Mark Hollis*, unambiguously clarifying the fact that he had always regarded it as a solo record. No one seems to know what happened to calling it *Mountains of the Moon*. 'A couple of times [in later years] we talked about packaging the albums together,' says Nigel Reeve. 'Mark was always very clear that the solo album shouldn't be in the set because, quite simply, it was not a Talk Talk record.'

It was sent out into the world with little enthusiasm, the third consecutive album of his to meet such a fate. A short time before the release of *Mark Hollis* was confirmed, Phill Brown was working with Dido and her brother Rollo, from the group Faithless. One day, Rollo told him that a member of their management team had recently gone into the Polydor office to meet Lucian Grainge. The Polydor MD had played him one of the more challenging tracks from the as yet unreleased Hollis album and asked his visitor what he thought.

'Yeah, I like it,' he replied. 'It's really good.'

'What, *really* good?' said Grainge.

'Yeah, really good. I think it sounds great.'

Grainge peered over the desk.

'Is it worth a million?'[10]

iii

*(Mark Hollis was not Talk Talk and
Talk Talk was not Mark Hollis)*

While Hollis beavered away, the estranged ex-members of Talk Talk moved on.

Harris reconvened with Paul Webb to form a new hydra-headed creative outlet called 'O'rang. Tim Friese-Greene went back to producing other bands before making music as a solo artist under the banner Heligoland.

The creativity that was poured into the records they had all made together originated from several sources. It should not be surprising that a lot of very good music flowed from each member of the group, official or otherwise, following the end of Talk Talk. Threads teased out in 1986 are even today still being pulled.

Harris and Webb formed 'O'rang in the months following the release of *Laughing Stock*. The pair had never been out of touch and had recently begun demoing new material they had written together. With Phill Brown joining as an affiliate member, the project became a form of therapy for all three of them – or at least a shot at catharsis. 'It was very much Lee's project,' says Brown. 'The three of us met up in Stoke Newington, a year after finishing *Laughing Stock*, and we got together and said, "You know, making records can be fun!" Because I don't think anyone thought *Laughing Stock* was fun. We had this idea of putting a little studio together and just going in and having fun again.'

They invested in building their own self-contained studio/clubhouse in an industrial unit in Tottenham, nicknamed The Slug. The strobes, oil projector and disco lights were dusted down, sacred relics from the heady days of *Spirit of Eden*, although with 'O'rang there was less emphasis on psychological vibe-disturbance and more on kicking back and having a party. According to Webb, Harris came up with the 'genius idea' of inviting a graffiti artist into the live room to paint a large exotic mural in fluorescent colours that glowed in the dark under ultraviolet light. 'The result wasn't unlike the passing walls found on fairground ghost train rides,' said Webb. 'This provided a great backdrop when recording our long jamming sessions for those albums.'[1] The twin engines of creativity were weed and drums. They wanted to work fast and spontaneously, to capture the magic in the moment and move on quickly to the next.

The creative ethos was collegiate. An array of friends and musicians were invited over to add to the music, including Talk Talk alumni Martin Ditcham, Mark Feltham and Simon Edwards, as well as former Waterboy Anthony Thistlethwaite, The The's Matt Johnson, Portishead's Beth Gibbons and Graham Sutton, the guitarist of the expansive rock collective Bark Psychosis. All contributed something to what Brown calls a 'library of instruments, performances and sounds comprising over eight hours of continuous music'.[2] This sprawling sonic collage was in time chopped up and subjected to a long and intensely complex process of computer-aided editing by Harris. It made Brown wonder whether Hollis hadn't been the only obsessive in Talk Talk. 'O'rang was largely Harris's project and completing it to his satisfaction after the trials and humiliations of *Laughing Stock* was clearly deeply important to him. 'He had something personal to prove to Mark and was determined to get everything just right and sounding just as he heard it in his head,' says Brown.[3]

There was another direct connection back to the mothership. On *Laughing Stock*, they had tried out six drum patterns in the studio, one of which they titled 'Swabi'. It was never mastered and therefore never used. 'We never got a take that Mark was happy with when we were doing it at that time,' says Brown. 'So Lee used the "Swabi" pattern for 'O'rang.' It was the least Harris deserved for his efforts. 'O'rang made the most of the eerily off-centre 'Swabi' rhythm on 'Little Brother', perhaps the standout piece on their debut album, *Herd of Instinct*, released in 1994. It is a startling track, the sound of a mutant musical army chopping its way through dense vegetation somewhere in the Tropics.

The band name was onomatopoeic. This was colourful, concentric head music, deep, dense and groove-based, picking up signals from all over the world. *Herd of Instinct* is a sometimes overloaded melange of global influences and instrumentation – musical anthropology, the sound of 'Talk Talk gone *Lord of the Flies*'.[4] It is also the sound of Talk Talk had they ditched the erase button and let loose jams reduce into a thick, soupy texture. The results drew on familiar touchstones, such as krautrock, folk and progressive rock, and continued with the ethos of making music rooted in improvisation. In a line Hollis might have appreciated, Webb said the album was 'recorded before it was written'.[5] They incorporated their youthful love of dub, reggae and soul, as well as the rhythmic complexity of Afrobeat. For all that Harris revered Can's Jaki Liebezeit, here his fealty to another stand-alone drummer, Tony Allen, is apparent, as the wild contours of Fela Kuti's febrile '70s funk are flung into the broth.

'O'rang distilled a range of interesting influences in ways that make their records feel conceptually connected to the sound-world of the latter Talk Talk albums, but also seem very prescient. Viewed from today, when it is routine to receive daily emails announcing the latest record from an Indonesian psych-folk band, they were arguably ahead of the game. And for all its strange throbbing humidity, the music's anchor was forged in Essex, courtesy of a rhythm section that had been playing together since their early teens. Webb and Harris locked in tight. This was still family business. When the record was finally finished, Harris gave *Herd of Instinct* to a mutual friend to pass on to Hollis. When he received word back that his old band mate had enjoyed it, he seemed overjoyed.

'O'rang released one more album, *Field of Waves* in 1996, before dissolving. Ever since, Webb and Harris have continued to work together sporadically, though never again as a defined unit. Both have made records with Beth Gibbons, another idiosyncratic and deeply emotional artist, as well as a somewhat elusive figure who delivers beauty with an unsettling undertow through her voice and in her music.

Webb now records under the name Rustin Man. It is the title of the final song on *Out of Season*, the contemplative yet spiky album of folk-centric songs, touched by jazz and chanson, that he co-wrote and co-produced with Gibbons in 2002, and on which he also played multiple instruments. It was by far his most successful record since Talk Talk, charting in several European countries and featuring famil-iar faces such as Simon Edwards, Mark Feltham and Harris.

Neill MacColl recorded with both Webb and Harris on the first Rustin Man album. 'It was a kind of perfect storm getting members of Talk Talk and Portishead together,' he says. 'I got a bit of insight into how Talk Talk might have worked, although we never talked about it. At the session I was on, Mark Feltham came in. His first take was the best thing I have ever heard on harmonica. It was riveting. He came back to the control room and Paul and Beth said, "Let's try a few more takes to see what happens." Mark spent the next half-hour playing it over and over, and it never got any better. But, of course, they had wiped the first take! I wouldn't call it an illness. It's just a different approach. It's that school where you work it and work it and work it, and that's how you get what you want. It was brilliant playing with Lee on Rustin Man. We played live together in the studio and I was just so in awe because as soon as he hits a drum, he's got that feel – you're on a Talk Talk record! He was such a huge part of their sound.'

In 2006, Webb played on and produced James Yorkston's album, *The Year of the Leopard*. Since then, working out of his own studio in a converted barn at his home in rural Essex, Rustin Man has released two more fine albums. On the largely self-played *Drift Code*, parts of which dated back to the turn of the millennium, but which was only released in 2019, Lee Harris played drums and co-wrote two songs. In 2020 came *Clockdust*, a related album of songs recorded during the same sessions. These are textured and enjoyably timeless albums of not-quite-folk, full of intimations both of wyrd old England and dustbowl America, with an abundance of graceful and unexpected moments. Webb's singing voice is odd but appealing. Of late, he has been collaborating with Steve Cradock of Ocean Colour Scene.

Lee Harris, meanwhile, swam a little further out from the shore. After the end of 'O'rang, he collaborated with Bark Psychosis on their 2004 album *Codename: Dustsucker*, a full, free-flowing work which had at least some interest in the terrain Talk Talk explored on their later records. He also contributed to Magnetik North, a collaborative project between Jaki Liebezeit and the producer and film/TV composer Ian Tregoning. *Evolver* was a frenetic fusion of live drums, acoustic instruments and electronic sequencing, each track recorded in a single key and drawing on industrial, classical, krautrock and Detroit electronica. It was, said the press bumf, like listening to a 'raga in an earthquake'.[6] Harris played on a track called 'Fuck the Napkin'. No one was expecting much drivetime radio play; this was very firmly in the realm of outsider music. Over Liebezeit's brooding tattoo, Harris added remarkable peals of Chinese percussion and hard, polyrhythmic djembe.

Neither he nor Webb are what you might call prolific, but Harris in particular appeared at times to be drifting around the far edges of a music career. With the passing years, he also seemed to grow almost as remote and publicity-shy as Hollis once was. Happily, he re-emerged in 2024 as an integral part of an album that enjoyed a higher profile than any he had been involved in since the days of Talk Talk. As well as playing drums, percussion and harmonium on Beth Gibbons' *Lives Outgrown*, he co-wrote four songs and also arranged and produced parts of it.

It was a record Harris had worked on from the ground up. 'It began by looking for sounds,' he said. 'Beth had a few things, but it was all too normal … We went through loads of stages, gradually building up our palette.'[7] Only then did they start writing tracks. It was somehow pleasing to discover that the dedication to take as much time as was needed to find just the right kind of 'not normal' had not dissipated. It took four years to form ten songs which shared the mood of 'a psychedelic pastoral, soft explosion'.[8] A seriously substantial piece of work, *Lives Outgrown* was Harris's most sustained creative output in decades.

Tim Friese-Greene, meanwhile, waved goodbye to Mark Hollis and, in the 1990s, produced two albums with Catherine Wheel, a British guitar band heavy on woozy texture, drones, feedback and effects. Shoegaze-adjacent, at the very least. He also recorded Sidi Bou Said, who sounded a little like a slightly more twee Anglo iteration of Throwing Muses – off-kilter indie-folk, literate lyrics, inventive, unusual arrangements. Guitarist Lee Howton later became Mrs Friese-Greene.

In time, he created Heligoland as a vehicle for his own musical endeavours. He sang lead vocals for the first time and played every instrument he could – which was most of them – and to all intents and purposes became an independent solo artist. 'I rented a very small hut on an island in the middle of the Blackwater Estuary in Essex,' he said, 'The island was called Osea Island. I went there with a four-track and worked out exactly what it was that I wanted to do and how I wanted to sing – if indeed I did want to sing because I wasn't even sure of that … It is totally a solo project … I don't get people in, except when absolutely necessary.'[9]

The first dark fruits appeared on *Creosote & Tar*, a four-track EP released as a limited edition in 1997. The title track was lo-fi, abrasive, both cacophonous and melodic, and broadly attuned to contemporary trends in alt.rock and indie music. The layering of instruments was clearly considered, but deliberately imprecise. There was an American bent to the noisy guitars and overloaded harmonicas, as well as Friese-Greene's small but complementary voice, with its faint echoes of Elliott Smith.

On the EP, there are threads, should you seek them out, that connect back to the more strident elements of *Laughing Stock* – not least a closing barrage of almost insolent noise on the song 'Creosote & Tar'. Everywhere there is the love of the unusual sound, the frayed texture. A wildly warped saxophone howls over a deadened drum beat on 'Blued', while the entrance of what sounds like Variophon against a raw bluesy guitar on 'Dreaming of Persephone' has the distinctive DNA of a musical fingerprint.

The EP was followed by two full-length albums, *Heligoland* in 2000 and *Pitcher, Flask & Foxy Moxie* in 2006, the latter a more distilled affair, at least for an album recorded in a disused mattress factory. By now, Friese-Greene had become a confident and engaging vocalist.

Since then, his creativity has continued in scattershot style. He lives in Devon and works independently. He appears to have fully embraced the freedoms of the internet age, taking the opportunity to release diverse output via multiple outlets. He runs his own label, Calcium Chloride, and makes his releases available via Soundcloud and Bandcamp – nowadays under his own name, rather than Heligoland. There are experimental pieces, improvisations and 'undocumented performances'. The music is diverse and eclectic – and done, one suspects, for the love of it; nothing is polished. The mischievous joie de vivre Friese-Greene always seemed to find in making loud and interesting noises has survived through the decades and negates any sense of preciousness. His love of a crackling electric guitar appears not to have diminished. His is the kind of interesting, marginal music that creative people make when earning a living from it is not really a consideration.

Friese-Greene is now seventy. Webb and Harris are approaching their mid-sixties.

All three are principal characters when it comes to the sound and spirit of most of the music discussed in this book and all three have stayed the course. From the unpromising origins of Southend ska bands and novelty hits with Tight Fit, they have remained committed not just to working with high-calibre artists, but also to a higher ideal of what music can be: surprising, beautiful, aggressive, experimental, ugly, spiritual, rough, transporting. And different. A certain purity of intent is evident in each man's work and in that, if not in the more prosaic specifics of song and sound, they have kept alive a connection to the open-hearted beauty of *Spirit of Eden*.

Perhaps that is why none of them talk about Talk Talk.

interlude 5

(The Dreaming)

In August 1993, Kate Bush appeared via telephone on Simon Mayo's Radio 1 Breakfast Show. She was gearing up to release her seventh album, *The Red Shoes*. During the conversation, Mayo asked what she had been listening to. 'I don't listen to very much, because I spend most of my time making music,' Bush responded. 'I like Talk Talk a lot.'[1]

Bush's long-term bass player, engineer and former boyfriend, the late Del Palmer, made an even closer connection during an interview the same year. 'At the moment, she's really into Talk Talk,' he said. 'She finds a real affinity with them.'[2]

This was post-*Spirit of Eden*, post-*Laughing Stock*. Hollis had headed for the hills. It was also the beginning of the period leading into Bush's lengthy absence from making new music, or at least releasing it, which stretched from early 1994 to the end of 2005.

Hollis and Tim Friese-Greene were admirers of hers stretching back to the 1980s. The influence of *Hounds of Love* on *The Colour of Spring* was perhaps more a matter of osmosis than anything more overt, even if 'Running Up That Hill' provided a rough template for the writing of 'Life's What You Make It'. Consciously or not, Talk Talk and Bush were operating in similar ways at the time in terms of layering, manoeuvring and manipulating individual parts into a carefully constructed soundscape that was heavily reliant on the Fairlight.

Killing Joke's bass player Youth, who worked with Bush on

Hounds of Love, recalled that 'every individual musician would come down [to the studio] and play their parts separately – drums, guitars, bass. I don't think she had them all performing together, which was weird, and gives the album a slightly futuristic atmosphere. I put down some basslines. She let me do what I liked, gave me some direction, and said, "Thanks very much. Off you go." Then she chopped it all up and arranged it in the Fairlight. I learned a lot from that, how to put a record together. It's more about selection than musicianship. She's after the currency of ideas that's reflected in the music rather than academic virtuosity.' Hollis and Friese-Greene, too, traded freely in the 'currency of ideas'. Bush's working methods were strikingly similar to their own, though entirely without that very male desire to bring friction into the creative process.

The masterful building and sustaining of atmosphere (during 'The Ninth Wave' suite on *Hounds of Love* in particular), the linking passages and the natural but audacious sonic shifts between the very beautiful and the deeply unsettling may later have partially illuminated the path towards *Spirit of Eden*.

During those sessions, chief engineer Stuart Stawman recalls work stopping at Wessex Studios when they somehow got hold of a very early pre-release version of Bush's song, 'The Sensual World'. 'They played it for the first time through the main monitors in the control room,' he says. 'I can still remember the bated breath of a room full of respect for Kate Bush as the church bells that open the track started playing.'

This was an unusual display of reverence for a contemporary artist.

They did not send her back to James Joyce.

As Bush confided to Radio 1, the respect was mutual and, in time, the influence swung back in the other direction. In the music Bush has made since 2005 in particular, it is not hard to hear the influence of Talk Talk and Mark Hollis. It is not always – or even often – overt, and Bush has always displayed less tolerance for the extreme sonic moment, but the space and silence she has increasingly built into her music feels affiliated, somehow, to the records in this book. I can imagine her listening to *Mark Hollis* during the time she spent away from releasing music and consciously or otherwise allowing some of its intense serenity to flow into her own music.

It started, perhaps, with a shift in her use of rhythm. She began working with American drummers with an intuitive jazz feel. First the great Peter Erskine, on *Aerial*, which remains perhaps Bush's underacknowledged masterpiece. The 'Sky of Honey' suite was as ambitious as 'The Ninth Wave' had been twenty years earlier, but this was arguably an even more expansive undertaking, sensitive to the touch and with a calm, opened-out cohesion.

Then came Steve Gadd. He first played for Bush on *Director's Cut*, in 2011, on which she re-recorded songs from her albums *The Sensual World* and *The Red Shoes* partly because she felt in hindsight the originals sounded too uptight, too compressed. Guided by Gadd, already-fine songs such as 'Never Be Mine' and 'Song of Solomon' opened up and breathed in a way that recalled the more flowing pastoral textures on the second side of *Spirit of Eden*. The wholesale deconstructions of 'This Woman's Work' and 'Moments of Pleasure' – ambient, glacial, with huge reverb-heavy notes clanging into silence – were even more radical. 'I achieved space in those tracks,' she said, and carried it forward.[3]

Bush used Steve Gadd again on her next record. *50 Words For Snow* is, to date, her last album of new music. Drawing on ECM, chamber jazz, blues and contemporary classical music, the diffuse melodies ebb and flow, meander and evolve. What hadn't worked for Hollis at Master Rock worked for Bush; Gadd's playing is the golden thread that binds it all together. The pitter-patter of drums, brushes and cymbals slide around her piano on these strange, arrhythmic songs, long, loose and linear.

Reviewers mentioned Eno, Scott Walker, Joni Mitchell and Michael Nyman. Few if any reached for Mark Hollis, yet in some ways *50 Words For Snow* can be regarded as a companion piece to Hollis's solo record. Listen to the final sections of 'Lake Tahoe', to the roll of the rhythm, the fluffed 'ghost' note and sudden gasp of silence, the low strings and steadily building textures. Then listen to 'The Watershed', the way the drums flutter and then fall like a sigh back into the piano melody just before the three-and-a-half minute mark. I hear a very present connection. There is also, on tracks such as 'Snowflake' and 'Lake Tahoe', a deep appreciation of the way silence can never ever be *just* silence.

An 'affinity', said Bush, and that is what it sounds like.

The connection crossed over into real life. Unsurprisingly, given we are discussing two artists who guarded their privacy with extreme care, we do not know much about what passed between Hollis and Bush, but they certainly met as like-minded artists with a view to perhaps working together.

'Kate mentioned it to me,' says David Rhodes, who was the guitarist in Bush's band when she returned to the stage in London in 2012 for the *Before the Dawn* series of shows. 'She met him and liked him. And then it didn't really get any further and I'm not quite sure why. I can't even remember precisely what Kate said … She did mention that there had been a little hook-up, but nothing came of it. I don't think there is anything in the vault! But what an intriguing idea.'

Mark Feltham attempted to divine more information from the Hollis side. 'I would try and drag it out of him,' he says. 'We would often meet up in London for a beer. He'd say to me, "Come on, let's get up to Waterloo." We would both travel in on the train and meet … We'd get in the pub and I'd say, "Well, come on, what's happening? Are you working?" I think he had become friends with Kate Bush. He used to see her socially now and again. I always thought there may be something that he would write, possibly with Kate. I used to try and get inside his head, [but] he didn't want to talk about it … I really couldn't get too much out of him. You know, he held things very close to his chest.'

Mark Hollis writing and recording with Kate Bush.

Kate Bush producing Mark Hollis.

It could never have worked. Could it?

iv

Mark Hollis fulfilled the second and final obligation in the artist's two-album, £2 million deal with Polydor. It is perhaps the world's least likely million-dollar record. It entered the UK album charts at number fifty-three on Valentine's Day 1998 and was gone by the following week. The final accounting must have made the record company's eyes bleed.

The reviews, of which there were many in the UK and Europe, were respectful and often reverent, engaging with the music seriously and with knowledge. Hollis had become a figure of substance. Most acknowledged that this was a record that existed so far inside its own world and so far outside of the current times that the two elements barely brushed against each other. If he even considered it, Hollis could hardly have fancied that this music stood any chance of connecting with a mainstream audience. He also knew that such things only count in the short term. What lasts is what matters, and what matters is what lasts.

Mark Hollis has lasted. It is a stunningly beautiful record: intimate without ever being soft or slushy, challenging and wilful without denying us the pleasure of melody or rhythm, structured and intentional without feeling overly composed or strait-jacketed. The sound it captures is astonishing; natural, tangible, realer than real. We hear the nuance of the bass and the brilliant treble high tones of the cymbals. There are acres of depth and yards of foreground. It pulls off its stated aim of transporting the listener directly to the recording studio, where we can hear, and perhaps see, these musicians fanned out before us in a circle.

It is tempting sometimes to wonder whether Hollis treated music as a puzzle, an academic pursuit, and then you hear the results and realise all he wanted to do was create music that was, emotionally speaking, absolutely true. As Paul Webb put it, in a warm statement following Hollis's death, 'he knew how to create depth of feeling with sound and space like no other'.[1] Warne Livesey, who has sufficient cause, perhaps, to feel a little sore about the solo album, is instead generous and perceptive. 'Mark had a magical ability to spend a huge amount of time working on music in a very intense and exacting way, but come up with something that sounds fresh, simple, economic and emotionally powerful, and as if it was effortless.'

The highwire sense of lightness, extreme quiet and fragility noted previously on 'Westward Bound' is characteristic of the album, though not entirely defining. There are songs here that kick up a fuss, where the drums click-clack, trumpets flare and harmonicas warp and wail. (As a sidenote, we would all do well in life to find someone who loves us the way Mark Hollis loved Mark Feltham's harmonica playing.)

But the dynamics defer to silence.

Think back to the start of *The Colour of Spring*, to that almost indecently alive drum fanfare proudly leading a new vision of the band into battle. How potent and spring-like it felt, how crisp and loud.

Only a dozen years later, the song of the same name which begins *Mark Hollis* starts with silence, as though establishing the base line for this music, the core principle against which everything must be measured. If there is a maxim which sums up Hollis's artistic stance, at least in his later years of making music, it is this: 'I would rather hear one note than I would two, and I would rather hear silence than I would one note.'[2]

'The Colour of Spring' begins with almost twenty seconds of not-quite nothingness, the silence scored with a smear of tape hiss which runs like a subterranean seam through the whole record. Then the faintest squeak of a piano stool, and the resonance of two hands placed on the keys, followed by a high, tremulous human hum, the sound of a soul taking a reading and locating its bearings. What is most striking about the music is its calmness, its beatific simplicity as it moves in the most easeful way between the two most primitive piano chords imaginable. These chords are primordial. They are 'Imagine' chords, 'Don't Look Back in Anger' chords. Gospel chords. Church chords. King David would recognise them.

The sound is warm and immediate. We are welcome, but keep the noise down and pay attention. Hollis's vocal enters the picture almost immediately. So clear, so pure, nothing forced. He sings the verse melody twice, before finding the chorus, if that is what it is. There is a soft, scattered Ravelian piano interlude, a kind of elegant loosening, and then a final chorus. It would have been easy – too easy, no doubt – to return for a third and final verse and those deeply satisfying gospel changes. But, still, this is a *song*, open and access-ible. At fewer than four minutes, it is the shortest track Hollis had recorded in a dozen years, and perhaps also the most direct. *Where has this guy been hiding?* It sometimes seems a shame that Hollis fell out of love with songcraft. He was very good at it. In my alternative fantasy Talk Talk universe, and with a little light dusting, 'The Colour of Spring' could have been a modest hit single.

We will never know whether *Mark Hollis* was consciously con-ceived as a final statement – whether something profound was being resolved in these clear, airy, alternately restful and disjointed, determinedly ludic songs. In interviews to promote the record, he spoke in qualified terms about the future: 'if I make another album…'; 'any album I might make…'.[3] Dominic Miller says Hollis 'told me after we did that record that he wasn't going to do any more'. There is certainly plenty of meat here for those who wish to read his last work as the parable of a man who had struggled to make meaningful and lasting art in the face of many trials and indignities. While the first verse of 'The Colour of Spring' recognises regret – 'Set up to sell my soul / I've lived a life for wealth to bring' – the second finds redemption through the eternal 'now' of the moment of creation. The chorus simply cries freedom: 'Soar the bridges that I burned.' We might read it as a testament that the prize was worth all those scattered bodies left along the way, but now? Now he was done.

There are many lines on the record which seem to explicitly reference the hard bargains struck in order for Hollis to commercialise the music he had been compelled to create. The virtue/disgust binary is boiled down to a series of stark professional epitaphs.

'Set up to sell my soul.'

'A song asale / Sold heart.'

'So sold out.'

'Left no life no more.'

'Sown my money / Sold my shirt.'

'Sun eclipsed to shame.'

Sale, sell, sold. The transactional blues. The bare bones of flogging your art. The final verse of 'Westward Bound' can be interpreted as a farewell to the whole sorry business. The first verse harks back to *The Colour of Spring* and 'April 5th', and the woman, the wife, the mother, the spirit 'born' – not 'borne' – 'on the April tide'. But the mood of regeneration doesn't hold. The bounty of domestic bliss in the first verse yields to the 'weight' and compromises demanded by the world beyond the front door. The song ends with the protagonist silenced, walking into the sinking sun. 'Migrate / Job on the threshing line / Mute I walk / Idle ground / Westward bound.' The sense of finality and departure is not quite explicit, perhaps, but keenly felt.

The other recurrent theme, also not a new one for Hollis, is that of promises broken, fresh chances squandered to the same old mistakes and mendacity, youth hamstrung. 'I think of it as being to do with compassion,' he said once of his worldview.[4] The bracketed subtitle of 'A Life (1895–1915)' directs us to a very specific time period. The song was loosely inspired by the short life of Roland Leighton, the fiancé of the feminist, scholar, socialist and pacifist Vera Brittain, who served as a voluntary nurse during the First World War. She wrote about Leighton in her 1933 memoir *Testament of Youth*. He died in the war, as did Brittain's brother and several other friends. Given the title, Hollis was very probably stirred into action by the publication in 1995 of *Vera Brittain: A Life*, a new biography by Paul Berry.

Hollis is using war to again address virtue: virtue roused – this time in the name of a seemingly just and noble cause – exploited and finally crushed. 'That was someone born before the turn of the century and dying within one year of the First World War at a young age,' he said. 'It's the expectation that must have been in existence at the turn of the century, the patriotism that must have existed at the start of the war and the disillusionment that must have come immediately afterwards. It's the very severe mood swings that fascinated me.'[5]

'A New Jerusalem' explores a similar idea using a similar context. The Blakean title also echoes a phrase – 'We see the new Jerusalem' – from Van Morrison's hymn-like 'Haunts of Ancient Peace', on

Common One, an album I suspect Hollis knew pretty well. In this case, the words are unambiguous. Living can be another kind of death. The young soldier has fought and survived and is 'home again' but alone, and 'dead to love', a pawn, second guessing his patriotism in the face of a nation failing to keep its promise. 'Heaven, burn me / Should I swear to fight once more?' It is worth remembering that the timelessness Hollis sought in his music encompasses the words. There is not a syllable in any of these eight songs that would date-stamp them.

Even so, *Mark Hollis* is not set adrift from his previous work. There are obvious connections between it and the final two Talk Talk albums. Beyond the identifying sound of his voice, there are sonic leitmotifs, stylistic flourishes and structural elements that recur. On 'A New Jerusalem', the opening organ wash establishes an enveloping atmosphere akin to 'Wealth' and 'I Believe in You', with which it shares a similar hymnal stillness. Later in the song comes an odd, abrasive scraping sound at two minutes, on the phrase 'and so the sea…' The song pauses, as though itself surprised, and breaks down into a drifting passage of piano and harmonium, before being jolted forward by a crisp roll of drums. I can imagine Tim Friese-Greene hearing it and raising his hat.

The closing harmonium figure on 'Inside Looking Out', which might just be the quietest, saddest music ever made, sounds like the analogue version of a classic Talk Talk Variophon part. The lyric, meanwhile, is a blues, plain and simple: 'Feel my skin, Lord / Feel my luck tumbling down'. The song ends on a rogue note, resisting easy resolution, while 'The Gift' works up from the rhythm, à la *Laughing Stock*. The Puckish guitar solo by Miller sounds at least partly improvised. The harmonica buzzes away, rushing forward then falling back, hovering around like a bad debt. The song swings but then stutters to a close, as though suddenly out of ideas.

'The Watershed' returns to a recurring theme, the futility of direct communication – 'Should have said so much, makes it harder, the more you love' – and decency destroyed: 'For the good has bled to dust / Departed, the morning sun.' It is a fabulous piece which begins before it starts, with a brief preparatory scuffle smuggled into the mix. There is a hint of John Fahey's folk blues in the rolling, guttural guitar riff. The lolloping string bass and campfire harmonica all feels appealingly close to the touch. The rhythm recalls the rainfall-pattering ride cymbal on 'Astral Weeks', bright and celestial. We can hear the strings squeak, the drawn breath behind the art. Four minutes in comes a drum roll and Henry Lowther's exquisite trumpet fire.

Oh yes, we recognise this music.

In broader terms, the idea of pushing the extremes of silence, from beauty to violence and back again, goes back to *Spirit of Eden* at least. 'It probably peaked on the solo album,' says Phill Brown, 'because everyone is just playing so quietly. His voice is *just about* there. If he sang any quieter, it wouldn't actually resonate anything [at all].'

Neither is this music without any rock or pop touchstones. As we have seen, there are further echoes of Kate Bush in this work, though they are more often pre-echoes, the sound of Bush albums to come. The spirit of Nick Drake rises on 'Westward Bound', both in the guitar playing and its non-standard tuning, as well as its air of *Pink Moon* spareness. The two shuffling guitar chords on 'The Gift' echo Neil Young's 'Down By the River'. It's not all Schoenberg and Feldman.

•

Music can be more than one thing at any one time. The solo album is a beautiful achievement. It is also a deeply strange record. It belongs nowhere. Certainly not in any popular music landscape, but likewise the modern jazz and contemporary classical touches are also skewed off-centre.

Hollis was using textures that he loved and understood – he even took lessons on the clarinet to learn the rudiments – but he was now writing in modes that can take decades of dedicated study to master. It is to his credit that there are times when it all blends beautifully, when all the many worlds of music he loved fold together. On the Feldmanesque 'The Daily Planet', the woodwind parts are a perfect organic fit with the music around which they are placed, developing a repetitive, almost funky backline riff. The drums establish a snappy pulse. With its splashy rhythm, the song could be an unplugged cousin to 'After the Flood', moving with a similar sense of propulsion. This is a swinging tune, with hints of wildness. Robbie McIntosh's big open guitar chords sit either side in the mix, giving the sound a wide-screen cinematic drama. It's a gutsy song. It sounds convincingly like a real band playing in a room. I wouldn't change a bassoon burp of it.

Then there are other occasions when, to my ear, the woodwind never successfully integrates with the music. 'Inside Looking Out' is one of two or three songs on the record where the creaks and squeaks feel strangely alienating, distracting if not superfluous. I'm not sure they bring much to the party. 'A Life (1895–1915)' begins with a short figure in the twelve-note style, everything determinedly atonal and unresolved. Listening to it, I sometimes wonder, *Is this really what Hollis wanted? Or did he fall short?*

'A composer has to be able to really understand the instrument to write for it,' says Laurence Pendrous. 'When I've heard clarinets, and the bassoon as well, it's always been in the very, very capable hands of the greats of the classical repertoire – and even among those, there are those that don't write very well for the instruments. With the woodwind on the solo album, I find there is a kind of starkness to it. I find it doesn't fit the way other clarinet use in the classical repertoire sits. Maybe what I'm saying is that I don't feel that Mark's writing for the wind instruments was particularly skilfully done, him not coming from that background. But then I don't know if that's a fair thing to say, because it could be exactly what he wanted. He did always know what he wanted. But [the album] doesn't really seem like anything else … I've always felt that. When I first got the CD, the demo, I *really* didn't know what to make of it. I really didn't. It just seemed so different. Maybe he just wanted that sound on the record. [For Mark], it had to be something new in order for it to be worth doing.'

When bassoon player Margaret Pollock spoke to the *Guardian* shorty after Hollis's death in 2019, she said something interesting about the way she was told these elements on the record were intended to work. 'Mark [and Livesey] had written short "sequences" of music that he planned to insert between tracks to link the whole album together, or to use as a backing for parts of the tracks,' recalled Pollock. 'He knew exactly the sounds he wanted, so we recorded different versions of each section to make it sound happy, angry, lost…'[6]

This suggests that the woodwind parts were fully scored, but not necessarily with the intention always of being a fixed part of one particular song. Hollis, as was his custom, was collecting parts to drop in where desired. It sounds that way, too. The woodwind elements make more sense in light of understanding this more fluid approach to placement. *Mark Hollis* was released in the era when the compact disc had more or less killed the vinyl album. The eight tracks are a sequence, rather than two sides. Heard that way, the linking passages between the end of 'The Gift' and the beginning of 'A Life (1895–1915)', and again between 'Westward Bound' and 'The Daily Planet', call back to the first side of *Spirit of Eden*. And like those passages, the music was written with that connective idea in mind.

For Hollis, the process of creating music was not just to make it different every time, but for it to be an informative and educational experience; it had to move the whole business of creativity forward, somehow. 'Working with Mark was always an education, because you sometimes didn't know what he was after,' says Robbie McIntosh. 'But then when you hear the finished result, you go, *Right, that was it,* and it made it all worthwhile. That's how you learn in this business, by sometimes having to do things that you don't quite understand. When you do, you've learned something.' He is speaking about himself, but the lesson applies to Hollis as much as anyone.

There is another related point to make about this music, and which is perhaps most applicable to the solo album. It was consciously intended to be a gift to the people playing it. Those who didn't see or hear that tended not to last the distance; those who did were cherished, and cherished Hollis in return. 'I've come to realise that Mark on every level was one of the most generous human beings I've ever met,' says Pendrous. 'What I think the most of Mark is his generosity. He was so meticulous. The planning that he put into his music he put into his expressions of generosity and friendship. It is really extraordinary. Just what he did for me!'

'The music was so gorgeous and so beautiful and so *playable* as a player,' says Dominic Miller. 'It's just such a joy to play music like that … It was an incredible experience. I have never worked with anyone like that.'

The price of such rewards was that it required huge leaps into the unknown. In some ways, on *Mark Hollis* we hear an artist very stubbornly playing against his strengths. It would feel dishonest not to recognise the occasionally attritional nature of the listening experience. That it is sometimes hard work. 'A Life (1895–1915)' is the album's longest track and its steepest ascent, its most daunting challenge. It's not an easy climb. There is little to hold on to but dissonance. A single note shades around silence and stretches out. The vocal melody isn't really a melody; it's just a means of reciting an unsettling litany: 'Avow / Relent.' The asymmetric jabs of woodwind feel almost performatively intrusive. Yes, the way Hollis sings 'Such suffering / Few certain' is like hearing a passing car playing some beautiful lost jazz standard. And, yes, the arrangement of the overlapping voices is mesmeric. *Who are they?* No singers are credited on the album sleeve (not even Hollis). And what are they saying?

The track isn't short of rich, engaging moments, but the goal that 'A Life (1895–1915)' is ultimately striving to reach feels elusive. One imagines this might be the track Lucian Grainge played before asking whether it was worth a million pounds.

•

As late as November 1997, Hollis told Rob Young that he didn't want the words included on the album sleeve, but come January there they were. He must have changed his mind. I doubt the marketing men at Polydor were begging for these terse, clenched verses to be laid bare. This time, the lyrics were rendered in crisp typeface, rather than his own curled handwriting. This was in keeping with the album's plain minimalism, but also a conscious severing from the Talk Talk aesthetic. As James Marsh has explained, he was not asked to create any artwork for the record. For the first time, a photograph was used on the cover, although Hollis's initial plans may have been somewhat more ambitious.

'I remember Mark asking me if I could design something,' says Mark Feltham with a laugh. 'I remember him saying, "Could you make some kind of clay sculpture? I want everyone to contribute a piece of their artwork to the album." I said, "Oh Mark, I can't! You're having a laugh, aren't ya!" I'm not an artistic guy outside of what I do. All of a sudden, he wanted me to be some kind of sculptor. That's what he was like.'

Instead, the album cover was framed by the same white border as both *Spirit of Eden* and *Laughing Stock*, only this time the centrepiece was not a painting but a black-and-white photograph. The image was at first indecipherable: grotesque, comedic, sad, vaguely unsettling without it quite being clear why. The photograph had been taken in Sicily in 1990 by Stephen Lovell-Davis, an old friend of Hollis's who had once auditioned to play bass in the Reaction but didn't get the job. He may have ended up with the better deal. 'This picture was chosen by my friend Mark Hollis for the cover of his solo album, much to the consternation of the record company,' Lovell-Davis wrote many years later. 'It is an almond Easter cake.'[7]

It wasn't any old almond cake; it was one depicting the lamb of God. *Pecorelle Pasquali* – marzipan lambs – are a traditional southern Italian confectionery commonly baked during regional festivals to celebrate Easter. Hollis was an Italophile, but it was more that he felt the photograph presented a suitably ambiguous and open-ended image to convey the music within. 'I like the way something appears to come out of his head. It makes me think of a fountain of ideas,' he said. 'Also the [way] the eyes are positioned fascinates me.

When I saw the picture for the first time, I had to laugh, but there is something very tragic about it at the same time.'[8]

·

'A New Jerusalem' is the final song worthy of the description that Mark Hollis ever released. It ends with a positively Ligetian flourish of clarinet: high, skittish, terribly sad. The effect is of a shrill 'Last Post'. It is followed by almost two minutes of raked silence. They are part of the song, as the album's muted opening preface is also part of the song. I like to think of this as the final playing out of Hollis's immense generosity. He is taking care to ease our transition back into real life, delivered safe from this other world.

The last words we ever hear him sing are, 'Do you see?'

Do we?

I listen to *Mark Hollis* now and I mostly think that he probably stopped releasing music at the right time. I'm not sure the solo album hints at any great riches lying ahead. For all its beauty, it can feel as though every last drop of something – inspiration, love, sheer cussedness – is being simultaneously poured into and drained out of the process of making this music. One feels, I suppose, that it shouldn't really be this hard. Perhaps he came to a similar conclusion. Like James Joyce, Hollis and his collaborators played ceaselessly with the form, taking familiar, even traditional or folkloric elements and subjecting them to rigorous processes of modernist experimentation. *Mark Hollis* might be his *Ulysses*. He spared us his *Finnegans Wake*.

He may have realised that he had nowhere all that interesting left to travel, at least by his own exacting and undoubtedly eccentric standards. He frequently said he would never make, or release, music for the sake of it. Apart from stopping, perhaps the only truly radical act at this stage in the game would have been returning to first principles: going back to the song, sitting down at the piano or with a guitar and a notepad. But, by now, that place had vanished from view. These extraordinary final four records – *The Colour of Spring, Spirit of Eden, Laughing Stock* and *Mark Hollis* – had involved a journey to a point where he could no longer see from where he had come.

'Through these albums, for me, each one has felt like a very natural progression from where the one before was,' he said shortly before the release of his final work. 'But [from] this one to the first one, there's no relationship at all.'[9] Job done, perhaps. Point proven. Time to soar those burned bridges.

The world turned; the seasons clicked through.

Spring again.

ENDINGS

(Wealth of Love)

There is a truism about the people Leonard Cohen once termed 'workers in song' and it is this: nobody ever walks away for good. The urge to create and share (and be loved for it) is ultimately too strong. David Bowie, Scott Walker, Kate Bush and Cohen all vanished for extended spells, but eventually re-emerged.

Part of the fascination with Mark Hollis is that he left and never came back.

Industrial quantities of what-ifs have been poured into the space left by his absence from the music industry in the years between the release of *Mark Hollis* in 1998 and his death from cancer in 2019.

There are a few things that happened afterwards and many, many more things that never happened. The things that never happened have tended to attract more interest than the things that did. They often sound very alluring: a soundtrack for the Wim Wenders' movie *Everything Will Be Fine*; a collaboration with Kate Bush; arthouse film scores.

They are ghost projects. None of them happened.

Very little did. Three things, in total.

Under the pseudonym John Cope, Hollis wrote and played 'Piano', a fourteen-minute exercise in extreme instrumental minimalism which appeared as a track on *AV 1*, an album by Dave Allinson and Phill Brown, released in March 1998. He also contributed uncredited piano to 'Chaos', a track on *Psyence Fiction* by James Lavelle's UNKLE, released in August 1998. Both these cameos belong to the same timeframe as the solo album, when Hollis remained more or less a public artist, and were recorded before it had even been released.

Then nothing for almost fifteen years. Not so much silence as absence. No music, no interviews, no public appearances.

Hollis no longer had a manager. The only regular contact he had with a 'record company' in later years was not discussing new projects in the boardroom, but going to the pub with Nigel Reeve, director of repertoire at Parlophone, for what they called their 'Dog & Duck evenings'. They talked about, well, many things, but part of their shared goal was to ensure that the music Hollis had been a part of between 1982 and 1998 was being appropriately looked after.

When he and Reeve were curating the Talk Talk compilation *Natural Order*, Reeve recalled that Hollis put almost as much thought into the gaps between the tracks as the songs themselves. 'For Mark,' he said, 'as much as anything it was about how it flowed.' I imagine him looking back at all the records he had made and seeing it as a single body of work. It 'flowed', too, and he may have recognised that the sequencing, which was immaculate, had now brought him to the end of the second side.

The mythology around what was perceived as a 'withdrawal' coincided with – and perhaps helped feed – an attendant rise in Talk Talk's status, as *Spirit of Eden* in particular began to grow into its standing as a classic album. How gratifying it was for him to see the music he had made, particularly since 1986, find its place in a glow of appreciation, as new fans not only recognised its special qualities but evangelised about them, is hard to say. He never spoke about it, but one imagines there was at least a quiet sense of fulfilment.

And still no music. As the lore around Hollis became more

intense, rumours grew arms and legs. Some people became amateur sleuths. To quote Tom Waits, *What was he building in there?*

Not a lot, is the answer.

In the context of such a deep and determined vacuum, the tendency to get over-excited about any hint of new music was perhaps understandable.

In 2012, an almost unseemly fuss was made when a Mark Hollis instrumental piece lasting ninety-two seconds was licensed to an American TV show. 'Arb Section 1' was made available on the *Boss* soundtrack album, overseen by Hollis's friend Brian Reitzell. A slight but beguiling confection of synthetic 'voice', tinkling pulse and simulated woodwind, it was indicative of the form Hollis latterly worked in. When Reitzell sent Hollis a copy of the *Boss* soundtrack on vinyl, he received a prompt response saying how much he loved 'the sound, artwork and track layout'. The 'flow', clearly, was still important.

The excitement that 'Arb Section 1' generated had very little to do with the content (it was quite fun to see music critics earnestly analyse a ninety-two-second fragment of weird art-music shorn of any wider context) and everything to do with where it might lead.

In the event, it led nowhere but to a continued absence. No music, no interviews, no public appearances.

Hollis died in February 2019 without any further work appearing.

'Instead of one note, I would rather hear silence.' He wasn't kidding. After January 1998, there are only footnotes. When it comes to the music of Talk Talk and Mark Hollis, the solo album is the full stop in the sentence.

•

We won't ever really know why Mark Hollis stopped actively making music for public release, and it isn't terribly important. Playing the great guessing game around the motives of a man who is sadly no longer here is fruitless but somewhat inevitable. All we can do is look to those two constants: character and virtue. They guided every creative decision he made. We must presume they played a part in the ones he chose not to make, too.

He was a domestic creature, seemingly very happily married, with many interests outside music. He had two children to whom he was devoted and who, by the millennium, were approaching their teenage years.

The practicalities made stepping back very easy. His contract with Polydor had an option to run to four albums, but the only contractual commitment was to make two. These were *Laughing Stock* and *Mark Hollis*. In terms of his obligations to the industry, he was done. There was certainly no financial incentive to continue, particularly after No Doubt had a huge international hit with 'It's My Life' in 2003. This development, I imagine, also freed up the song's co-writer Tim Friese-Greene to pursue his own interests a little more wilfully. The Talk Talk 'best of', *Natural History*, continued ticking over. 'The publishing always brought income,' says Nigel Reeve, 'and he didn't live an extravagant life.'

He had long ago relinquished any interest in performing live. The indignities surrounding the release of *Spirit of Eden*, *Laughing Stock* and, perhaps most of all, the solo record had been acute, if not all that unusual. He may have decided enough was enough on that score. 'I think he just hated the music industry,' says Dominic Miller. 'He hated it. I made the mistake a couple of times of talking about the industry and he was just shut off.' Perhaps he also had enough objectivity to recognise that in fact he'd had a decent run; the days of a record label handing out huge sums to make niche, challenging, determinedly non-commercial albums had passed. He had certainly made the most of them. Hereon, the budgets would be more modest, his ambitions, perhaps, circumscribed.

Despite serial drama with record labels, there would have been no shortage of suitors more than willing to take on a new Mark Hollis record. Had he created music that he wanted to release, presumably he could and would have, and done it on his own terms. 'The only thing that I can ever hope is that I would never make an album for the wrong reasons and just stay with that ethic,' he said in 1991. 'I can't see the point of making an album for the sake of it. There's nothing that I would get from it.'[1]

It's a clear statement. 'I think he got to the end of the solo record and thought, *Where do I go from here?*' says Mark Feltham, who remained a family friend. *'I've produced what I feel is the best work I can offer.'* For a man with a dread of repeating himself, stepping away may have seemed a very active and positive choice.

There is no suggestion that, at any time after 1998, Hollis seriously considered undertaking a recording project of any substance. 'We never really discussed it,' says Reeve. 'He might say he had been tinkering, if he had time on his hands he might head towards the piano and do something, but there was never any discussion of a new project or an album or, "Who should I sign with?" Absolutely nothing like that whatsoever. I genuinely think he had done what he had set out to do, and anything else that he would have done, or did, was pure hobby.'

'Arb Section 1' sounds like hobby music, or at least music made entirely for the composer's own pleasure – and almost certainly made at home. The journey leading to its public release was organic rather than strategic, growing from Hollis's friendship with the American film composer, producer and musician Brian Reitzell. Hollis had been a fan of the previous film Reitzell had worked on, *Lost in Translation*, and after some back and forth correspondence, in 2006 they met in London and a friendship developed, much of it based on a mutual love of music and, especially, film. 'He loved Andrey Zvyagintsev's films, especially *The Banishment*,' says Reitzell. 'I told him about Oskar Fischinger's animations and old Japanese films I liked. We had a shared love of Yasujirō Ozu. Alejandro Iñárritu's films, especially *21 Grams*, and Pawel Pawlikowski's *Ida* were other favourites.'

Hollis had been talking about his desire to make music for 'European' cinema since the mid-'80s, citing his admiration for Marcel Carné, Fellini and '50s and '60s English films such as *Whistle Down the Wind* – another religious allegory. There had been a brief notion to make some kind of a film based on *Spirit of Eden*. Encouraged by Reitzell's enthusiasm, Hollis provided music for consideration for Michael Lander's 2010 psychological thriller, *Peacock*. It was not accepted but that one piece, 'Arb Section 1', ended up being used in the second season of *Boss*, the political drama starring Kelsey Grammer on which Gus Van Sant was one of the producers and Reitzell composer. 'Mark was a fan of Gus's work, especially *Elephant*,' he says. 'He told me how much he loved the show and that being attached to it had been an honour for him.'

Peacock to *Boss*. There was never any great sense that Hollis was scoring seriously for specific individual projects. It was more likely he was hoping directors he admired would use his pieces – most likely the same or similar ones each time – but on his own terms. He was, in effect, asking them to subjugate their vision to his music. He enjoyed the idea of his work being used by a master filmmaker, but the reality of being a composer for film, which is that they must bend their will to that of the director, for an artist as controlled as Hollis was never going to work.

And indeed it didn't. In spring 2014, he responded 'very' positively to an invitation made via Reitzell to write music for Wim Wenders' next film, *Everything Will Be Fine*. 'A meeting was set up for Wim and Mark to discuss further,' says Reitzell. 'This was supposed to happen in Berlin but moved to London in April. Mark read the script and then he gave Wim three selections of music as audio files when they met. This was to give Wim an idea of the style and scale that Mark would write for the film. He said to Wim to let him know in his own time as to whether or not he felt it suitable and that meanwhile he would continue to carry on composing anyway.'

In the end, Wenders went with something different, following his initial instincts for a more classical approach à la Vaughan Williams. On another proposed film project, Hollis got as far as supplying short instrumentals with precise points indicating where he wanted the music to be used. After the pieces had been synced to the film, however, Hollis withdrew. 'The concept had been sold to him that the music was going to be used in a non-emotionally manipulative fashion,' says a source who was involved on the project. 'That was part of what he found very appealing about it. When he heard the music in the film, he realised that it had an emotional impact; therefore he withdrew.'

What he needed, perhaps, was a filmmaker who was devoted to an ongoing partnership that framed Hollis's work in a genuinely empathetic and collaborative way: arthouse film's very own Tim Friese-Greene – two auteurs dovetailing in sound and image. Would it have worked? Probably not. But film seemed the only context in which making music still even remotely interested him.

It may simply have been that Hollis finally ran out of willing accomplices. He even fell out with Phill Brown in the end. By early 1999, Brown recalls, Hollis had 'decided to retire as a recording artist and suggested that we team up and co-produce other artists'.[2] They worked together at Pete Townshend's Eel Pie Island studio on an album by Norwegian singer-songwriter Anja Garbarek called *Smiling and Waving*, which was released in 2001. The partnership yielded two tracks before it fell apart. 'During a string and woodwind overdub session, it all started to get rather difficult,' Brown recalled. 'Mark was not communicating well with the session musicians and I found it all incredibly stressful … After the musicians had left, I told Mark, unfortunately in a rather aggressive and rude tone, that I too was heading home.'[3] Hollis left the project. He and Brown became estranged. There was no further talk of being a producer, and no more collaborations.

It is the one great anomaly, perhaps, of Hollis's creative life. He simply could not do it alone. We must remember that the best music he made, he made in extremely close collaboration with others. Hearing 'Arb Section 1' does little to suggest he worked better by himself. It gives the distinct impression, in fact, that Hollis had more or less written himself to a standstill. 'He has never been a solo artist,' says Laurence Pendrous. 'Even with a solo album, he was working with the other musicians, so it was a necessity.'

Perhaps Hollis stopped making records because ultimately he found that 'necessity' too testing – for him and for others. The list of exhausted, frustrated or exiled partners is a long one. Hollis wore people out. He lacked the ability to clearly articulate his vision. He simply knew what he wanted when he heard it. 'It's all chance,' he told Phill Brown. This method took an inevitable toll – and may plausibly have ultimately dampened down any desire to keep making music in the way that he once had.

Friends sometimes enquired gently and were left none the wiser. 'A few times in the pub, with trepidation, I would say [something] to Mark,' says Dominic Miller. 'Actually, the last conversation I had with him, about three or four years [before he died], I had a coffee with him and I said, "Hey, Mark, you know, do you fancy coming up with something?" He just looked at me and laughed and said, "Are you fucking kidding?" I thought, *Okay, let's forget it. Let's just talk about football or just not talk at all.* He said the only thing that he was interested in doing was something for a movie or TV. "That's all I want to do right now," he said, "But I don't even really want to do that."'

Perhaps Hollis came close to doing something new and remarkable.

Perhaps he was firmly resolved not to even try.

It doesn't really matter. There is nothing for us to hear, not even the merest hint of some great lost work, no *Spirit of Eden II* lingering in the vaults.

Talking to friends and close collaborators, it's clear that Hollis did not spend his last two decades in a state of tortured isolation. He travelled widely, motorbiking through South America, Europe and the US. He loved his family, watched football and met friends in London and elsewhere for Guinness and cappuccino.

He was still a music fan, still curious. 'We would exchange CDs,' says Dominic Miller. 'Two he really liked were of orchestrated tango music, and a koto player from Korea, playing one note at a time. He loved that!'

'He would send me YouTube links to tracks, interesting music, older music, more obscure things,' says Nigel Reeve. 'He really liked John Lennon's "Steel and Glass" and I sent him an alternative version of "Steel and Glass" which was on [the Lennon compilation] *Menlove*

Avenue, which he thought was really cool.' His connection with modern music was less obvious. 'He never came and said, "There's this great new band I think you should sign." There was none of that.'

•

In the last two decades of his life, Hollis released precisely ninety-two seconds of music. Even the most devout fan would be hard pushed to call it a comeback. A seductive mystique grew up around his silence; it is easy to get swayed by all the might-have-beens, the rumours and speculation, to lose focus and forget they yielded nothing but air.

This is not a biography of a person or a band, but of four records. They are real and they are enough.

Mark Hollis was the full stop at the end of the sentence.

The story ended there and yet continues each time we play the music.

What was it all about?

We should give Mark Hollis the final word.

'Sometimes I don't know what to say when I get asked all these questions, because for me the music says it all. I'm not the important thing. You have to concentrate to understand it and I don't think that's too much to ask, really. Asking me questions isn't going to get things any clearer, because there really is no grand scheme behind any of this.

'I suppose, if you want to see where it all comes from, it's a rebelling again conventions that constrict the form. We go against what's established and open things out a little. It's only because the form is so narrow at the moment, we stand out. We're breaking the unspoken rules about what's expected.

'But then nobody likes rules, do they?'[4]

NOTES AND SOURCES

Numerous books, newspapers, magazines, online articles, websites, radio broadcasts, albums, TV shows and films proved of great value during the researching and writing of this book. Given the impossibility of listing them all, I'll simply note that particular credit is due to *Snow in Berlin*, an exhaustive and venerable online Talk Talk resource: www.snowinberlin.com. Many of the other most useful resources are mentioned below.

All quotations in the book are taken from my own interviews, except where otherwise indicated in the text or in the reference information that follows. Writers are credited wherever possible, but occasionally I came across articles which had no byline or where accurate information on the author was not available.

BEGINNINGS

1. Cliff Jones, *Melody Maker*, 26 October 1991
2. Taken from the full transcript of an interview with Paul Webb by Wyndham Wallace conducted for *Uncut*, December 2018
3. ibid

SPRING

i

1. Jim Irvin, *MOJO*, March 2006
2. Neville Unwin and Tim Goodyer, *Home & Studio Recording*, April 1986
3. Cliff Jones, *International Musician*, October 1991

4. Betty Page, *Record Mirror*, 1 February 1986
5. Corné Evers, *Oor*, April 1986. English translation on Snow in Berlin: snowinberlin.com
6. Rob Young, *The Wire*, January 1988
7. Jim Irvin, *MOJO*, March 2006

ii

1. *Kim*, 22 January 1983
2. Jean-Daniel Beauvallet, *Les Inrockuptibles*, September/October 1991
3. Jim Irvin, *MOJO*, March 2006
4. Richard Skinner, BBC Radio 1 interview, October 1988
5. History of Eddie & the Hot Rods, Punk 77: punk77.co.uk/band/eddie-the-hot-rods
6. Taken from the full transcript of an interview with Paul Webb by Wyndham Wallace conducted for *Uncut*, December 2018
7. Jim Irvin, *MOJO*, May 2019
8. James Marsh, Chris Roberts and Toby Benjamin, *Spirit of Talk Talk* (Rocket 88 Books, 2011)
9. Betty Page, *Noise!*, 11 November 1982
10. Simon Williams, *NME*, 23 September 1988
11. Adrian Thrills, *NME*, 16 January 1982
12. Marianne Ebertowski, *ZigZag*, July 1982
13. Simon Tebbutt, *Record Mirror*, 8 May 1982
14. Ben Wardle, *Mark Hollis: A Perfect Silence* (Rocket 88 Books, 2022)

interlude 1

1. John Clarkson, Penny Black Music: pennyblackmusic.co.uk/Home/Details?id=13729, 24 May 2006
2. ibid
3. ibid
4. ibid
5. ibid
6. Jim Irvin, *MOJO*, March 2006
7. Corné Evers, *Oor*, April 1986. English translation on Snow in Berlin: snowinberlin.com

iii

1. James Marsh, Chris Roberts and Toby Benjamin, *Spirit of Talk Talk*, p. 126
2. *Hitkrant*, 11 January 1986. English translation on Snow in Berlin: snowinberlin.com

3. John Clarkson, Penny Black Music: pennyblackmusic.co.uk/Home/ Details?id=13729, 24 May 2006

4. James Marsh, Chris Roberts and Toby Benjamin, *Spirit of Talk Talk*, p. 221

5. Cliff Jones, *International Musician*, October 1991

6. Richard Walmsley, *International Musician & Recording World*, April 1986

7. Bob Dickinson, *NME*, 24 May 1986

8. Andy Strickland, *Record Mirror*, 15 February 1986

iv

1. William Shaw, *Smash Hits*, 4 June 1986

2. James Marsh, Chris Roberts and Toby Benjamin, *Spirit of Talk Talk*, p. 113

3. ibid, p. 73, quote attributed to Keith Aspden

4. Joost Niemöller, *Vinyl*, 2 February 1986

5. Simon Williams, *NME*, 12 October 1991

6. Jim Irvin, *MOJO*, March 2006

7. Dave Sexton, *Record Mirror*, 24 May 1986

8. William Shaw, *Smash Hits*, 4 June 1986

9. James Marsh, Chris Roberts and Toby Benjamin, *Spirit of Talk Talk*, p. 215–6

10. ibid

11. ibid

12. ibid

SUMMER

i

1. Paul Webb, rustinman.com: rustinman.com/about-1-1

2. Tim Friese-Greene: soundcloud.com/user-947232876/eden-rehearsal-cassette

3. Andrew Smith, *International Musician & Recording World*, November 1988

4. James Marsh, Chris Roberts and Toby Benjamin, *Spirit of Talk Talk*, p. 222

5. John Clarkson, Penny Black Music: pennyblackmusic.co.uk/Home/ Details?id=13729, 24 May 2006

6. ibid

7. ibid

8. Adrian Deevoy, *Q*, October 1988

9. The Bowie Bible: bowiebible.com/songs/dj

10. Andrew Smith, *International Musician & Recording World*, November 1988

11. Steve Sutherland, *Melody Maker*, 7 September 1991
12. James Marsh, Chris Roberts and Toby Benjamin, *Spirit of Talk Talk*, Mark Hollis interview with Rob Young, p. 212
13. Steve Sutherland, *Melody Maker*, 7 September 1991
14. Jack Chambers, *Milestones: The Music and Times of Miles Davis* (Da Capo Press, 1988)

ii

1. Andrew Smith, *International Musician & Recording World*, November 1988

iii

1. James Marsh, Chris Roberts and Toby Benjamin, *Spirit of Talk Talk*, p. 221
2. *Sounds*, 24 September 1988
3. Simon Williams, *NME*, 24 September 1988
4. David Sinclair, *The Times*, 24 September 1988
5. Mark Cooper, *Q*, October 1988
6. Adrian Deevoy, *Q*, October 1988
7. Graham Coxon, 'My Music', *NME*, 22 September 2009: nme.com/blogs/nme-blogs/graham-coxon-my-music-45260
8. Laura Snapes, *The Guardian*, 26 February 2019: theguardian.com/music/2019/feb/26/musicians-on-mark-hollis-he-found-hooks-in-places-im-still-trying-to-fathom
9. ibid
10. *Guy Garvey's Finest Hour*, *Spirit of Eden* special, BBC Radio 6 Music, 15 October 2018

iv

1. Paul Webb on Instagram @rustinmanofficial, 25 August 2025: instagram.com/p/DM8Tt9YsDMZ/?hl=en
2. EMI Records Limited v Mark David Hollis, Lee David Harris, Paul Douglas Webb in the Supreme Court of Judicature Court of Appeal (Civil Division) on Appeal from the High Court of Justice, Chancery Division, 23 May 1989
3. Paul Webb on Instagram @rustinmanofficial, 25 August 2025: instagram.com/p/DM8Tt9YsDMZ/?hl=en
4. Chris Pope, *For The Record*, 10 November 1988
5. Paul Webb on Instagram @rustinmanofficial, 25 August 2025: https://www.instagram.com/p/DM8Tt9YsDMZ/?hl=en
6. Steve Sutherland, *Melody Maker*, 7 September, 1991

7.   ibid
8.   ibid
9.   ibid
10. Ben Wardle, *Mark Hollis: A Perfect Silence*, p. 255

AUTUMN

i

1.   David Quantick, *NME*, 28 September 1991
2.   John Clarkson, Penny Black Music: pennyblackmusic.co.uk/Home/Details?id=13729, 24 May 2006
3.   ibid
4.   Phill Brown, *Are We Still Rolling?: Studios, Drugs and Rock 'n' Roll – One Man's Journey Recording Classic Albums* (Tape Op, 2011)
5.   Steve Sutherland, *Melody Maker*, 7 September 1991
6.   Cliff Jones, *Melody Maker*, 26 October 1991
7.   John Clarkson, Penny Black Music: pennyblackmusic.co.uk/Home/Details?id=13729, 24 May 2006
8.   James Marsh, Chris Roberts and Toby Benjamin, *Spirit of Talk Talk*, p. 222
9.   Cliff Jones, *International Musician*, November 1991
10. ibid
11. Cliff Jones, *Melody Maker*, 26 October 1991
12. Jim Irvin, *MOJO*, March 2006
13. John Clarkson, Penny Black Music: pennyblackmusic.co.uk/Home/Details?id=13729, 24 May 2006

ii

1.   John Clarkson, Penny Black Music: pennyblackmusic.co.uk/Home/Details?id=13729, 24 May 2006
2.   Steve Sutherland, *Melody Maker*, 7 September 1991
3.   John Clarkson, Penny Black Music: pennyblackmusic.co.uk/Home/Details?id=13729, 24 May 2006
4.   Bradley J. Birzer, *Progarchy*, 18 June 2018: progarchy.com/2018/06/18/seven-sacraments-to-song-talk-talks-laughing-stock-1991
5.   Steve Sutherland, *Melody Maker*, 7 September 1991
6.   John Clarkson, Penny Black Music: pennyblackmusic.co.uk/Home/Details?id=13729, 24 May 2006
7.   Steve Sutherland, *Melody Maker*, 7 September 1991

8. *Guy Garvey's Finest Hour*, *Spirit of Eden* special, BBC Radio 6 Music, 15 October 2018

9. Betty Page, *Vox*, November 1991

iv

1. Joost Niemöller, *Vinyl*, 2 February 1986

2. Rob Young, *The Wire*, January 1998

3. Steve Sutherland, *Melody Maker*, 7 September 1991

4. *Haagsche Courant*, September 1988; English translation on Snow in Berlin: www.snowinberlin.com

5. Rob Young, *Electric Eden: Unearthing Britain's Visionary Music* (Faber & Faber, 2010)

6. Bradley J. Birzer, *The Imaginative Conservative*, 17 December 2024: theimaginativeconservative.org/2024/12/mark-hollis-christianity-either-real-or-real-bradley-birzer

7. Corné Evers, *Oor*, April 1986

8. Steve Sutherland, *Melody Maker*, 7 September 1991

9. James Marsh, Chris Roberts and Toby Benjamin, *Spirit of Talk Talk*, Mark Hollis interview with Rob Young, p. 214

10. Nick Cave and Seán O'Hagan, *Faith, Hope and Carnage* (Canongate, 2022)

11. James Marsh, Chris Roberts and Toby Benjamin, *Spirit of Talk Talk*, Mark Hollis interview with Rob Young, p. 213

12. James MacMillan, 'Diary', *The Spectator*, 10 May 2025

WINTER

i

1. Andy Gill, *Independent*, 20 September 1991

2. Phill Brown, *Are We Still Rolling?*

3. Steve Sutherland, *Melody Maker*, 7 September 1991

4. John Clarkson, Penny Black Music: pennyblackmusic.co.uk/Home/Details?id=13729, 24 May 2006

5. Mugram Thesic, *Bombay Arts Review*, 2000

6. ibid

7. Jim Irvin, *MOJO*, March 2006

8. ibid

9. David Stubbs, *Vox*, February 1998

10. James Marsh, Chris Roberts and Toby Benjamin, *Spirit of Talk Talk*, Mark Hollis interview with Rob Young, p. 212

11. *Music Minded*, April 1998: web.archive.org/web/20091009000251/http:/
    www.palyniam.co.uk/content.php?page=interview-mark
12. James Marsh, Chris Roberts and Toby Benjamin, *Spirit of Talk Talk*, Mark
    Hollis interview with Rob Young, p. 212
13. ibid, p. 217
14. ibid, p. 211
15. ibid, p. 101

ii

1. Les Tomkins, *Jazz Professional*, January 1978, c/o National Jazz Archive
2. James Marsh, Chris Roberts and Toby Benjamin, *Spirit of Talk Talk*, Mark
   Hollis interview with Rob Young, p. 217
3. Phill Brown, *Are We Still Rolling?*
4. ibid
5. ibid
6. ibid
7. Laura Snapes, *The Guardian*, 26 February 2019: theguardian.com/music/
   2019/feb/26/musicians-on-mark-hollis-he-found-hooks-in-places-im-still-
   trying-to-fathom
8. Phill Brown, *Are We Still Rolling?*
9. ibid
10. ibid

iii

1. Paul Webb, rustinman.com: rustinman.com/about-1-1
2. Phill Brown, *Are We Still Rolling?*
3. ibid
4. Rob Young, *Electric Eden*
5. Dave Robinson, 'Of Masks and Men', *Future Music*, October 1994
6. https://magnetiknorth.bandcamp.com/album/e-v-o-l-v-e-r
7. Ian Harrison, *MOJO*, April 2024
8. ibid
9. John Clarkson, Penny Black Music: pennyblackmusic.co.uk/Home/
   Details?id=13729, 24 May 2006

interlude 5

1. Kate Bush interview with Simon Mayo, BBC Radio 1, 16 August 1993
2. Tony Horkins, *Rock Compact Disc*, November 1993
3. OutQ, Sirius XM, 8 December 2011

iv

1. Paul Webb on Instagram @rustinmanofficial, 25 February 2019: instagram.com/p/BuUWCVah_8J/?hl=en
2. Richard Skinner, BBC Radio 1 interview, September 1991
3. James Marsh, Chris Roberts and Toby Benjamin, *Spirit of Talk Talk*, Mark Hollis interview with Rob Young, p. 217
4. ibid
5. Mark Beaumont, *NME*, 14 February 1998
6. Laura Snapes, *The Guardian*, 26 February 2019: theguardian.com/music/2019/feb/26/musicians-on-mark-hollis-he-found-hooks-in-places-im-still-trying-to-fathom
7. Stephen Lovell-Davis, Instagram, 21 August 2021: instagram.com/p/CS5A86wI3gg/?hl=en
8. *Music Minded*, April 1998: web.archive.org/web/20091009000251/http:/www.palyniam.co.uk/content.php?page=interview-mark
9. James Marsh, Chris Roberts and Toby Benjamin, *Spirit of Talk Talk*, Mark Hollis interview with Rob Young, p. 213

ENDINGS

1. Steve Sutherland, *Melody Maker*, 7 September 1991
2. Phill Brown, *Are We Still Rolling?*
3. ibid
4. Cliff Jones, *International Musician*, October 1991

SELECTED BIBLIOGRAPHY

Birch, Will, *No Sleep Till Canvey Island: The Great Pub Rock Revolution* (Virgin Books, 2000)

Brown, Phill, *Are We Still Rolling?: Studios, Drugs and Rock 'n' Roll – One Man's Journey Recording Classic Albums* (Tape Op, 2011)

Cave, Nick; O'Hagan, Séan, *Faith, Hope and Carnage* (Canongate, 2022)

Chambers, Jack, *Milestones: The Music and Times of Miles Davis* (Da Capo Press, 1988)

Higgs, John, *William Blake vs the World* (Weidenfeld & Nicolson, 2021)

Leech, Jeanette, *Fearless: The Making of Post-Rock* (Jawbone, 2017)

Marsh, James; Roberts, Chris; Benjamin, Toby, *Spirit of Talk Talk* (Rocket 88 Books, 2012)

Morrison, Van, *Lit Up Inside / Keep 'Er Lit: The Collected Lyrics* (Faber & Faber, 2025)

Palmer, Christopher, *Impressionism in Music* (Hutchinson University Library, 1973)

Steel, Gary, *Talk Talk on Track: Every Album, Every Song* (Sonicbond Publishing, 2023)

Thomson, Graeme, *Under the Ivy: The Life and Music of Kate Bush* (Omnibus Press, 2012)

Twain, Mark, *Life on the Mississippi* (SeaWolf Press, 2018)

Wardle, Ben, *Mark Hollis: A Perfect Silence* (Rocket 88 Books, 2022)

Young, Rob, *Electric Eden: Unearthing Britain's Visionary Music* (Faber & Faber, 2010)

Young, Rob; Schmidt, Irmin, *All Gates Open: The Story of Can* (Faber & Faber, 2018)

ACKNOWLEDGEMENTS

I am grateful to all the artists, musicians, writers, producers and engineers, as well as the friends and associates of Talk Talk, who spoke to me about the band and their music, whether in 2012, 2019 or at any time between 2022 and 2025. Although not everybody is quoted directly in the book, all these conversations and contributions were of value and greatly appreciated.

Thanks to Matthew Hamilton at the Hamilton Agency and to Pete Selby and James Lilford at New Modern. I owe a particular debt of gratitude to Pete for his patience and understanding, and for always believing in the book.

I am much obliged to my old *Word* magazine comrade Nige Tassell for his meticulous and improving copy-editing. Any mistakes that remain are my own.

Thanks also to…

Paul Palmer-Edwards for his terrific work designing the cover, and to Steve Lovell-Davis for allowing his elegantly abstract photograph of the band, taken in 1988, to grace it.

Toby Benjamin and Wyndham Wallace for Talk Talk talk and for kindly sharing their insights and much useful information.

David Joseph for a number of enjoyable exchanges. David's band Held By Trees have performed and recorded with many notable Talk Talk alumni and their music is well worth investigating.

Bristol Dave, wherever he may be, for sitting me in front of *Spirit of Eden* at precisely the right time – *the when, the where and the who.*

And, as ever and for always, I send a wealth of love to my family.

The team at New Modern would like to thank the following individuals:

Nige Tassell for copy-editing
Marie Doherty for typesetting
Jo Mortimer for proofreading
Paul Palmer-Edwards for cover design
Stephen Lovell-Davis for cover photograph
Dusty Miller for publicity
Marie Lecouturier, Charlotte Rose, Andreina Brezzo
and the team at Simon & Schuster UK for sales and distribution